THE SONNETS

OF

WILLIAM SHAKSPERE

EDITED BY

EDWARD DOWDEN

Elibron Classics
www.elibron.com

SHAKSPERE'S SONNETS

THE SONNETS

OF

WILLIAM SHAKSPERE

EDITED BY

EDWARD DOWDEN

ARBOR SCIENTIÆ

ARBOR VITÆ

LONDON

KEGAN PAUL, TRENCH & CO., 1, PATERNOSTER SQUARE

1881

CONTENTS.

—•◇•—

Contents.

NOTE.

The present Edition differs from that in the Parchment Series in having fuller notes, and Part II. of the Introduction, giving a survey of the Literature of the Sonnets.

The best counsel to a reader of Shakspere is to cling close to the text of plays and poems, and remain with it long. Notes are made to be used, and then cast aside. But the careful student knows how presumptuous a mistake it is to suppose that an offhand reader will always take up the meaning rightly. The study of each line and each sentence on this side and on that is like the preliminary posturings of wrestlers before the grapple and the tug. To those unversed in the art it is foolishness; but others know the uses of the wary eye and slow approach.

INTRODUCTION.

PART I.

No edition of Shakspere's Sonnets,[1] apart from his other writings, with sufficient explanatory notes, has hitherto appeared. Notes are an evil, but in the case of the Sonnets a necessary evil, for many passages are hard to understand. I have kept beside me for several years an interleaved copy of Dyce's text, in which I set down from time to time anything that seemed to throw light on a difficult passage. From these jottings, and from the Variorum Shakspere of 1821,[2] my annotations have been chiefly drawn. I have had before me in preparing this volume the editions of Bell, Clark and Wright, Collier, Delius, Dyce, Halliwell, Hazlitt, Knight, Palgrave, Staunton, Grant White; the translations of François-Victor Hugo, Bodenstedt, and others; and the greater portion of the extensive Shakspere Sonnets literature,

[1] The poet's name is rightly written *Shakespeare*, rightly also *Shakspere*. If I err in choosing the form *Shakspere*, I err with the owner of the name.

[2] To which this general reference may suffice. I often found it convenient to alter slightly the notes of the Variorum Shakspere, and I have not made it a rule to refer each note from that edition to its individual writer.

English and German.   It is sorrowful to consider of how
small worth the contribution I make to the knowledge
of these poems is, in proportion to the time and pains
bestowed.

To render Shakspere's meaning clear has been my aim.
I do not make his poetry an occasion for giving lessons
in etymology.   It would have been easy, and not useless,
to have enlarged the notes with parallels from other
Elizabethan writers; but they are already bulky.   I
have been sparing of such parallel passages, and have
illustrated Shakspere chiefly from his own writings.
Repeated perusals have convinced me that the Sonnets
stand in the right order, and that sonnet is connected
with sonnet in more instances than have been observed.
My notes on each sonnet commonly begin with an
attempt to point out the little links or articulations in
thought and word which connect it with its predecessor
or the group to which it belongs.   I frankly warn the
reader that I have pushed this kind of criticism far, per-
haps too far.   I have perhaps in some instances fancied
points of connection which have no real existence; some
I have set down which seem to myself conjectural.
After this warning, I ask the friendly reader not to
grow too soon impatient; and if, going through the text
carefully, he will consider for himself the points which
I have noted, I have a hope that he will in many in-
stances see reason to agree with what I have said.

The text here presented is that of a conservative
editor, opposed to conjecture, unless conjecture be a
necessity, and desirous to abide by the Quarto (1609),
unless strong reasons appear for a departure from it.

Sonnets by Shakspere are first mentioned in Meres's *Palladis Tamia*, 1598: "The sweete wittie soule of *Ovid* lives in mellifluous and hony-tongued Shakespeare, witnes . . . his sugred Sonnets among his private friends." In the following year, 1599, Sonnets CXXXVIII. and CXLIV. were printed in the bookseller Jaggard's surreptitious miscellany, *The Passionate Pilgrim* (see Notes on these Sonnets). Both of these refer to a woman beloved by the writer: the second is that remarkable poem beginning

Two loves I have of comfort and despair.

For ten years we hear no more of the Sonnets. On May 20, 1609, *A book called Shakespeares Sonnettes* was entered on the Stationers' Register by Thomas Thorpe, and in the same year the Quarto edition appeared: " *Shake-speares Sonnets.* Never before Imprinted. At London by G. Eld for T. T. [Thomas Thorpe] and to be solde by William Apsley. 1609." [1] Edward Alleyn notes in that year that he bought a copy for fivepence. The Sonnets had not the popularity of Shakspere's other poems. No second edition was published until 1640 (printed 1639), when they formed part of " *Poems:* written by Wil. Shake-speare, Gent," a volume containing many pieces not by Shakspere. Here the Sonnets are printed with small regard to their order in the edition of 1609, in groups, with the poems of *The Passionate Pilgrim* interspersed, each group bearing a fanciful title. The bookseller Benson introduced the Poems with an address to The Reader, in which he

[1] Some copies instead of "William Apsley" have "John Wright, dwelling at Christ Churchgate."

asserts that they are "of the same purity the Authour then living avouched," and that the reader will find them "seren, clear, and elegantly plain." The titles given to the groups carry the suggestion that the Sonnets, with few exceptions, were addressed by a lover to his lady.

This edition of 1640 was reprinted several times in the eighteenth century; the text of the quarto 1609, by Lintott 1711, in Steevens's *Twenty Plays*, 1766, and by Malone. Gildon and Sewell, editors of the first half of the century, having the 1640 text before them, assumed that the Sonnets were addressed to Shakspere's mistress. It remained for the editors and critics of the second half of the century to discover that the greater number were written for a young man. To a careful reader of the original it needed small research to ascertain that a friend is addressed in the first hundred and twenty-five sonnets, to which the poem in twelve lines, numbered CXXVI., is an *Envoy*; while the Sonnets CXXVII.–CLIV. either address a mistress, or have reference to her and to the poet's passion for her.

The student of Shakspere is drawn to the Sonnets not alone by their ardour and depth of feeling, their fertility and condensation of thought, their exquisite felicities of phrase, and their frequent beauty of rhythmical movement, but in a peculiar degree by the possibility that here, if nowhere else, the greatest of English poets may —as Wordsworth puts it—have " unlocked his heart "[1]

---

[1] Poets differ in the interpretation of the Sonnets as widely as critics.

> " ' *With this same key*
> *Shakespeare unlocked his heart'* once more !
> Did Shakespeare ? If so, the less Shakespeare he !"

It were strange if his silence, deep as that of the secrets of Nature, never once knew interruption. The moment, however, we regard the Sonnets as autobiographical, we find ourselves in the presence of doubts and difficulties, exaggerated, it is true, by many writers, yet certainly real.

If we must escape from them, the simplest mode is to assume that the Sonnets are " the free outcome of a poetic imagination " (Delius). It is an ingenious suggestion of Delius that certain groups may be offsets from other poetical works of Shakspere. Those urging a beautiful youth to perpetuate his beauty in offspring may be a derivative from *Venus and Adonis;* those declaring love for a dark - complexioned woman may rehandle the theme set forth in Berowne's passion for the dark Rosaline of *Love's Labour's Lost;* those which tell of a mistress resigned to a friend may be a non-dramatic treatment of the theme of love and friendship

So, Mr. Browning; to whom replies Mr. Swinburne, " No whit the less like Shakespeare, but undoubtedly the less like Browning." Some of Shelley's feeling with reference to the Sonnets may be guessed from certain lines to be found among the *Studies for Epipsychidion and Cancelled Passages* (Poetical Works: ed. Forman, vol. ii. pp. 392, 393), to which my attention has been called by Mr. E. W. Gosse :—

> " If any should be curious to discover
> Whether to you I am a friend or lover,
> Let them read Shakspeare's sonnets, taking thence
> A whetstone for their dull intelligence
> That tears and will not cut, or let them guess
> How Diotima, the wise prophetess,
> Instructed the instructor, and why he
> Rebuked the infant spirit of melody
> On Agathon's sweet lips, which as he spoke
> Was as the lovely star when morn has broke
> The roof of darkness, in the golden dawn,
> Half-hidden and yet beautiful."

presented in the later scenes of *The Two Gentlemen of Verona.* Perhaps a few sonnets, as CX., CXI., refer to circumstances of Shakspere's life (Dyce). The main body of these poems may still be regarded as mere exercises of the fancy.

Such an explanation of the Sonnets has the merit of simplicity; it unties no knots but cuts all at a blow. If the collection consists of disconnected exercises of the fancy, we need not try to reconcile discrepancies, nor shape a story, nor ascertain a chronology, nor identify persons. And what indeed was a sonneteer's passion but a painted fire? What was the form of verse but an exotic curiously trained and tended, in which an artificial sentiment imported from Italy gave perfume and colour to the flower?

And yet, in this as in other forms, the poetry of the time, which possesses an enduring vitality, was not commonly caught out of the air, but—however large the conventional element in it may have been—was born of the union of heart and imagination: in it real feelings and real experience, submitting to the poetical fashions of the day, were raised to an ideal expression. Spenser wooed and wedded the Elizabeth of his *Amoretti.* The *Astrophel and Stella* tells of a veritable tragedy, fatal perhaps to two bright lives and passionate hearts. And what poems of Drummond do we remember as we remember those which record how he loved and lamented Mary Cunningham?

Some students of the Sonnets, who refuse to trace their origin to real incidents of Shakspere's life, allow that they form a connected poem, or at most two connected poems;

and these, they assure us, are of deeper significance than any mere poetical exercises can be. They form a stupendous allegory; they express a profound philosophy. The young friend whom Shakspere addresses is in truth the poet's Ideal Self or Ideal Manhood, or the Spirit of Beauty, or the Reason, or the Divine Logos; his dark mistress, whom a prosaic German translator (Jordan) takes for a mulatto or quadroon, is indeed Dramatic Art, or the Catholic Church, or the Bride of the Canticles, black but comely. Let us not smile too soon at the pranks of Puck among the critics; it is more prudent to move apart and feel gently whether that sleek nole with fair large ears may not have been slipped upon our own shoulders.

When we question saner critics why Shakspere's Sonnets may not be at once *Dichtung und Wahrheit*, poetry and truth, their answer amounts to this: Is it likely that Shakspere would so have rendered extravagant homage to a boy patron? Is it likely that one, who so deeply felt the moral order of the world, would have yielded, as the poems to his dark lady acknowledge, to a vulgar temptation of the senses? or, yielding, would have told his shame in verse? Objections are brought forward against identifying the youth of the Sonnets with Southampton or with Pembroke. It is pointed out that the writer speaks of himself as old, and *that* in a sonnet published in Shakspere's thirty-fifth year. Here evidently he cannot have spoken in his own person, and if not here, why elsewhere? Finally, it is asserted that the poems lack internal harmony: no real person can be—what Shakspere's friend is described as being—true and false, constant and fickle, virtuous and vicious, of hopeful expectation and publicly blamed for careless living.

Shakspere speaks of himself as old. True, but in the sonnet published in *The Passionate Pilgrim* (CXXXVIII.), he speaks as a lover, contrasting himself skilled in the lore of life with an inexperienced youth. Doubtless at thirty-five he was not a Florizel nor a Ferdinand. In the poems to his friend, Shakspere is addressing a young man perhaps of twenty years, in the fresh bloom of beauty ; he celebrates with delight the floral grace of youth, to which the first touch of time will be a taint; those lines of thought and care, which his own mirror shows, bear witness to time's ravage. It is as a poet that Shakspere writes, and his statistics are those not of arithmetic but of poetry.

That he should have given admiration and love without measure to a youth high born, brilliant, accomplished, who singled out the player for peculiar favour, will seem wonderful only to those who keep a constant guard upon their affections, and to those who have no need to keep a guard at all. In the Renascence epoch, among natural products of a time when life ran swift and free, touching with its current high and difficult places, the ardent friendship of man with man was one. To elevate it above mere personal regard a kind of Neo-Platonism was at hand, which represented Beauty and Love incarnated in a human creature as earthly vicegerents of the Divinity. " It was then not uncommon," observes the sober Dyce, " for one man to write verses to another in a strain of such tender affection as fully warrants us in terming them amatory." Montaigne, not prone to take up extreme positions, writes of his dead Estienne de la Boëtie with passionate tenderness which will not hear of moderation. The haughtiest spirit of Italy, Michael Angelo, does homage to the worth and beauty of young Tommaso Cavalieri in such words as these:

> *Heavenward your spirit stirreth me to strain ;*
> *E'en as you will I blush and blanch again,*
> *Freeze in the sun, burn 'neath a frosty sky,*
> *Your will includes and is the lord of mine.*

The learned Languet writes to young Philip Sidney : " Your portrait I kept with me some hours to feast my eyes on it, but my appetite was rather increased than diminished by the sight." And Sidney to his guardian friend : " The chief object of my life, next to the everlasting blessedness of heaven, will always be the enjoyment of true friendship, and there you shall have the chiefest place." The writer of amatory sonnets was expected as a matter of course to express an extravagance of sentiment. But friendship—a marriage of soul with soul—was looked upon as even a more ardent and more transcendent power than love. In Allot's *Wit's Commonwealth* (1598) we read : " The love of men to women is a thing common and of course, but the friendship of man to man infinite and immortal."[1] " Some," said Jeremy Taylor, " live under the line, and the beams of friendship in that position are imminent and perpendicular. Some have only a dark day and a long night from him [the Sun], snows and white cattle, a miserable life and a perpetual harvest of Catarrhes and Consumptions,

---

[1] I find this quotation in Elze's *William Shakespeare*, p. 497.

apoplexies and dead palsies : but some have splendid fires
and aromatick spices, rich wines and well-digested fruits,
great wit and great courage, because they dwell in his
eye and look in his face and are the Courtiers of the Sun,
and wait upon him in his Chambers of the East.   Just so
it is in friendship." Was Shakspere less a courtier of
the sun than Languet or Michael Angelo ?

If we accept the obvious reading of the Sonnets, we
must believe that Shakspere at some time of his life was
snared by a woman, the reverse of beautiful according to
the conventional Elizabethan standard — dark-haired,
dark-eyed, pale-cheeked (CXXXII.); skilled in touching the
virginal [1] (CXXVIII.); skilled also in playing on the heart
of man ; who could attract and repel, irritate and soothe,
join reproach with caress (CXLV.) ; a woman faithless to
her vow in wedlock (CLII.).   Through her no calm of joy
came to him ; his life ran quicker but more troubled
through her spell, and she mingled strange bitterness
with its waters.   Mistress of herself and of her art, she
turned, when it pleased her, from the player, to capture a

---

[1] In *Much Ado about Nothing* (II. iii.), Benedick describes the woman
whom he may love: " Of good discourse, an excellent musician, and her
hair shall be of what colour it please God." Hermann Isaac notices that
in the old play, *The Taming of a Shrew*, Katharine is a blonde beauty.
Ferando (Shakspere's Petruchio) describes her :

> Whiter than are the snowie Apenis,
> Or icie hair that grows on Boreas chin.
>
> *   *   *   *   *
>
> More faire and radiente is my bonie Kate
> Than silver Xanthus.

But Shakspere's Petruchio :

> Kate, like the hazel twig,
> Is straight and slender, and *as brown in hue*
> *As hazel nuts.*

more distinguished prize, his friend. For a while Shak-
spere was kept in the torture of doubt and suspicion ; then
confession and tears were offered by the youth. The
wound had gone deep into Shakspere's heart :—

> *Love knows it is a greater grief*
> *To bear love's wrong than hate's known injury.*

But, delivering himself from the intemperance of wrath,
he could forgive a young man beguiled and led astray.
Through further difficulties and estrangements their
friendship travelled on to a fortunate repose. The series
of Sonnets, which is its record, climbs to a high sunlit
resting-place. The other series, which records his passion
for a dark temptress, is a whirl of moral chaos. Whether
to dismiss him, or to draw him farther on, the woman had
urged upon him the claims of conscience and duty. In
the latest sonnets—if this series be arranged in chrono-
logical order — Shakspere's passion, grown bitter and
scornful (CLI., CLII.), strives, once for all, to defy and
wrestle down his better will.

Shakspere of the Sonnets is not the Shakspere serenely
victorious, infinitely charitable, wise with all wisdom of
the intellect and the heart, whom we know through *The
Tempest* and *King Henry VIII.* He is the Shakspere of
Venus and Adonis and *Romeo and Juliet,* on his way to
acquire some of the dark experience of *Measure for Mea-
sure,* and the bitter learning of *Troilus and Cressida.*
Shakspere's writings assure us that in the main his eye
was fixed on the true ends of life, but they do not lead
us to believe that he was inaccessible to temptations of
the senses, the heart, and the imagination. We can only

guess the frailty that accompanied such strength, the
risks that attended such high powers; immense demands
on life, vast ardours, and then the void hour, the deep
dejection.   There appears to have been a time in his life
when the springs of faith and hope had almost ceased to
flow; and he recovered these, not by flying from reality
and life, but by driving his shafts deeper towards the
centre of things.   So Ulysses was transformed into
Prospero, worldly wisdom into spiritual insight.   Such
ideal purity as Milton's was not possessed nor sought by
Shakspere.   Among these Sonnets, one or two might be
spoken by Mercutio, when his wit of cheveril was stretched
to an ell broad.   To compensate—Shakspere knew men
and women a good deal better than did Milton, and
probably no patches of his life are quite as unprofitably
ugly as some which disfigured the life of the great
idealist.   His daughter could love and honour Shakspere's
memory.   Lamentable it is, if he was taken in the toils,
but at least we know that he escaped all toils before the
end.   May we dare to conjecture that Cleopatra, queen
and courtesan, black from " Phœbus' amorous pinches," a
" lass unparalleled," has some kinship through the imagi-
nation with the dark lady of the virginal?   " Would I
had never seen her," sighs out Antony; and the shrewd
onlooker Enobarbus replies, " O sir, you had then left
unseen a wonderful piece of work, which not to have
been blest withal would have discredited your travel."

Shakspere did not, in Byron's manner, invite the
world to gaze upon his trespass and his griefs.   Setting
aside two pieces printed by a pirate in 1599, not one
of these poems, as far as we know, saw the light until

long after they were written, according to the most probable chronology; and when in 1609 the volume entitled *Shakespeare's Sonnets* was issued, it had, there is reason to believe, neither the superintendence nor the consent of the author.[1] Yet their literary merits entitled these poems to publication, and Shakspere's verse was popular. If they were written on fanciful themes, why were the Sonnets held so long in reserve ? If, on the other hand, they were connected with real persons and painful incidents, it was natural that they should not pass beyond the private friends of their possessor.

But the Sonnets of Shakspere, it is said, lack inward unity. Some might well be addressed to Queen Elizabeth, some to Anne Hathaway, some to his boy Hamnet, some to the Earl of Pembroke or the Earl of Southampton. It is impossible to make all these poems (I.–CXXVI.) apply to a single person. Difficulties of this kind may perplex a painful commentator, but would hardly occur to a lover or a friend living "where the beams of friendship are imminent." The youth addressed by Shakspere is "the master-mistress of his passion" (XX.); summing up the perfections of man and woman, of Helen and Adonis (LIII.); a liege, and yet through love a comrade; in years a boy, cherished as a son might be; in will a man, with all the power which rank and beauty give. Love, aching with its own monotony, invites imagination to invest it in changeful forms. Besides, the varying feelings of at least three years.

---

[1] The Quarto of 1609, though not carelessly printed, is far less accurate than *Venus and Adonis.* See note on CXXVI. for a curious error of printer or editor.

(CIV.)—three years of loss and gain, of love, wrong, wrath, sorrow, repentance, forgiveness, perfected union — are uttered in the Sonnets. When Shakspere began to write, his friend had the untried innocence of boyhood and an unspotted fame; afterwards came the offence and the dishonour. And the loving heart practised upon itself the piteous frauds of wounded affection.

> *How oft have poor abusèd I took part*
> *With Falsehood, only for to make thee true!*
> *How oft have I argued against my heart,*
> *Not suffering it to know that which it knew!*
> *And for I would not have thee what thou art,*
> *I made myself unto myself untrue.*[1]

Now he can credit no evil of the beloved, now he must believe the worst. While the world knows nothing but praise of one so dear, a private injury goes deep into the soul; when the world assails his reputation, straightway loyalty revives, and even puts a strain upon itself to hide each imperfection from view.

A painstaking student of the Sonnets, Henry Brown, was of opinion that Shakspere intended in these poems to satirize the sonnet-writers of his time, and in particular his contemporaries, Drayton and John Davies of Hereford. Professor Minto, while accepting the series I.–CXXVI. as of serious import, regards the sonnets addressed to a woman, CXXVII.–CLII., as "exercises of skill undertaken in a spirit of wanton defiance and derision of commonplace." Certainly if Shakspere is a satirist in I.–CXXVI., his irony is deep; the malicious smile was not noticed during

---

[1] Daniel: The letter of Octavia to Marcus Antonius. Stanza v.

two centuries and a half. The poems are in the taste of the time; less extravagant and less full of conceits than many other Elizabethan collections, more distinguished by exquisite imagination, and all that betokens genuine feeling; they are, as far as manner goes, such sonnets as Daniel might have chosen to write if he had had the imagination and the heart of Shakspere. All that is quaint or contorted or "conceited" in them can be paralleled from passages of early plays of Shakspere, such as *Romeo and Juliet* and *The Two Gentlemen of Verona*, where assuredly no satirical intention is discoverable. In the Sonnets CXXVII.–CLIV. Shakspere addresses a woman to whom it is impossible to pay the conventional homage of sonneteers: he cannot tell her that her cheeks are lilies and roses, her breast is of snow, her heart is chaste and cold as ice. Yet he loves her, and will give her tribute of verse. He praises her precisely as a woman who without beauty is clever and charming, and a coquette, would choose to be praised. True, she owns no commonplace attractions; she is no pink and white goddess; all her imperfections he sees. Yet she can fascinate by some nameless spell; she can turn the heart hot or cold. If she is not beautiful, it is because something more rare and fine takes the place of beauty. She angers her lover; he declares to her face that she is odious, and at the same moment he is at her feet.

A writer whose distinction it is to have produced the largest book upon the Sonnets, Mr. Gerald Massey, holds that he has rescued Shakspere's memory from shame by the discovery of a secret history legible in these

poems to rightly illuminated eyes.[1] In 1592, according
to this theory, Shakspere began to address pieces in
sonnet-form to his patron Southampton. Presently the
Earl engaged the poet to write love sonnets on his behalf
to Elizabeth Vernon; assuming also the feelings of
Elizabeth Vernon, Shakspere wrote dramatic sonnets, as
if in her person, to the Earl. The table-book containing
Shakspere's autograph sonnets was given by Southampton
to Pembroke, and at Pembroke's request (yet with a half-
satirical intention) was written the dark-woman series;
for Pembroke, although . history knows nothing of the
facts, was enamoured of Sidney's Stella, now well advanced
in years, the unhappy Lady Rich. A few of the sonnets
which pass for Shakspere's are really by Herbert, and
he, the "Mr. W. H." of Thorpe's dedication, is the "only
begetter," that is, procurer of these pieces for the
publisher. The Sonnets require rearrangement, and are
grouped in an order of his own by Mr. Massey.

Mr. Massey writes with zeal; with a faith in his own
opinions which finds scepticism hard to explain except on
some theory of intellectual or moral obliquity; and he
exhibits a wide, miscellaneous reading. The one thing
Mr. Massey's elaborate theory seems to me to lack is
some evidence in its support. His arguments may well
remain unanswered. One hardly knows how to tug at
the other end of a rope of sand.

With Wordsworth, Sir Henry Taylor, and Mr. Swin-
burne; with François-Victor Hugo, with Kreyssig, Ulrici,
Gervinus, and Hermann Isaac;[2] with Boaden, Armitage

---

[1] The first hint of this theory was given by Mrs. Jameson.
[2] A learned and thoughtful student of the Sonnets to whom I am

Brown, and Hallam; with Furnivall, Spalding, Rossetti, and Palgrave, I believe that Shakspere's Sonnets express his own feelings in his own person. To whom they were addressed is unknown. We shall never discover the name of that woman who for a season could sound, as no one else, the instrument in Shakspere's heart from the lowest note to the top of the compass. To the eyes of no diver among the wrecks of time will that curious talisman gleam. Already when Thorpe dedicated these poems to their "only begetter," she perhaps was lost in the quick-moving life of London, to all but a few in whose memory were stirred, as by a forlorn, small wind, the grey ashes of a fire gone out. As to the name of Shakspere's youthful friend and patron, we conjecture on slender evidence at the best. Setting claimants aside on whose behalf the evidence is absolutely none, except that their Christian name and surname begin with a W and an H, two remain whose pretensions have been supported by accomplished advocates. Drake (1817), a learned and refined writer, was the first to suggest that the friend addressed in Shakspere's Sonnets was Henry Wriothesley, Earl of Southampton, to whom *Venus and Adonis* was dedicated in 1593, and in the following year *Lucrece*, in words of strong devotion resembling those of the twenty-sixth Sonnet.[1] B. Heywood Bright (1819) and James Boaden (1832) in-dependently arrived at the conclusion that the Mr. W. H.

indebted for some valuable notes. See his Articles in *Archiv für das Studium der Neueren Sprachen und Literaturen*, 1878—9.

[1] Drake did not, as is sometimes stated, suppose that Mr. W. H. was Southampton. He took "begetter" to mean *obtainer*, and left Mr. W. H. unidentified. Others hold that "W. H." are the initials of South-ampton's names reversed as a blind to the public.

of the dedication, the " begetter " or inspirer of the
Sonnets, was William Herbert, Earl of Pembroke, to
whom with his brother, as two well-known patrons of
the great dramatist, his fellows Heminge and Condell
dedicated the First Folio. Wriothesley was born in 1573,
nine years after Shakspere; Herbert in 1580. Wriothes-
ley at an early age became the lover of Elizabeth Vernon,
needing therefore no entreaties to marry (I.-XVII.); he was
not beautiful; he bore no resemblance to his mother (III.
9); his life was active, with varying fortunes, to which
allusions might be looked for in the Sonnets, such as may
be found in the verses of his other poet, Daniel. Further,
it appears from the punning Sonnets (CXXXV. and CXLIII.,
see Notes), that the Christian name of Shakspere's friend
was the same as his own, *Will,* but Wriothesley's name
was Henry. To Herbert the punning Sonnets and the
" Mr. W. H." of the dedication can be made to apply.
He was indeed a nobleman in 1609, but a nobleman might
be styled *Mr.*; Lord Buckhurst is entered as *M.* Sack-
ville in *England's Parnassus* (Minto); or the *Mr.* may
have been meant to disguise the truth. Herbert was
beautiful; was like his illustrious mother; was brilliant,
accomplished, licentious; " the most universally beloved
and esteemed," says Clarendon, " of any man of his age."
Like Southampton, he was a patron of poets, and he loved
the theatre. In 1599 attempts were unsuccessfully made
to induce him to become a suitor for the hand of the Lord
Admiral's daughter. So far the balance leans towards
Herbert. But his father lived until 1601 (see XIII. and
Notes); Southampton's father died while his son was a
boy; and the date of Herbert's birth (1580), taken in

connection with Meres's mention of Sonnets, and the "Two loves" of the *Passionate Pilgrim* Sonnet (1599), CXLIV., may well cause a doubt.

A clue, which promises to lead us to clearness, and then deceives us into deeper twilight, is the characterisation (LXXVIII.–LXXXVI.) of a rival poet who for a time supplanted Shakspere in his patron's regard. This rival, the "better spirit" of LXXX., was learned (LXXVIII); dedicated a book to Shakspere's patron (LXXXII. and Notes); celebrated his beauty and knowledge (LXXXII.); in "hymns" (LXXXV.); was remarkable for "the full proud sail of his great verse" (LXXXVI., LXXX.); was taught "by spirits" to write "above a mortal pitch;" was nightly visited by "an affable familiar ghost," who "gulled him with intelligence" (LXXXVI.). Here are allusions and characteristics which ought to lead to identification. Yet in the end we are forced to confess that the poet remains as dim a figure as the patron.

Is it Spenser? He was learned, but what ghost was that which gulled him? Is it Marlowe? His verse was proud and full, and the creator of Faustus may well have had dealings with his own Mephistophelis; but Marlowe died in May, 1593, the year of *Venus and Adonis*. Is it Drayton, or Nash, or John Davies of Hereford? Persons in search of an ingeniously improbable opinion may chose any one of these. Is it Daniel? Daniel's reputation stood high; he was regarded as a master by Shakspere in his early poems; he was brought up at Wilton, the seat of the Pembrokes, and in 1601 he inscribed his *Defence of Ryme* to William Herbert; the Pembroke family favoured astrologers, and the ghost

that gulled Daniel may have been the same that gulled
Allen, Sandford, and Dr. Dee, and through them gulled
Herbert.   Here is at least a clever guess, and Boaden is
again the guesser.   But Professor Minto makes a guess
even more fortunate.   No Elizabethan poet wrote ampler
verse, none scorned " ignorance " more, or more haughtily
asserted his learning, than Chapman.   In *The Tears of
Peace* (1609), Homer as a spirit visits and inspires him:
the claim to such inspiration may have been often made
by the translator of Homer in earlier years.   Chapman
was pre-eminently the poet of Night.   *The Shadow of
Night*, with the motto, *Versus mei habebunt aliquantum
Noctis*, appeared in 1594 ; the title-page describes it as
containing " two poeticall *Hymnes.*"   In the dedication
Chapman assails unlearned " passion-driven men," " hide-
bound with affection to great men's fancies," and ridicules
the alleged eternity of their "idolatrous platts for riches."
" Now what a supererogation in wit this is, to think Skill
so mightily pierced with their loves, that she should
prostitutely show them her secrets, when she will scarcely
be looked upon by others, but with invocation, fasting,
watching ; yea, not without having drops of their souls
like a heavenly familiar."   Of Chapman's Homer a part
appeared in 1596 : dedicatory sonnets in a later edition
are addressed to both Southampton and Pembroke.

   Mr. W. H., the only begetter of the Sonnets, remains
unknown.   Even the meaning of the word " begetter " is
in dispute.   " I have some cousin-germans at court,"
writes Decker in *Satiromastix,* " shall *beget* you the
reversion of the master of the king's revels," where *beget*
evidently means *procure.*   Was the " begetter " of the

Sonnets, then, the person who procured them for Thorpe? I cannot think so. There is special point in the choice of the word "begetter," if the dedication be addressed to the person who inspired the poems and for whom they were written. Eternity through offspring is what Shakspere most desires for his friend. If he will not beget a child, then he is promised eternity in verse by his poet —in verse "whose influence is thine, and *born of thee*" (LXXVIII.). Thus was Mr. W. H. the begetter of these poems, and from the point of view of a complimentary dedication he might well be termed the *only* begetter.

I have no space to consider suggestions which seem to me of little weight—that W. H. is a misprint for W. S., meaning William Shakspere (Ingleby); that "W. H. all" should be read "W. Hall" (J. Forsyth); that W. H. stands for William Hammond (F. S. Ellis, Hazlitt),[1] or Henry Walker the godson of Shakspere, or William Houghton the dramatist, or William Hewes the musician;[2] that a full stop should be placed after "wisheth," making Mr. W. H., perhaps William Herbert or William Hathaway, the wisher of happiness to Southampton, the only begetter (Ph. Chasles and Bolton Corney); nor do I think we need argue for or against the supposition of a painful German commentator (Barnstorff), that Mr. W. H. is none other than Mr. William Himself. When Thorpe uses the words "the adventurer in setting forth," perhaps he meant to compare himself to one of the young

---

[1] *Notes and Queries*, Dec. 2, 1865.

[2] See Mr. C. Elliott Browne's letters in *The Athenæum*, 1873, ii. p. 277 and p. 336, who however does not maintain that this William Hewes was Mr. W. H.

volunteers in the days of Elizabeth and James, who embarked on naval enterprises, hoping to make their fortunes by discovery or conquest; so he with good wishes took his risk on the sea of public favour in this light venture of the Sonnets.[1]

The date at which the Sonnets were written, like their origin, is uncertain. Individual sonnets have been indicated as helping to ascertain the date.

I.—It has been confidently stated that CVII., containing the line,

> *The mortal moon hath her eclipse endured,*

must refer to the death of Elizabeth (1603), the poet's Cynthia; but the line may well bear another interpretation. (See Notes.)

II.—Mr. Tyler (*Athenæum*, Sept. 11, 1880) ingeniously argues that the thought and phrasing of lines in Sonnet LV. are derived from a passage in Meres's *Palladis Tamia*, 1598, where Shakspere among others is mentioned with honour:

"As Ovid saith of his worke:—

> *Jamque opus exegi, quod nec Jovis ira, nec ignis,*
> *Nec poterit ferrum, nec edax abolere vetustas :*

And as Horace saith of his:—

> *Exegi monumentum aere perennius,*
> *Begalique situ pyramidum altius ;*
> *Quod non imber edax, non Aquilo impotens*
> *Possit diruere, aut innumerabilis*
> *Annorum series et fuga temporum :*

---

[1] See Dr. Grosart's *Donne*, vol. ii. pp. 45, 46.

So say I severally of Sir Philip Sidney's, Spenser's, Daniel's, Drayton's, Shakespeare's, and Warner's worke:—

Nec Jovis ira, imbres, Mars, ferrum, flamma, senectus,
Hoc opus unda, lues, turbo, venena ruent.

Et quanquam ad pulcherrimum hoc opus evertendum tres illi Dii conspirabunt, Chronus, Vulcanus, et Pater ipse gentis;

Nec tamen annorum series, non flamma, nec ensis,
Aeternum potuit hoc abolere decus."

III.—The last line of Sonnet XCIV.,

Lilies that fester smell far worse than weeds,

occurs also in the play *King Edward III.* (printed 1596), in a part of the play ascribed by some critics to Shakspere. We cannot say for certain whether the play borrows from the sonnet, or the sonnet from the play. The latter seems to me the more likely supposition of the two.

The argument for this or that date from coincidences in expression between the Sonnets and certain plays of Shakspere has no decisive force. Coincidences may often be found between Shakspere's late and early plays. But the general characteristics of style may lead us to believe that some Sonnets, as I.–XXIV., belong to a period not later than *Romeo and Juliet;* others, as LXIV.–LXXIV., seem to echo the sadder tone heard in *Hamlet* and *Measure for Measure.* I cannot think that any of the Sonnets are earlier than Daniel's *Delia*

(1592), which, I believe, supplied Shakspere with a model for this form of verse; and though I can allege no strong evidence for the opinion, I should not be disposed to place any later than 1605.

Various attempts have been made by English, French, and German students to place the Sonnets in a new and better order, of which attempts no two agree between themselves. That the Sonnets are not printed in the Quarto, 1609, at haphazard, is evident from the fact that the *Envoy* (CXXVI.) is rightly placed; that poems addressed to a mistress follow those addressed to a friend; and that the two Cupid and Dian Sonnets stand together at the close. A nearer view makes it apparent that in the first series, I.-CXXVI., a continuous story is conducted through various stages to its termination; a more minute inspection discovers points of contact or connection between sonnet and sonnet, and a natural sequence of thought, passion and imagery. We are in the end convinced that no arrangement which has been proposed is as good as that of the Quarto. But the force of this remark seems to me to apply with certainty only to Sonnets I.-CXXVI. The second series, CXXVII.-CLIV., although some of its pieces are evidently connected with those which stand near them, does not exhibit a like intelligible sequence; a better arrangement may perhaps be found; or, it may be, no possible arrangement can educe order out of the struggles between will and judgment, between blood and reason; tumult and chaos are perhaps a portion of their life and being.

A piece of evidence confirming the opinion here advanced will be found in the use of *thou* and *you* by

Shakspere as a mode of address to his friend. Why *thou* or *you* is chosen, is not always explicable. Sometimes the choice seems to be determined by considerations of euphony, sometimes of rhyme; sometimes intimate affection seems to indicate the use of *you*, and respectful homage that of *thou;* but this is by no means invariable. What I would call attention to, however, as exhibiting something like order and progress in the arrangement of 1609, is this: that in the first fifty sonnets *you* is of extremely rare occurrence; in the second fifty *you* and *thou* alternate in little groups of sonnets, *thou* having still a preponderance, but now only a slight preponderance; in the remaining twenty-six *you* becomes the ordinary mode of address, and *thou* the exception. In the sonnets to a mistress, *thou* is invariably employed. A few sonnets of the first series, as LXIII.-LXVIII., have " my love," and the third person throughout.

The table on next page presents the facts. *Thou* and *you* are considered only when addressing friend or lover, not Time, the Muse, etc. Five sets of sonnets may then be distinguished, as in the table. I had hoped that this investigation was left to form one of my gleanings. But Professor Goedeke in the *Deutsche Rundschau,* March 1877, looked into the matter. His results seem to me vitiated by an arbitrary division of the sonnets using neither *thou* nor *you* into groups of eleven and twelve, and by a fantastic theory that Shakspere wrote his sonnets in books or groups of fourteen each.

A.	B.	C.	D.	E.
1–4	5			
6–12		13		
14		15–17		
18	19			
20	21			
22	23			24
	25			
26–32	33			
34–51		52–55	56	
		57–59		
60–62	63–68			
69–70		71–72		
73–74		75–76		
77–79		80–81		
82		83–86		
87–93	94			
95–97		98		
99			100–101	
		102–104	105	
		106		
107–110		111–115	116	
		117–118	119	
		120	121 (?)	
122	123–124			
125–126				

A.—Sonnets using *thou.* B.—Sonnets using neither *thou* nor *you*, but belonging to a *thou* group. C.—Sonnets using *you.* D.—Sonnets using neither *thou* nor *you*, but belonging to a *you* group. E.—Sonnet using both *thou* and *you.*

All Sonnets after the *Envoy*, 126, *i.e.*, all the Sonnets to a Mistress, use *thou.*

Whether idealising reality or wholly fanciful, an Elizabethan book of sonnets was—not always, but in many instances—made up of a chain or series of poems, in a designed or natural sequence, viewing in various aspects a single theme, or carrying on a love story to its issue, prosperous or the reverse. Sometimes advance is made through the need of discovering new points of view, and the movement, always delayed, is rather in a circuit than straight forward. In Spenser's *Amoretti* we read the progress of love from humility through hope to conquest.

In *Astrophel and Stella,* we read the story of passion struggling with untoward fate, yet at last mastered by the resolve to do high deeds.

> *Sweet ! for a while give respite to my heart,*
> *Which pants as though it still would leap to thee ;*
> *And on my thoughts give thy Lieutenancy*
> *To this great Cause.*

In *Parthenophil and Parthenophe* the story is of a new love supplanting an old, of hot and cold fevers, of despair, and, as last effort of the desperate lover, of an imagined attempt to subdue the affections of his cruel lady by magic art. But in reading Sidney, Spenser, Barnes, and still more Watson, Constable, Drayton, and others, although a large element of the art-poetry of the Renascence is common to them and Shakspere, the student of Shakspere's Sonnets does not feel at home. It is when we open Daniel's *Delia* that we recognize close kinship. The manner is the same, though the master proves himself of tardier imagination and less ardent temper. Diction, imagery, rhymes, and, in sonnets of like form, versification, distinctly resemble those of Shakspere. Malone was surely right when he recognized in Daniel the master of Shakspere as a writer of sonnets—a master quickly excelled by his pupil. And it is in Daniel that we find sonnet starting from sonnet almost in Shakspere's manner, only that Daniel often links poem with poem in more formal wise, the last or the penultimate line of one poem supplying the first line of that which immediately follows.

Let us attempt to trace briefly the sequence of in-

cidents and feelings in the Sonnets I.-CXXVI. A young
man, beautiful, brilliant, and accomplished, is the heir
of a great house: he is exposed to temptations of youth
and wealth and rank.   Possibly his mother desires to
see him married; certainly it is the desire of his friend.
" I should be glad if you were caught," writes Languet
to Philip Sidney, "that so you might give to your
country sons like yourself."   "If you marry a wife, and if
you beget children like yourself, you will be doing better
service to your country than if you were to cut the throats
of a thousand Spaniards and Frenchmen."   "'Sir,' said
Crœsus to Cambyses,' Languet writes to Sidney, now aged
twenty-four, 'I consider your father must be held your
better, because he was the father of an admirable prince,
whereas you have as yet no son like yourself.'"   It is in
the manner of Sidney's own Cecropia that Shakspere
urges marriage upon his friend.[1]   "Nature, when you
were first born, vowed you a woman, and as she made
you child of a mother, so to do your best to be mother
of a child" (Sonnet XIII. 14); "she gave you beauty to
move love; she gave you wit to know love; she gave you
an excellent body to reward love; which kind of liberal
rewarding is crowned with an unspeakable felicity. For
this as it bindeth the receiver, so it makes happy the
bestower; this doth not impoverish, but enrich the giver
(VI. 6) . . . O the comfort of comforts, to see your chil-
dren grow up, in whom you are as it were eternized! . . .
Have you ever seen a pure Rose-water kept in a crystal
glass? how fine it looks, how sweet it smells, while that

---

[1] *Arcadia,* lib. iii. Noticed by Mr. Massey in his *Shakespeare's Sonnets
and his Private Friends,* pp. 36, 37.

beautiful glass imprisons it! Break the prison and let the water take his own course, doth it not embrace dust, and lose all his former sweetness and fairness? Truly so are we, if we have not the stay, rather than the restraint of Crystalline marriage (v.). . . . And is a solitary life as good as this? Then, can one string make as good music as a consort. (VIII.) "[1]

In like manner Shakspere urges the youth to perpetuate his beauty in offspring (I.-XVII.).[2] But if *Will* refuses, then his poet will make war against Time and Decay, and confer immortality upon his beloved one by Verse (XV.-XIX.) *Will* is the pattern and exemplar of human beauty (XIX.), so uniting in himself the perfections of man and woman (XX.). This is no extravagant praise, but simple truth (XXI.). And such a being has exchanged love with Shakspere (XXII.), who must needs be silent with excess of passion (XXIII.), cherishing in his heart the image of his friend's beauty (XXIV.), but holding still more dear the love from which no unkind fortune can ever separate him (XXV.). Here affairs of his own compel Shakspere to a journey which removes him from *Will* (XXVI., XXVII.). Sleepless at night, and toiling by day, he thinks of the absent one (XXVII., XXVIII.); grieving for his own poor estate (XXIX.), and the death of friends, but finding in the one beloved amends for all (XXX., XXXI.); and so Shakspere commends to his friend his poor verses as a token of affection which may survive if

---

[1] For additional parallels from Sidney, see the article by Fritz Krauss, "Die schwarze Schöne der Shakespeare-Sonette," in *Shakespeare Jahrbuch*, 1881.

[2] In what follows, to avoid the confusion of *he* and *him*, I call Shakspere's friend, as he is called in CXXXV., *Will.*

he himself should die (XXXII.). At this point the mood changes—in his absence his friend has been false to friendship (XXXIII.); now, indeed, *Will* would let the sunshine of his favour beam out again, but that will not cure the disgrace; tears and penitence are fitter (XXXIV.); and for sake of such tears *Will* shall be forgiven (XXXV.); but henceforth their lives must run apart (XXXVI.); Shakspere, separated from *Will*, can look on and rejoice in his friend's happiness and honour (XXXVII.), singing his praise in verse (XXXVIII.), which he could not do if they were so united that to praise his friend were self-praise (XXXIX.); separated they must be, and even their loves be no longer one; Shakspere can now give his love, even her he loved, to the gentle thief; wronged though he is, he will still hold *Will* dear (XL.); what is he but a boy whom a woman has beguiled (XLI.)? and for both, for friend and mistress, in the midst of his pain, he will try to feign excuses (XLII.). Here there seems to be a gap of time. The Sonnets begin again in absence, and some students have called this, perhaps rightly, the Second Absence (XLIII., *sqq.*). His friend continues as dear as ever, but confidence is shaken, and a deep distrust begins to grow (XLVIII.). What right indeed has a poor player to claim constancy and love (XLIX.)? He is on a journey which removes him from *Will* (L., LI.). His friend perhaps professes unshaken loyalty, for Shakspere now takes heart, and praises *Will's* truth (LIII., LIV.)—takes heart, and believes that his own verse will for ever keep that truth in mind. He will endure the pain of absence, and have no jealous thoughts (LVII., LVIII.); striving to honour his friend in song better than ever man was honoured before (LIX.); in song which

shall outlast the revolutions of time (LX.). Still he cannot
quite get rid of jealous fears (LXI.); and yet, what right
has one so worn by years and care to claim a young man's
love (LXII.)? *Will*, too, in his turn must fade, but his
beauty will survive in verse (LXIII.). Alas! to think that
death will take away the beloved one (LXIV.); nothing
but Verse can defeat time and decay (LXV.). For his
own part Shakspere would willingly die, were it not that,
dying, he would leave his friend alone in an evil world
(LXVI.). Why should one so beautiful live to grace this
ill world (LXVII.), except as a survival of the genuine
beauty of the good old times (LXVIII.); yet beautiful as
he is, he is blamed for careless living (LIX.); but surely
this must be slander (LXX.). Shakspere here returns to
the thought of his own death When I leave this vile
world let me be forgotten (LXXI., LXXII.); and my
death is not very far off (LXXIII.); but when I die my
spirit still lives in my verse (LXXIV.). A new group
seems to begin with LXXV. Shakspere loves his friend as
a miser loves his gold, fearing it may be stolen (fearing a
rival poet?). His verse is monotonous and old-fashioned
(not like the rival's verse?) (LXXVI.); so he sends *Will*
his manuscript book unfilled, which *Will* may fill, if he
please, with verse of his own; Shakspere chooses to sing
no more of Beauty and of Time; *Will's* glass and dial
may inform him henceforth on these topics (LXXVII.). The
rival poet has now won the first place in *Will's* esteem
(LXXVIII.-LXXXVI.). Shakspere must bid his friend fare-
well (LXXXVII.) If *Will* should scorn him, Shakspere will
side against himself (LXXXVIII., LXXXIX.). But if his
friend is ever to hate him, let it be at once, that the

bitterness of death may soon be past (XC.). He has dared
to say farewell, yet his friend's love is all the world to
Shakspere, and the fear of losing him is misery (XCI.);
but he cannot really lose his friend, for death would come
quickly to save him from such grief; and yet *Will* may be
false and Shakspere never know it (XCII.); so his friend,
fair in seeming, false within, would be like Eve's apple
(XCIII.); it is to such self-contained, passionless persons
that nature entrusts her rarest gifts of grace and beauty ;
yet vicious self-indulgence will spoil the fairest human
soul (XCIV.). So let *Will* beware of his youthful vices,
already whispered by the lips of men (XCV.); true, he
makes graces out of faults, yet this should be kept within
bounds (XCVI.). Here again, perhaps, is a gap of time.[1]
Sonnets XCVII.-XCIX. are written in absence, which some
students, perhaps rightly, call Third Absence. These
three sonnets are full of tender affection, but at the close
of XCIX. allusion is made to *Will's* vices, the canker in
the rose. After this followed a period of silence. In C.
love begins to renew itself, and song awakes. Shakspere
excuses his silence (CI.); his love has grown while he was
silent (CII.); his friend's loveliness is better than all song
(CIII.); three years have passed since first acquaintance ;
Will looks as young as ever, yet time must insensibly
be altering his beauty' (CIV.). Shakspere sings with a
monotony of love (CV.). All former singers praising
knights and ladies only prophesied concerning *Will*

---

[1] The last two lines of XCVI.—not very appropriate, I think, in that
sonnet—are identical with the last two lines of XXXVI. It occurs to me
as a possibility that the MS. in Thorpe's hands may here have been im-
perfect, and that he filled it up so far as to complete XCVI. with a couplet
from an earlier sonnet.

(CVI.); grief and fear are past; the two friends are reconciled again; and both live for ever united in Shakspere's verse (CVII.). Love has conquered time and age, which destroy mere beauty of face (CVIII.). Shakspere confesses his errors, but now he has returned to his home of love (CIX.), he will never wander again (CX.); and his past faults were caused by his temptations as a player (CXI.); he cares for no blame and no praise now except those of his friend (CXII.). Once more he is absent from his friend (Fourth Absence ?), but full of loving thought of him (CXIII., CXIV.). Love has grown, and will grow yet more (CXV.). Love is unconquered by Time (CXVI.). Shakspere confesses again his wanderings from his friend; they were tests of *Will's* constancy (CXVII.); and they quickened his own appetite for genuine love (CXVIII.). Ruined love rebuilt is stronger than at first (CXIX.); there were wrongs on both sides, and must now be mutual forgiveness (CXX.). Shakspere is not to be judged by the report of malicious censors (CXXI.); he has given away his friend's present of a table-book, because he needed no remembrancer (CXXII.); records and registers of time are false; only a lover's memory is to be wholly trusted, recognizing old things in what seem new (CXXIII.); Shakspere's love is not based on self-interest, and therefore is uninfluenced by fortune (CXXIV.); nor is it founded on external beauty of form or face, but is simple love for love's sake (CXXV.). *Will* is still young and fair, yet he should remember that the end must come at last (CXXVI.). ·

Thus the series of poems addressed to his friend closes gravely with thoughts of love and death. The Sonnets may be divided at pleasure into many smaller groups, but

I find it possible to go on without interruption from I. to
XXXII.; from XXXIII. to XLII.; from XLIII. to LXXIV.; from
LXXV. to XCVI.; from XCVII. to XCIX.; from C. to CXXVI.[1]

I do not here attempt to trace a continuous sequence in
the Sonnets addressed to the dark-haired woman (CXXVII.-
CLIV.); I doubt whether such continuous sequence is to
be found in them; but in the Notes some points of con-
nection between sonnet and sonnet are pointed out.

If Shakspere "unlocked his heart" in these Sonnets,
what do we learn from them of that great heart? I can-
not answer otherwise than in words of my own formerly
written. "In the Sonnets we recognise three things:
that Shakspere was capable of measureless personal devo-
tion; that he was tenderly sensitive, sensitive above all
to every diminution or alteration of that love his heart
so eagerly craved; and that, when wronged, although he
suffered anguish, he transcended his private injury, and
learned to forgive. . . . The errors of his heart originated
in his sensitiveness, in his imagination (not at first inured
to the hardness of fidelity to the fact), in his quick con-
sciousness of existence, and in the self-abandoning devo-
tion of his heart. There are some noble lines by Chapman
in which he pictures to himself the life of great energy,
enthusiasms, and passions, which for ever stands upon the
edge of utmost danger, and yet for ever remains in ab-
solute security :—

> *Give me a spirit that on this life's rough sea*
> *Loves to have his sails fill'd with a lusty wind*

---

[1] Perhaps there is a break at LVIII. The most careful studies of the
sequence of the Sonnets are Mr. Furnivall's in his preface to the *Leopold
Shakspere*, and Mr. Spalding's in *The Gentleman's Magazine*, March, 1878.

Even till his sail-yards tremble, his masts crack,
And his rapt ship runs on her side so low
That she drinks water, and her keel ploughs air ;
There is no danger to a man that knows
What life and death is,—there's not any law
Exceeds his knowledge ; neither is it lawful
That he should stoop to any other law.

Such a master-spirit, pressing forward under strained canvas, was Shakspere. If the ship dipped and drank water, she rose again ; and at length we behold her within view of her haven, sailing under a large, calm wind, not without tokens of stress of weather, but if battered, yet unbroken by the waves." The last plays of Shakspere, *The Tempest, Cymbeline, Winter's Tale, Henry VIII.,* illuminate the Sonnets and justify the moral genius of their writer.

I thank Professor Atkinson for help given in reading the proof-sheets of my Introduction ; Mr. W. J. Craig, for illustrations of obsolete words ; Mr. Furnivall, for hints given from time to time in our discussion by letter of the grouping of the Sonnets ; Mr. Edmund Gosse and Dr. Grosart, for the loan of valuable books ; Mr. Halliwell-Phillipps, for a note on the date of Lintott's reprint ; Prof. Hales and Mr. Hart, for several ingenious suggestions ; and Mr. L. C. Purser, for translations of the Greek epigrams connected with Sonnets CLIII., CLIV.

PART II.

WHILE reading or glancing through various books, review articles, and scattered fragments of criticism on the Sonnets, I made notes of their contents. These, being now put together, form a history of opinion respecting Shakspere's Sonnets as curious and perhaps as edifying as a history of opinion respecting the Apocalyptic number 666 might be. My notes may at least serve the useful purpose of helping students to avoid certain false guides. But it will be seen that among the writers on the Sonnets are several both learned and judicious.

I do not attempt a Bibliography of the Editions of the Sonnets, for with the materials at my disposal such a bibliography would be far from complete. Nor do my notes give a view of the entire critical literature of the subject. Still, they do not omit a great deal, and I fear they are amply sufficient to exhaust the patience of a well-disposed reader who should try to make his way straight through them, and not use them (as I have hoped that they may be used) rather for the purpose of reference.[1]

---

[1] Mr. Swinburne, in his "full and heightened style," writes : "Upon the Sonnets such a preposterous pyramid of presumptuous commentary has long since been reared by the Cimmerian speculation and Bœotian 'brain-sweat' of Sciolists and Scholiasts, that no modest man will hope, and no wise man will desire, to add to the structure or subtract from it one single brick of proof or disproof, theorem or theory."

Among books or pamphlets which I have not seen are the following:—Albert (Rev. John Armstrong), *Sonnets from Shakespeare*, 8vo, 1791; Alger (W. R.), *Shakespeare's Sonnets and Friendship;* Donnelly (I.), *The Sonnets of Shakspeare;* Hillard (K.), *The Study of Shakespeare's Sonnets;* Richardson (D. L.), *Literary Leaves; Shakspeare's Sonnets* (American Review, 1847). I shall be glad if any reader will favour me with notes on any of these or other studies unknown to me which illustrate the Sonnets, and should this book reach a second edition, I will make use of such information.

Tieck's novel (1829), *Der Dichter und sein Freund*, and the romance by H. König (1839), *William's Dichten und Trachten*, I have not read.

Of translations of the Sonnets my knowledge is very imperfect. I have selected for notice two as distinguished for high literary merits—that of Bodenstedt into German, and that of F. Victor-Hugo into French. I am not able to furnish a complete list of translations, but I may mention the French translation by Lafont (1856), and those in German by Lachmann (1820), Wagner (1840), Jordan (1861), Gelbcke (1867), Simrock (1867), H. von Friesen (1869), Tschischwitz (1870), Gildemeister (1871), Krauss (1872), Neidhardt (no date on title-page). Gildemeister in the main agrees with Delius in his view of the Sonnets; Krauss and Gelbcke follow Massey. The Sonnets have been translated into Dutch by Professor Burgersdijk (1879).

I have to acknowledge my obligations to Mr. Justin Winsor's *Bibliography of the Earlier Editions of Shakespeare's Poems* (Cambridge, Mass., 1879); and to Mr. Hubbard's valuable *Catalogue of Works relating to William Shakespeare and his Writings, in the Barton Collection, Boston Public Library.*

THE SONNETS BEFORE 1609.

The first mention of sonnets by Shakspere occurs in the *Palladis Tamia* of Francis Meres, 1598. " As the soule of *Euphorbus* was thought to liue in *Pythagoras*, so the sweete wittie soule of *Ovid* liues in mellifluous and hony-tongued Shakespeare, witnes his *Venus and Adonis*, his *Lucrece*, his sugred Sonnets among his priuate friends." In the following year (1599) the bookseller Jaggard published *The Passionate Pilgrim. By W. Shakespeare* —a surreptitious collection, of which few pieces are by Shakspere. It opens with two sonnets, those numbered CXXXVIII. and CXLIV. in the edition of 1609. In one of these sonnets occur the words, " I know my years are past the best." Both refer to a woman beloved by the writer. The second is that remarkable sonnet opening with the lines :—

> *Two loves I have, of comfort and despair,*
> *That like two spirits do suggest me still ;*
> *My better angel is a man right fair,*
> *My worser spirit a woman colour'd ill.*

The text of these Sonnets varies slightly from that of the edition of 1609 ; the variations will be found in my notes on Sonnets CXXXVIII. and CXLIV.

In *Stationers' Register*, January 3, 1599-1600, we find, " Entred for his copye under the handes of the Warden

a book called Amours by J. D., with certen other son-
nettes by W. S." Possibly these are sonnets by Shak-
spere. No copy of the book is known.

WILLOBIE'S AVISA, 1594, AND ITS SUPPOSED CONNECTION
WITH SHAKSPERE'S SONNETS.

"Willobie his Avisa or the true Picture of a modest
maid, and of a chast and constant wife" was "imprinted
at London by John Windet, 1594." Hadrian Dorrell in
an epistle to the reader "from my chamber in Oxford"
states that not long since his friend and chamber fellow,
M. Henry Willobie, a young man and a scholar of
very good hope, being desirous to see the fashions of
other countries, departed voluntarily on her Majesty's
service. Among Willobie's papers this poem was found
by Dorrell, who took upon himself to publish it during
Willobie's absence. A second edition appeared in 1596,
to which Dorrell prefixed an "Apologie showing the true
meaning of Willobie his Avisa." Here, contradicting his
first statement, he says that this poetical fiction "was
penned by the Author at least for thirty and five years
since,". and speaks of Willobie as "now of late gone to
God."

A Henry Willobie, aged sixteen, matriculated in St.
John's College, Oxford, 1591. No Hadrian Dorrell is
known. Dr. Ingleby (New Shakspere Society's *Shak-
spere Allusion-books*, Part I., and General Introduction, pp.
xxviii.-xxxi.) supposes that Hadrian Dorrell was the real
author, and that in what he tells us of Willobie he is

hoaxing us. Dr. Grosart (Introduction to his edition of *Willobie's Avisa,* printed for the subscribers, 1880) is of opinion that some person unknown, assuming the name of Hadrian Dorrell, wrote the poem, and further to conceal his authorship ascribed it to a real Henry Willobie. "Willobie his Avisa" is a poem of seventy-two cantos in six-line stanzas, celebrating the chastity of Avisa as maid and wife. Whether Avisa was an ideal of the writer's imagination, or, as seems more likely, a living woman, we cannot be certain.

Some commendatory verses, signed "Contraria Contrariis, Vigilantius Dormitanus," contain the earliest printed mention of Shakspere by name yet discovered:—

> *Yet* Tarquyne *plucked his glistering grape,*
> *And* Shake-speare *paints poore* Lucreece *rape.*

The following passage in prose introduces Canto XLIV., and the W. S. of this curious passage has been supposed to mean William Shakspere.

> "*Henrico Willobego.   Italo-Hispalensis.*[1]

"H. W. being sodenly affected with the contagion of a fantasticall fit, at the first sight of A. [Avisa] pyneth a while in secret griefe, at length not able any longer to indure the burning heate of so fervent a humour, bewrayeth the secresy of his disease vnto his familiar frend

---

[1] The chastity of Avisa is tried by the assaults of passion as seen in men of various nations, French, German, etc. How Willobie can be "Italo-Hispalensis" remains unexplained, unless it has reference to his travels abroad.

W. S., who not long before had tryed the curtesy of the like passion, and was now newly recovered of the like infection; yet finding his frend let blood in the same vaine, he took pleasure for a tyme to see him bleed, and in steed of stopping the issue, he inlargeth the wound, with the sharpe rasor of a willing conceit, persuading him that he thought it a matter very easy to be compassed, and no doubt with payne, diligence, and some cost in tyme to be obtayned. Thus this miserable comforter comforting his frend with an impossibilitie eyther for that he now would secretly laugh at his frends folly, that had given occasion not long before vnto others to laugh at his owne, or because he would see whether an other could play his part better than himselfe and in vewing a far off the course of this louing Comedy, he determined to see whether it would sort to a happier end for this new actor, then it did for the old player. But at length this Comedy was like to haue growen to a Tragedy, by the weake and feeble estate that H. W. was brought vnto, by a desperate vewe of an impossibility of obtaining his purpose, til Time and Necessity, being his best Phisitions brought him a plaster, if not to heale, yet in part to ease his maladye. In all which discourse is liuely represented the vnrewly rage of vnbrydeled fancy, hauing the raines to roue at liberty, with the dyuers and sundry changes of affections and temptations, which Will, let loose from Reason, can devise," etc. From Canto XLIV. to XLVIII. W. S. addresses H. W. on his love-affair, and H. W. replies.

As affording presumptions that W. S. may be William Shakspere, we may notice:—

1st.—The fact that Shakspere is mentioned in the commendatory poem.

2nd.—The fact that Shakspere was, by virtue of *Venus and Adonis,* an authority on love and how to woo.

3rd.—The theatrical phraseology in the passage, " the new actor," " the old player," " Tragedy," and " Comedy." [1]

4th.—The fact that Canto XLVII. of " Willobie his Avisa," W. S.'s advice to Willobie as to how to compass his desire, strikingly resembles the poem in the same stanza, No. 19 of *The Passionate Pilgrim,* beginning :—

When as thine eye hath chose the dame, etc.

Dr. Grosart is " inclined to conjecture that Shakespeare may have sent his friend H. W., or Dorrell, this identical poem (19 of Pass. Pilg.), while in *Avisa* we have recollections of actual conversations between Shakespeare and his love-lorn friend."

Assuming that W. S. is William Shakspere, we learn that he had loved and recovered from the infection of his passion before the end of 1594. The chaste Avisa is as unlike as possible the dark woman of the Sonnets ; nor does anything appear which can connect Henry Willobie with Shakspere's young friend of the Sonnets, except the fact that the initials of the only begetter's name were W. H., those of Henry Willobie reversed, and that Henry

---

[1] The force of the allusion to tragedy and comedy is weakened by the fact that we find in *Alcilia* (1595) the course of love spoken of as a tragi-comedy, where no reference to a real actor on the stage is intended : *Sic incipit stultorum Tragicomoedia.*

Willobie assails the chastity of a married woman. He is, however, repulsed by the chaste Avisa.

Except in the reference to W. S.'s love, and his recovery from passion, I see no possible point of connection between *Willobie's Avisa* and Shakspere's Sonnets. The book, even as reprinted by Dr. Grosart, is not accessible to all readers, and the curiosity of some has perhaps been quickened by Mr. Swinburne's reference to it as "the one contemporary book which has ever been supposed to throw any direct or indirect light on the mystic matter [of the Sonnets];" while of Dr. Grosart's promised reprint, Mr. Swinburne spoke as of "the one inestimable boon long hoped for against hoping, and as yet but 'a vision of a dream' to the most learned and most loving of true Shakespearean students" (*A Study of Shakespeare*, pp. 62, 63). The literary merits of *Willobie's Avisa* are few and slight.

THE QUARTO EDITION OF 1609, AND REPRINTS OF THE SAME.[1]

Shakspere's Sonnets are entered on the Stationers' Registers in the following words :—

"20 maii [1609]. Thomas Thorpe entred for his copie vnder th[e h]andes of master Wilson and master Lownes warden, a Booke called Shakespeare's Sonnetes." vjd.

In that year, 1609, appeared the first edition :—

Shake-speares Sonnets. Neuer before Imprinted. At London. By G. Eld for T. T., and are to be solde by William Apsley, 1609.

[1] Partly from Mr. Justin Winsor's Bibliography.

Some copies instead of " William Apsley " have " Iohn Wright, dwelling at Christ Churchgate."

Description.—Sig. A, two leaves; text B to K, in fours; L, two leaves; forty leaves in all. The book contains one hundred and fifty-four Sonnets, ending on the recto of K 1, and on the verso begins A louers Complaint. By William Shakespeare.

Reprints.—I. A Collection of poems, in two volumes; being all the miscellanies of Mr. William Shakespeare, which were publish'd by himself in the year 1609, and now correctly printed from those editions. The first volume contains : I. Venus and Adonis. II. The rape of Lucrece. III. The passionate pilgrim. IV. Some sonnets set to sundry notes of musick. The second volume contains—I. One hundred and fifty-four Sonnets, all of them in praise of his mistress. II. A lover's complaint of his angry mistress. London : B. Lintott. [No date.] This reprint—Lintott's *second* volume—is advertised in the Post Boy of 24th–27th Feb., 1710-11. The copy Lintott used was furnished by Congreve (according to Malone, *An Inquiry into the authenticity of certain miscellaneous papers*, etc., p. 28).

II.—In vol. iv. of Steevens's " Twenty Plays," 1766.

III.—A lithographic fac-simile of the copy with Wright's imprint, found by Professor Mommsen in the dispersed Bentinck Library at Varel, near Oldenburg, was made in 1857.

IV.—In 1862 Lovell Reeve issued, under Staunton's direction, a fac-simile by photo-zincography of the Ellesmere (Apsley imprint) copy.

V.—In 1870, John Russell Smith issued an Apsley reprint "in the orthography and punctuation of the original."

BEN JONSON.

Some critics have supposed that Ben Jonson alludes to Thorpe's dedication of Shakspere's Sonnets in the following words of his own dedication of "Epigrams" to William Herbert, Earl of Pembroke. "My Lord,—While you cannot change your merit, *I dare not change your title;* it was that made it and not I. Under which name I here offer to your Lordship the ripest of my studies, my Epigrams; which though they carry danger in the sound, do not therefore seek your shelter; for, when I made them, I had nóthing in my conscience, to expressing of which I did need a cypher."

The following from *Bartholomew Fair* (Act v. Scene 3) has also been pointed out as perhaps referring to the Sonnets. "*Cokes.* A motion! What's that? [*Reads.*] *The ancient modern history of Hero and Leander, otherwise called the Touchstone of true Love, with as true a trial of friendship between Damon and Pythias, two faithful friends o' the Bankside.*" Damon and Pythias "have both but one drab."[1]

THE SONNETS IN "POEMS," 1640.[2]

Poems: Written by Wil. Shake-speare, Gent. Printed at *London* by *Tho. Cotes,* and are to be sold by *Iohn Benson,* dwelling in *St. Dunstan's* Church-yard. 1640.

[1] See Karl Elze: *William Shakespeare*, p. 499.
[2] Partly from Mr. Justin Winsor's Bibliography.

Description.—Opposite the title is a portrait of Shakespeare. " W. M[arshall] sculpsit."

Title, one leaf; To the Reader, signed I. B., two pages; Poems by L. Digges, three pages; Poem by John Warren, one page; a second title, omitting only the date; sig. A 1; text A 2 to M 4. At sig. L 2 is "an Addition of some Excellent Poems;" 191 pp. sm. 8vo.

Dr. Bliss had a leaf of this edition, with a contemporary manuscript note, showing that it was printed in 1639, and was sold bound for fifteen pence.

Contents.—To the reader, by I. B.; Verses by Leon. Digges and John Warren; Poems by Will. Shakespeare, Gent.; An addition of some excellent poems, to those precedent, of renowned Shakespeare, by other gentlemen: His mistresse drawn by B. I.; Her minde by B. I.; To Ben Johnson by F. B.; His mistres shade; Lavinia walking in a frosty morning; A sigh sent to his mistresse; An allegorical allusion of melancholy thoughts to bees by I. G.; The primrose; A sigh; A blush; Orpheus lute; Am I dispised? Vpon a gentlewoman walking on the grasse; On his love going to sea; Aske me no more.

The poems ascribed to Shakespeare are the Sonnets, with the exception of Nos. 18, 19, 43, 56, 75, 76, 96, 126, rearranged under various titles. Interspersed with them are " A lover's complaint," and "The passionate pilgrim," together with the verses from " As you like it," commencing, " Why should this desart be." In addition to these are the following translations from Ovid: " The Tale of Cephalus and Procris, That Menelaus was cause of his owne wrongs, Vulcan was Iupiters Smith, The History how the Mynotaure was begot, This Myno-

taure, when hee come to growth, was incloased in the
Laborinth, Achilles his concealement of his sex, The
amorous Epistle of Paris to Hellen, Hellen to Paris."
Following these are Milton's "Epitaph," "On the death
of Shakespeare," by W. B., and "An elegie on the death
of that famous writer and actor, M. William Shakspeare."

The following is the arrangement of the Sonnets in
groups, with the poems of "The Passionate Pilgrim"
(marked P. P.) interspersed :—

The Glory of Beauty, LXVII., LXVIII., LXIX. ; Injurious
Time, LX., LXIII., LXIV., LXV., LXVI ; True Admiration,
LIII., LIV. ; The Force of Love, LVII., LVIII. ; The Beauty
of Nature, LIX. ; Love's Cruelty, I., II., III. ; Youthful
Glory, XIII., XIV., XV. ; Good Admonition, XVI., XVII. ;
Quick Prevention, VII. ; Magazine of Beauty, IV., V., VI. ;
An Invitation to Marriage, VIII., IX., X., XI., XII. ; False
Belief, CXXXVIII. ; A Temptation, CXLIV. ; Fast and
Loose, P. P. I. ; True Content, XXI. ; A bashful Lover,
XXIII.; Strong Conceit, XXII.; A sweet Provocation, P. P.
XI. ; A constant Vow, P. P. III.; The Exchange, XX. ; A
Disconsolation, XXVII., XXVIII., XXIX. ; Cruel Deceit, P. P.
IV. ; The Unconstant Lover, P. P. V. ; The Benefit of
Friendship, XXX., XXXI., XXXII. ; Friendly concord, P. P.
VI. ; Inhumanity, P. P. VII. ; A Congratulation, XXXVIII.,
XXXIX., XL. ; Loss and Gain, XLI., XLII. ; Foolish Disdain,
P. P. IX. ; Ancient Antipathy, P. P. X. ; Beauty's Valua-
tion, P. P. XI.; Melancholy Thoughts, XLIV., XLV. ; Love's
Loss, P. P. VIII. ; Love's Relief, XXXIII., XXXIV., XXXV. ;
Unanimity, XXXVI., XXXVII.; Loth to depart, P. P. XII.,
XIII. ; A Masterpiece, 24; Happiness in Content, XXV. ;
A Dutiful Message, XXVI; Go and come quickly, L., LI. ;

Two Faithful Friends, XLVI., XLVII.; Careless neglect, XLVIII.; Stout resolution, XLIX.; A Duel, P. P. XIV.; Love-sick, P. P. XV.; Love's Labour Lost, P. P. XVI.; Wholesome Counsel, P. P. XVII.; Sat fuisse, LXII.; A living Monument, LV.; Familiarity breeds Contempt, LII.; Patiens Armatus, LXI.; A Valediction, LXXI., LXXII., LXXIV.; Nil Magnis Invidia, LXX.; Love-sick, LXXX., LXXXI.; The Picture of true Love, CXVI.; In Praise of his Love, LXXXII., LXXXIII., LXXXIV., LXXXV.; A Resignation, LXXXVI., LXXXVII.; Sympathising Love, P. P. XVIII.; A Request to his Scornful Love, LXXXVIII., LXXXIX., XC., XCI.; A Lover's Affection, though his Love prove Unconstant, XCII., XCIII., XCIV., XCV.; Complaint for his Lover's Absence, XCVII., XCVIII., XCIX.; An Invocation to his Muse, C., CI.; Constant Affection, CIV., CV., CVI.; Amazement, CII., CIII.; A Lover's Excuse for his long Absence, CIX., CX.; A Complaint, CXI., CXII.; Self-flattery of her Beauty, CXIII., CXIV., CXV.; A Trial of Love's Constancy, CXVII., CXVIII., CXIX.; A good Construction of his Love's Unkindness, CXX.; Error in Opinion, CXXI.; Upon the Receipt of a Table-Book from his Mistress, CXXII.; A Vow, CXXIII.; Love's Safety, CXXIV.; An Entreaty for her Acceptance, CXXV.; Upon her playing upon the Virginals, CXXVIII.; Immoderate Lust, CXXIX.; In praise of her Beauty, though Black, CXXVII., CXXX., CXXXI., CXXXII.; Unkind Abuse, CXXXIII., CXXXIV.; Love-suit, CXXXV., CXXXVI.; His heart wounded by her Eye, CXXXVII., CXXXIX., CXL.; A Protestation, CXLI., CXLII; An Allusion, 143; Life and Death, CXLV.; A consideration of Death, CXLVI.; Immoderate Passion, CXLVII.; Love's powerful Subtilty, CXLVIII., CXLIX., CL.;

Retaliation, XXXVIII., LXXIX.; Sunset, LXXIII., LXXVII.; A Monument to Fame, CVII., CVIII.; Perjury, CLI., CLII.; Cupid's Treachery, CLIII., CLIV.

I. B.'s, that is the bookseller Benson's, curious address " To the Reader," is as follows:—

"I here presume (under favour) to present to your view some excellent and sweetly composed Poems, of Master *William Shakespeare*, Which in themselves appeare of the same purity, the Authour himselfe then living avouched; they had not the fortune by reason of their Infancie in his death, to have the due accomodation of proportionable glory, with the rest of his ever-living Workes, yet the lines of themselves will afford you a more authentick approbation than my assurance any way can, to invite your allowance, in your perusall you shall find them *Seren,* cleere and eligantly plaine, such gentle straines as shall recreate and not perplexe your braine, no intricate or cloudy stuff to puzzell intellect,[1] but perfect eloquence, such as will raise your admiration to his praise: this assurance I know will not differ from your acknowledgement. And certaine I am, my opinion will be seconded by the sufficiency of these ensuing Lines; I have been some what solicitus to bring this forth to the perfect view of all men; and in so doing glad to be serviceable for the continuance of glory to the deserved Author in these his Poems."

Reprints.—In the editions of Shakspere's works published in 1709–10 (Rowe's ed.; in the vol. of *Poems* with remarks by Gildon), 1714, 1725, in Ewing's Dublin

---

[1] Perhaps referring to the obscurity of the reigning " metaphysical " school of poetry."

edition (1771), and those published at Boston, U.S.A., 1807, 1810.

In the editions of Shakspere's Poems (Bell), 1774 ; (Murden, etc.) ? about 1780 ; (Chapple) 2 vols., 1804.

HISTORY OF OPINION ON THE SONNETS DURING THE EIGHTEENTH CENTURY.

[From Shakspeare and his Times. By Nathan Drake. 2 vols. 1817. Vol. ii. pp. 59–61.]

When Gildon reprinted the Sonnets in 1710, he gives it as his opinion that they were *all of them in praise of his* [Shakspere's] *mistress* ;[1] and Dr. Sewell, when he edited them in 1728, had embraced a similar idea, for he tells us, in reference to our author's example, that " A young muse must have *a mistress,* to play off the beginning of fancy ; nothing being so apt to elevate the soul to a pitch of poetry as the passion of love." [2]

The conclusion of these editors remained undisputed for more than half a century, when Mr. Malone, in 1780, published his Supplement to the Edition of Shakspeare's Plays of 1778, which includes the Sonnets of the poet, accompanied by his own notes and those of his friends. Here, besides the opinion which he has himself avowed, he has given the conjectures of Dr. Farmer and Mr. Tyrwhitt, and the decision of Mr. Steevens.

[1] Rowe writes (1709): " There is a Book of Poems publish'd in 1640, under the name of Mr. William Shakespeare, but as I have but very lately seen it without an opportunity of making any judgment upon it, I won't pretend to determine whether it be his or no."

[2] Preface to his revised and corrected edition of Shakspeare's Works, p. 7.

All these gentlemen concur in believing that more than one hundred of our author's sonnets are addressed to a *male object.* Dr. Farmer, influenced by the *initials* in the dedication, supposes that Mr. William Harte, the poet's nephew, was the object in question; but a reference to the Stratford Register completely overturns this hypothesis, for it there appears that William, the eldest son of William Harte, who married Shakspere's sister Joan, was baptized August 28th, 1600, and consequently could not be even in existence when the greater part of these compositions was written.

Mr. Tyrwhitt, founding his conjecture on a line in the twentieth Sonnet, which is thus printed in the old copy,

A man in hew all Hews *in his controlling,*

conceives that the letters W. H. were intended to imply *William Hughes.* . . . When Mr. Steevens, in 1766, annexed a reprint of the Sonnets to Shakspere's plays, from the quarto editions, he hazarded no observations on their scope or origin;[1] but in Malone's Supplement he ventured, in a note on the Twentieth Sonnet, to declare his conviction that it was addressed to a *male object.*

Lastly, Mr. Malone, in the Supplement just mentioned, after specifying his concurrence in the conjecture of Mr. Tyrwhitt, adds:—" To this person, whoever he was, one hundred and twenty-six of the following poems are addressed; the remaining twenty-eight are addressed to a lady."[2]

[1] Steevens's remark that an Act of Parliament could not compel the perusal of the Sonnets is indignantly commented on by Wordsworth.

[2] Malone's Supplement, vol. i. p. 579.

Thus the matter rested on the decision of these four celebrated commentators, who were uniform in asserting their belief that Shakspeare had addressed the greater part of his Sonnets to a man, when Mr. George Chalmers in 1797, in his "Apology for the Believers in the Shakspeare Papers," attempted to overturn their conclusion, by endeavouring to prove that the whole of the Sonnets had been addressed by Shakspere to Queen Elizabeth; a position which he labours to strengthen by additional research in his "Supplemental Apology" of 1799! ["I mean to prove," writes Chalmers (*Supplemental Apology*, p. 21), "1st, that Spenser addressed his *Amoretti* to Elizabeth; 2ndly, that Shakspeare was ambitious of emulating Spenser; and 3rdly, that Shakspeare was thus induced to address *his Sonnets* to the same Queen."]

WORDSWORTH.

[Poems, 1815. Essay supplementary to the Preface. Vol. i. p. 353.]

There is extant a small volume of miscellaneous poems, in which Shakspeare expresses his own feelings in his own person. It is not difficult to conceive that the editor, George Steevens, should have been insensible to the beauties of one part of that volume, the Sonnets; though in no part of the writings of this poet is found, in an equal compass, a greater number of exquisite feelings felicitously expressed. But, from regard to the critic's own credit, he would not have ventured to talk of an [1]

---

[1] This flippant insensibility was publicly reprehended by Mr. Coleridge in a course of Lectures upon Poetry given by him at the Royal Institution.

Act of Parliament not being strong enough to compel the
perusal of those little pieces, if he had not known that
the people of England were ignorant of the treasures
contained in them ; and if he had not, moreover, shared
the too common propensity of human nature to exult
over a supposed fall into the mire of a genius whom
he had been compelled to regard with admiration, as
an inmate of the celestial regions—" there sitting where
he durst not soar."

NATHAN DRAKE.

[Shakespeare and his Times. 2 vols. 4to. London, 1817. Vol. ii.
pp. 50-86.]

Lord Southampton is the subject of the Sonnets I.-
CXXVI. They are addressed to a man; in the age of Shak-
spere the language of *love* and *friendship* was mutually
convertible ("love" and "lover" = friend). The language
of the *Lucrece* Dedication to Southampton and that of
part of the 26th Sonnet are almost precisely the same
(see notes on the 26th Sonnet) ; the language of both
is amatory. To whom except Southampton could the
101st and 110th Sonnets be addressed ? But why should
Shakspere urge marriage on Southampton, who from 1594
to 1599 was the lover of Elizabeth Vernon? Drake believes
there is reason to think the Earl's engagement was twice
given up to please the Queen. Southampton, when the

For the various merits of thought and language in Shakspeare's Sonnets
see Numbers XXVII., XXIX., XXX., XXXII., XXXIII., LIV., LXIV., LXVI., LXVIII.,
LXXIII., LXXVI., LXXXVI., XCI., XCII., XCIII., XCVII., XCVIII., CV., CVII., CVIII.,
CIX., CXI., CXIII., CXIV., CXVI., CXVII., CXXIX., and many others (*Words-
worth's note*).

marriage seemed hopeless, may have said that if he could not marry the object of his choice he would die single. Hence, perhaps, Shakspere's expostulations. When in 1598 Southampton resolved to marry Elizabeth Vernon, Shakspere ceased to urge him; hence only the first seventeen sonnets are on this subject. These were naturally kept private until after the death of Elizabeth, who had opposed the Earl's marriage; hence Jaggard secured none of these for *The Passionate Pilgrim.*

The Sonnets were written at various periods before 1609.

Sonnet LXXVIII. refers to the Earl's well-known munificence as a literary patron. If Southampton be the subject of *one* sonnet, he is subject of *all*, for Sonnets LXXVI. and CV. speak of the monotonous praises of a single person in these poems. The 1st sonnet suits well Southampton, aged twenty-one in the year 1594; the 126th, written perhaps in 1609, still calls him "sweet boy," for Shakspere (Sonnet CVIII.) says that he is determined to consider him as young as when he first hallowed his fair name. He ends Sonnet CXXVI., however, with a warning that Time is creeping on and death approaching.

Of Sonnets CXXVII.–CLIV., two, CXXIX. and CXLVI., have no reference to any individual: four others have no very determinate application. Considering the general moral beauty of Shakspere's character, that he was a husband and a father, we cannot but feel the most entire conviction that the remaining twenty-two sonnets were never directed to a real object. They were solely intended to express the contrarieties, the inconsistencies, and the miseries of illicit love.

Mr. W. H. was the obtainer ("begetter") of the Sonnets for Thorpe. We know not his name.

COUNT PLATEN.

The following sonnet by Count Platen (1796–1835) I find quoted by Bodenstedt.

SHAKESPEARE IN SEINEN SONETTEN.

Du ziehst bei jedem Loos die beste Nummer;
  Denn wer, wie Du, vermag so tief zu dringen
  In's tiefste Herz? Wenn Du beginnst zu singen,
Verstummen wir als klägliche Verstummer.
Nicht Mädchenlaunen störten Deinen Schlummer,
  Doch stets um Freundschaft sahn wir warm Dich ringen:
  Dein Freund errettet Dich aus Weiberschlingen,
Und seine Schönheit ist Dein Ruhm und Kummer.
Bis auf die Sorgen, die für ihn Dich nagen,
  Erhebst Du Alles zur Apotheose,
Bis auf den Schmerz, den er Dich lässt ertragen!
  Wie sehr Dich kränken mag der Seelenlose,
Du lässest nie von ihm, und siehst mit Klagen
  Den Wurm des Lasters in der schönsten Rose.

BOADEN.

[On the Sonnets of Shakespeare identifying the person to whom they are addressed; and elucidating several points in the poet's history. By James Boaden, Esq. London, Thomas Rodd, 1837. (Reprinted from *The Gentleman's Magazine*, 1832.)]

1. In the dedication by "begetter," the *object* of the Sonnets, Mr. W. H., not their *bringer forth*, is intended.

2. Mr. W. H. cannot be William Harte.

3. Nor Queen Elizabeth.

4. The Sonnets do not at all apply to Lord Southampton—either as to his age, character, or the bustle and activity of a life distinguished by distant and hazardous services—to some of which they must have alluded had he been their object. Southampton in 1594 was twenty-one, and Shakspere only thirty; yet the Sonnets speak of one as in the spring and the other in the autumn of life. The initials W. H. do not apply to Henry Wriothesley. Southampton did not possess personal beauty. The Sonnets contain no allusion to his active life and his struggles with fortune, such as we would naturally look for, and such as we find in Daniel's verses addressed to him.

5. Shakspere's Sonnets I.–CXXVI. were addressed to Mr. William Herbert in his youth. To him the initials apply. We know from the dedication of the first folio that he was a patron of Shakspere. The Sonnets CXXVII.–CLIV., though not addressed, were sent to him, as alluding to matters mentioned in I.–CXXVI.; and it is probable the Earl sanctioned their publication in 1609 under his untitled initials.

. 6. The two biographers of Mr. William Herbert, afterwards Lord Pembroke, establish his right to the Sonnets by echoing the contents of them. He was born in April, 1580, became a nobleman of New College, Oxford, 1592, aged thirteen. "He was," says Antony à Wood, "not only a great favourer of learned and ingenious men, but was himself learned and endowed to admiration with a poetical genie, as by those *amorous* and not inelegant

Aires and Poems of his composition doth evidently appear." Lord Clarendon calls him "the most universally beloved and esteemed of any man of that age." " And as his conversation was most with men of the *most pregnant parts and understanding*, so towards any such, who needed support or encouragement, though unknown, if fairly recommended to him, *he was very liberal*. . . . Yet his memory must not be flattered that his virtues and good inclinations may be believed. He was not without some *alloy of vice*, nor without being clouded with great infirmities which he had in too exorbitant a proportion. *He indulged to himself the pleasures of all kinds, almost in all excesses. To women . . . he was immoderately given up.* But therein he likewise retained such a power and jurisdiction over his very appetite, that he was not so much transported with beauty and outward allurements, as with those advantages of the mind as manifested extraordinary *wit* and *spirit* and *knowledge*, and administered pleasure in the conversation. To these he sacrificed himself, his precious time, and much of his fortune."

From Antony à Wood we learn that Mr. Tho. Allen had calculated William Herbert's nativity and prognosticated the day of his death; from Clarendon, that his tutor Sandford had prognosticated the day of his death. His mother, the sister of Philip Sidney, was learned and beautiful (see Sonnet III.); all that the Sonnets express as to the beauty of his own person may be credited upon a sight of Vandyke's picture of him in his maturity.

7. The poet Daniel was the *better spirit* of whom Shakspere expresses his *jealousy* in the Sonnets (LXXX., LXXXII.,

LXXXV., LXXXVI.). Daniel's reputation stood high, next, perhaps, to that of Spenser. He was brought up at Wilton, the seat of the Pembrokes, and in 1601 inscribed his *Defence of Ryme* to William Herbert. (See Sonnet LXXXII., "*dedicated words* which writers use," etc.) Shakspere had imitated the style of Daniel's *Rosamond* in his *Lucrece;* in the Sonnets he has Daniel's *Delia* for a model.

8. Daniel lived among astrologers (see Sonnet LXXXVI.); for beside Allen and Sandford, there was Dr. Dee (who pretended intercourse with an angel and other familiar spirits), of whom Queen Elizabeth and the *Pembroke* family were chief patrons.

[Mr. B. Heywood Bright had anticipated Mr. Boaden in the alleged discovery that the Sonnets I.–CXXVI. are addressed to William Herbert, but had not made his conclusion public. On the appearance of Mr. Boaden's first article, 1832—and before William Herbert had been named—Mr. Bright, foreseeing what was coming, hastened to claim precedence; and in a letter to the Rev. Joseph Hunter announced his discovery, the progress of which he had detailed to Mr. Hunter in 1819.]

COLERIDGE (May 14, 1833).

[Table-Talk, pp. 244–246, ed. 1852.]

I believe it possible that a man may, under certain states of the moral feeling, entertain something deserving the name of love towards a male object—an affection beyond friendship, and wholly aloof from appetite. In Elizabeth's and James's time it seems to have been almost fashionable to cherish such a feeling; and perhaps we may account in some measure for it by considering how very inferior the women of that age, taken generally, were in education and accomplishment of mind to the men. Of course there were brilliant exceptions enough; but the plays of Beaumont and Fletcher—the most popular dramatists that ever wrote for the English stage—will show us what sort of women it was generally pleasing to represent. Certainly the language of the two friends, Musidorus and Pyrocles, in the Arcadia, is such as we could not now use except to women; and in Cervantes the same tone is sometimes adopted, as in the novel of the Curious Impertinent. And I think there is a passage in the New Atlantis of Lord Bacon, in which he speaks of the possibility of such a feeling, but hints the extreme danger of entertaining it, or allowing it any place in a moral theory. I mention this with reference to Shakspeare's Sonnets, which have been supposed, by some, to be addressed to William Herbert, Earl of Pembroke, whom Clarendon calls the most beloved man of his age, though his licentiousness was equal to his virtues. I doubt this. I do not think that Shakspeare, merely because he was an actor, would have thought it necessary to veil his emotions towards Pembroke under a disguise, though he might probably have done so if the real object had perchance been a Laura or a Leonora. It seems to me that the Sonnets could only have come from a man deeply in love, and in love with a woman; and there is one sonnet which, from its incongruity, I

take to be a purposed blind. These extraordinary Son-
nets form, in fact, a poem of so many stanzas of fourteen
lines each ; and, like the passion which inspired them,
the Sonnets are always the same, with a variety of ex-
pression—continuous, if you regard the lover's soul—
distinct, if you listen to him, as he heaves them sigh
after sigh.

These Sonnets, like the Venus and Adonis and the
Rape of Lucrece, are characterized by boundless fertility
and laboured condensation of thought, with perfection
of sweetness in rhythm and metre. These are the essen-
tials in the budding of a great poet. Afterwards habit
and consciousness of power teach more ease—*præcipi-
tandum liberum spiritum.*

CHARLES ARMITAGE BROWN.

[Shakespeare's Autobiographical Poems. Being his Sonnets clearly de-
veloped ; with his Character drawn chiefly from his works. London,
1838.]

The name of the individual to whom the Sonnets were
addressed is a matter of minor importance compared to
the unravelling of their meaning. Mr. W. H., to
whom they are addressed, is William Herbert. " Mr.
was not improperly applied to the eldest son of an earl,
there not having been, at that period, any grander title
of courtesy." Meres, in 1598, probably spoke only of
the first twenty-six sonnets. Herbert was then eighteen
years of age, the age at which Shakspere himself was
married.

The 153rd and 154th Sonnets are intruders, utterly

foreign to the rest. Sonnets I.–CLII. are six poems in sonnet-stanza, each poem concluding with an appropriate envoy.

FIRST POEM.—Stanzas I.–XXVI. *To his friend, persuading him to marry;* I.–XVI., arguments to this effect; XVII.–XXV., with the same arguments, the poet resolves, in case his friend will not perpetuate the beauty of his youth in offspring, to make him live for ever young in verse; XXVI., *L'Envoy.*

SECOND POEM.—Stanzas XXVII.–LV. *To his friend—who had robbed the poet of his mistress—forgiving him.* The poem was written when Shakspere was distant from London, possibly during one of his journeys to Stratford. Sonnet LV., *L'Envoy.*

THIRD POEM.—Stanzas LVI.–LXXVII. *To his friend, complaining of his coldness, and warning him of life's decay.* Soon after the reconciliation, the youth evinced a coldness towards his friend. In the first three stanzas Shakspere complains of this coldness; afterwards it is only once referred to (Stanza LXI.); and the remainder of the poem is filled with compliments and assurances of unaltered affection, mixed with warnings of the fleeting nature of youth—exemplified in the poet himself, now past his best days, and looking forward to age and death. When writing the poem he was, Mr. Brown believes, about five and thirty. In Stanzas LXIX. and LXX. he mentions his having heard his young friend's conduct blamed. This he supposes to be a slander, yet counsels him to beware of giving a likelihood to such talk. *L'Envoy* is curious. It appears that the poem was written in a book, leaving some blank leaves, which

Shakspere recommends his friend to occupy with his mind's imprint.

FOURTH POEM.—Stanzas LXXVIII.–CI. *To his friend, complaining that he prefers another poet's praises, and reproving him for faults that may injure his character.* Who this rival poet was is beyond my conjecture; nor does it matter. To point out how different Shakspere himself is from a servile poet, he now blames the youth for his faults—licentious conversation and fickleness in friendship—excusing himself for interference by alleging that a stain on the youth's character affects his friend. The *Envoy* (CI.), like that of the second poem, contains a promise of immortal fame in an address to his muse.

FIFTH POEM.—Stanzas CII.–CXXVI. *To his friend, excusing himself for having been some time silent, and disclaiming the charge of inconstancy.* Three years had elapsed between the first poem and the fifth. In the first three poems we find tenderness and integrity expressed, for the most part, in monotonous lines; the sentiment often disguised in conceits. The fourth is far less objectionable; but the fifth is full of varied, rich, and energetic poetry. In Stanza CXXI., " to be vile " means to be fickle in friendship, and yield to " affections new." The *Envoy* seems to take a poetical leave of the youth, and, to mark this, it is written not in sonnet-stanza but six couplets.

SIXTH POEM.—Stanzas CXXVII.–CLII. *To his mistress, on her infidelity.* The stanzas up to CXXVI. are in due order ; the same attention was not paid to this sixth poem. Some irrelevant stanzas (*e.g.*, the *Will* ones, CXXXV., CXXXVI.) have been introduced. Shakspere here contends with an unworthy passion, and conquers it, leaving his mistress (CLII.) with bitter words. The punning sonnets are too playful; CXLV. is octosyllabic; CXLVI. solemn, but not congruous with the rest. These must be expunged. They occur between two parts of the poem; the first part being written in doubt and jealousy, and the after part in certainty of the woman's infidelity. The feeling of the poem lacks continuity, being a stormy feeling buffeted to and fro; the poem presents an admirable picture of pain and distraction caused by an almost overwhelming passion for a worthless object. This poem was written just before the *second* one to his friend, or soon after, in dramatic retrospection. Mr. Brown gives a brief prose paraphrase of each of the Sonnets.

HALLAM.

[Introduction to the Literature of Europe. Part III. ch. v.]

No one, as far as I remember, has ever doubted their genuineness; no one can doubt that they express not only real but intense emotions of the heart; but when they were written, who was the W. H. quaintly called their begetter—by which we can only understand the cause of their being written—and to what persons or circumstances they allude, has of late years been the subject of much curiosity. These Sonnets were long overlooked; Steevens spoke of them with the utmost scorn, as productions which no one could read; but a very different suffrage is generally given by the lovers of poetry, and perhaps there is now a tendency, especially among young men of poetical tempers, to exaggerate the beauties of these remarkable productions. They rise indeed, in estimation, as we attentively read and reflect upon them; for I do not think that at first they give us much pleasure. No one ever entered more fully than Shakspeare into the character of this species of poetry, which admits of no expletive imagery, no merely ornamental line. But though each sonnet has generally its proper unity, the sense, I do not mean the grammatical construction, will sometimes be found to spread from one to another, independently of that repetition of the leading idea, like variations of an air, which a series of them frequently exhibits, and on account of which they have latterly been reckoned by some rather an integral poem than a collection of sonnets. But this is not uncommon among the Italians, and belongs, in fact, to those of Petrarch himself. They may easily be resolved into several series according to their subjects; but when read attentively, we find them relate to one definite, though obscure, period of the poet's life, in which an attachment to some female, which seems to have touched neither his heart nor his fancy very sensibly, was overpowered, without entirely ceasing, by one to a friend; and this last is of such an enthusiastic character, and so extravagant in the phrases which the author uses, as to have thrown an unaccountable mystery over the whole work. It is true that in the poetry as well as in the fictions of early ages we find a more ardent tone of affection in the language of friendship than has since been usual; and yet no instance has been adduced of such rapturous devotedness, such an idolatry of admiring love, as one of the greatest beings

whom Nature ever produced in the human form pours
forth to some unknown youth in the majority of these
Sonnets.

The notion that a woman was their general object is
totally untenable, and it is strange that Coleridge should
have entertained it. Those that were evidently addressed
to a woman, the person above hinted, are by much the
smaller part of the whole, but twenty-eight out of one
hundred and fifty-four. And this mysterious Mr. W. H.
must be presumed to be the idolised friend of Shakspeare.
But who could he be? No one recorded as such in
literary history or anecdote answers the description. But
if we seize a clue which innumerable passages give us,
and suppose that they allude to a youth of high rank as
well as personal beauty and accomplishment, in whose
favour and intimacy, according to the base prejudices of
the world, a player and a poet, though he were the author
of Macbeth, might be thought honoured, something of
the strangeness, as it appears to us, of Shakspeare's
humiliation in addressing him as a being before whose
feet he crouched, whose frown he feared, whose injuries—
and those of the most insulting kind, the seduction of the
mistress to whom we have alluded—he felt and bewailed
without resenting; something, I say, of the strangeness
of this humiliation, and at best it is but little, may be
lightened, and in a certain sense rendered intelligible.
And it has been ingeniously conjectured within a few
years by inquirers independent of each other that
William Herbert, Earl of Pembroke, born in 1580, and
afterwards a man of noble and gallant character, though
always of a licentious life, was shadowed under the initials

F

of Mr. W. H. This hypothesis is not strictly proved, but sufficiently so, in my opinion, to demand our assent.[1]

Notwithstanding the frequent beauties of these Sonnets, the pleasure of their perusal is greatly diminished by these circumstances; and it is impossible not to wish that Shakspeare had never written them. There is a weakness and folly in all excessive and misplaced affection, which is not redeemed by the touches of nobler sentiments that abound in this long series of sonnets. But there are also faults of a merely critical nature. The obscurity is often such as only conjecture can penetrate; the strain of tenderness and adoration would be too monotonous, were it less unpleasing; and so many frigid conceits are scattered around, that we might almost fancy the poet to have written without genuine emotion, did not such a host of other passages attest the contrary.

CHARLES KNIGHT.

[The Pictorial Edition of Shakspere. Edited by Charles Knight. Illustrations of the Sonnets in vol. ii. of Tragedies, pp. 453–488 (2nd edition revised).]

Mr. W. H. was the obtainer ("begetter") of the sonnets for Thorpe; the publication was not sanctioned by Shakspere, and the arrangement of Sonnets in the Quarto, 1609, is arbitrary.

A number of separate poems can be distinguished. Some, as that urging a friend to marry, and that com-

---

[1] Pembroke succeeded to his father in 1601. I incline to think that the Sonnets were written about that time, some probably earlier, some later.

plaining of the robbery of a mistress, are probably fictions in the Italian style; others express Shakspere's personal feelings.

Knight reconstructs from the Sonnets the following poems:—

I.—Relating to Love.

Three Juvenilia (the punning Sonnets), CXXXV., CXXXVI., CXLIII.

Black Eyes (to Anne Hathaway), CXXVII., CXXXI., CXXXII.

The Virginal (*vers de société*), CXXVIII.

False Compare (*vers de société*), CXXX., XXI.

Tyranny (to Anne Hathaway), CXXXIX., CXL., CXLIX.

Slavery (to Anne Hathaway), LVII., LVIII.

Coldness (to Anne Hathaway), LVI.

I hate—not you (playful), CXLV.

The little love-god, CLIII., CLIV.

Love and hatred (love incompatible with duty), CXXIX., CXXXVII., CXXXVIII., CXLI., CXLII., CXLVII., CXLVIII., CL.–CLII.

Infidelity (of a mistress), CXXXIII., CXXXIV., CXLIV.

Injury (robbery of a mistress), XXXIII.–XXXV., XL.–XLII.

A friend's faults, XCIV.–XCVI.

Forgiveness, CXVIII.–CXX.

II.—Relating to Friendship.

Confiding friendship, XXIX.–XXXII.

Humility, XXXVI.–XXXIX.

Absence, L.–LII., XXVII., XXVIII., LXI., XLIII.–XLV.

Estrangement, XLVIII., LXXV., XLIX., LXXXVIII.–XCIII.

A second absence, XCVII.–XCIX.

Fidelity, CIX.–CXXV. (omitting CXVIII.–CXXI).

Dedications, XXIII., XXV., XXVI.

The Picture, XXIV., XLVI., XLVII.

The Note-book, LXXVII.

Rivalry, LXXVI., LXXVIII.–LXXX., LXXXII.–LXXXVII.

Reputation, CXXI.

The Soul, CXLVI.

III.—To a beautiful youth (a real person, but the subject treated ideally).

I.–XIX. forming a complete poem; XX., LIII.–LV. fragments of a similar poem; C.–CVIII., LIX., LX., CXXVI., to the same friend; XXII., LXII.–LXXIV., LXXXI., Death and the youth (the sentiments dramatic, not personal).

Knight argues against the theory that Sonnets I.–CXXVI. are addressed to one person, on the ground of inconsistencies in the characterization of the person addressed.

G. G. GERVINUS.

[Shakespeare Commentaries. Translated by F. E. Bunnett (edition 1875). Shakespeare's Sonnets (pp. 441–474).]

The first 126 Sonnets addressed to a youth, probably the Earl of Southampton; CXXVII.–CLIV., to a woman connected with Shakespeare and his young friend. The initials "Mr. W. H." concealed and betrayed just as much of the truth as was intended by the dedication. "Begetter" means *inspirer*.

Groups I.–XVII. Urges his friend to marry, and praises
his beauty and truth.

  XVIII.–XL. The inequality of the position of the
two friends.

  XL.–XLII. The poet complains of the robbery
of his love.

  XLIII.–LXI. Written in absence; a serious mood;
jealousy.

  LXII.–LXXVII. The serious mood gains ground;
world-weariness.

  LXXVIII.–LXXXVI. A rival writer has gained his patron's
favour.

  LXXXVII.–XCV. Complete estrangement.

  C.–CXXVI. Reunion, and restored happiness.

  CXXVII.–CLIV. Relate the persons and incidents
treated of in Sonnets XL.–XLII.

CHARLES BATHURST.

[Remarks on Shakespeare's Versification in different periods of his Life.
London. 1857. Sonnets, pp. 110–115.]

The Sonnets give, but only in a general and mysterious
way, a picture of Shakspere's mind and disposition. A
melancholy character predominates. It cannot be that
Shakspere was a burden to himself. It must have been
that he was liable to great changes of temper, some
spontaneous, some brought on by external circumstances.
The style is founded on Spenser, but more enriched; and
a more *dwelling*, slow, full softness of verse. From the
connection of subjects they are, for the most part, evi-

dently in order, though not, as has been said, in the
nature of the continuous stanzas of entire poems. I see no
change in the *matter*. All beautiful verse, flowing, almost
entirely unbroken. They go more with the Poems than
with the early Histories. The following lines in the
Comedy of Errors are remarkably in the style of the
Sonnets :—

> *And may it be that you have quite forgot*
> *A husband's office ?*
>> (Sixteen lines, Act III. sc. 2, ll. 1–16.)

and

Teach me, dear creature, etc.   (Same scene, ll. 33–39.)

WESTMINSTER REVIEW.

[The Sonnets of Shakespeare. An article in the Westminster Review,
July, 1857.]

William Herbert (W. H.) addressed in the Sonnets ;
the story of the dark woman a real one. The "affable
familiar ghost" of Sonnet LXXXVI. is not Dr. Dee, who,
though favoured by the Herbert family, had for chief
patrons the Dudleys. From the life of the Earl of
Pembroke by Antony à Wood we learn that Mr. Tho.
Allen of Gloucester Hall had calculated the Earl's
nativity ; from Lord Clarendon, that Pembroke's tutor,
Sandford, had prognosticated upon his nativity the day
of his death. The Earl then was "mixed up with
astrologers, and it is undoubtedly to these the reference
is made in the Sonnet."

J. PAYNE COLLIER.

[Shakespeare's Comedies, Histories, Tragedies, and Poems. Second ed. 1858.]

It is evident that the Sonnets were written at very different periods of Shakespeare's life, and under very different circumstances—some in youth, some in more advanced age. "Begetter" means *procurer.* C. A. Brown goes far to prove that the Sonnets in the first five of· his divisions (*i.e.*, I.–CXXVI.) are consecutive. The thought that Shakspere may have written these Sonnets on behalf of friends had occurred long since to Collier, but he now entirely abandons the supposition.

R. CARTWRIGHT.

[The Sonnets of William Shakespeare. Rearranged and divided into Four Parts, with an Introduction and Explanatory Notes [by Robert Cart-wright]. London, J. R. Smith. 1859.]

Mr. W. H. [? William Herbert] the collector ["be-getter"] of the Sonnets. The young man of the Son-nets, and the Adonis of *Venus and Adonis*, is the Earl of Southampton; but he is also an ideal of beauty. Perhaps as a quiz on the follies of sonneteering, Shak-spere took a beautiful youth for his lady-love. The rival poet is Marlowe. The date of the earliest Sonnets, 1591–92; of the latest, spring of 1596. The first twenty sonnets are in right order; those which follow need re-arrangement. ("If music and sweet poetry agree," from "The Passionate Pilgrim," is introduced as Sonnet XXI. Sonnet CXLVI. is the last in order. Sonnet CVII.—being

XXXII. of the rearranged series—probably refers to the prosperity, conciliation of Catholics, freedom from fear of Spain, under Elizabeth.)

"Antony and Cleopatra" presents in dramatic disguise the persons of the Sonnets. Antony, the Shakspere of 1593; Cleopatra, the dark woman; Octavia, Mrs. W. Shakspere; Enobarbus, Lord Southampton; "Lepidus is evidently Marlowe; and strangest of all, Sextus Pompeius is William Herbert; and Menas, Thomas Thorpe."

D. BARNSTORFF.

[Schlüssel zu Shakspeare's Sonetten. Bremen, 1860. 179 pp. 8vo.
A Key to Shakespeare's Sonnets. By D. Barnstorff. Translated from the German by T. J. Graham. London, 1862. 215 pp. 8vo.]

Shakspere in the Sonnets (I.) presents his own spiritual self (Sonnets I.–CXXVI.) in an appeal from his mortal to his immortal part (under the symbol of a beautiful youth); secondly, Sonnets CXXVII.–CLIV., under the symbol of a mistress, in whom he would sow the seeds of his genius, he gives us his inmost thoughts on the drama. "From this point of view nothing remains obscure or doubtful." For example:—

> *Thou art thy mother's glass, and she in thee*
> *Calls back the lovely April of her prime.*

Thy mother = Nature; "glass" = his genius; "the lovely April" = the bloom of art in Greece.

W. H. probably means William Himself, Shakspere naturally dedicating to himself these poems which treat of his own genius and his art.

HOWARD STAUNTON.

[The Works of Shakespeare. 1861.]

"The truth we apprehend to be, that although these poems are written in the poet's own name, and are, apparently, grounded on actual incidents in his career, they are, for the most part, if not wholly, poetical fictions."

PHILARÈTE CHASLES AND BOLTON CORNEY.

M. Philarète Chasles regards the words, "To the onlie begetter," etc., not as a dedication, but as a monumental inscription consisting of two clauses. He places a period after the word "wisheth;" to this verb "wisheth" the nominative is "Mr. W. H.;" *i.e.*, Mr. W. H. [William Hathaway][1] wishes happiness and eternity to the only begetter of the Sonnets. Thomas Thorpe adds his own name as "the well-wishing adventurer in setting forth," *i.e.*, publisher.

Mr. Bolton Corney (*The Sonnets of William Shakespeare: a critical disquisition suggested by a recent discovery.* London, 1862. Privately printed.) accepts this reading. He supposes the Sonnets were written for Southampton, soon after 1594 (the date of the *Lucrece*), as mere poetical exercises. Mr. W. H., that is William Herbert, Earl of Pembroke, inscribes this copy to Southampton, the only

[1] M. Chasles supposed at first that W. H. was William Herbert. See *Athenæum*, Jan. 25, 1862, Feb. 16, 1867, and Feb. 23, 1867, where Mr Neil claims priority in the suggestion of William Hathaway. See M. Chasles on "begetter," in the *Athenæum*, 1867, vol. i. p. 662.

begetter.   Perhaps Southampton had lost his own copy,
or perhaps this one was presented as a remarkable speci-
men of penmanship.

F. BODENSTEDT.

[William Shakespeare's Sonette in Deutscher Nachbildung.   Von Fried-
rich Bodenstedt.   Berlin, 1862.]

The order of the Sonnets in ed. 1609 is accidental.
Many of the Sonnets are later than 1598, especially those
of great excellence.   The greater number of those written
for friends and patrons are addressed to Southampton.
" Begetter" perhaps means " obtainer."   The rival poet
is Spenser.

A large part of Bodenstedt's " Schlusswort " consists of
a reply to Barnstorff.

Bodenstedt's translation is in verse; the Sonnets are
arranged in a new order, and divided into four parts.

The order is as follows:—Part I. CXXVIII., CXXXV.,
CXXXVI., CXLIII., XXIII., CXXI., CLIII., CLIV., CLII., CXXXVII.,
CLI., CXLV., CXLIX., CL., CXLI., CXLII., LXXV., CXLVII.,
CXLVIII., CXXX., CXXVII., CXXXII., CXXXI., CXXXVIII.,
XLVI., XLVII., CXIII., CXIV., LVII., XCVII.–XCIX., LVI., XCVI.,
XCV., LXXXVIII., LXXXVII., LXXXIX., CXXXIX., CXL., CXXIX.
Part II. CXXXIII., CXXXIV., CXLIV., XXXIII.–XXXV., XL.–
XLII., XXVI., XX., XXIV., XXIX.–XXXI., XXXVI., LXVI.,
XXXIX., XXXVIII., XLVIII., LII., L., LI., XXVII., XXVIII.,
LXI., XLIII.–XLV., LIII., LXXX., LXXXII., LXXXV., LXXXVI.,
LXXVIII., LXXIX., XXXVII., LVIII., XLIX., LXII., LXXXIII.,
LXX., LXIX., LXVII., LXVIII., XCIII., LXXXI., LXXIV.,

XXXII. Part III. I.–XIX., XXII., XXI., CXXVI., CX.–CXII., LXXXIV., LXIV., LXV., CVII., CVIII. Part IV. C., CIX., CXVIII., XC., XCII., CXXV., CXIX., CXX., CXVII., CIII., LXIII., CIV.–CVI., CXXII., CXV., CXVI., LXXIII., LXXII., XCI., LXXVI., CI., CII., LIX., LX., LIV., LV., CXXIII., XCIV., CXLVI., CXXIV., LXXVII., XXV.

Nos. 1 and 3 of Bodenstedt's translation, preceding and immediately following Sonnet CXXVIII., are No. 3 of *Passionate Pilgrim*, "Let not the heavenly rhetoric of thine eye" (from *Love's Labour's Lost*), and No. 8 of the same, "If music and sweet poetry agree."

FRANÇOIS-VICTOR HUGO.

[Œuvres complètes de W. Shakespeare. Tome xv. Sonnets, Poëmes, Testament. Paris [1862].]

The Sonnets, arranged in a new order, are translated into prose. M. Hugo begins with Shakspere in love; the three punning sonnets (CXXXV., CXXXVI., CXLIII.) are placed first. The lady does not yield; Shakspere asks, "Do you love me?" she replies, "I hate—not you" (CXLV.). In the fifth sonnet (CXXVIII.) we see him seated by the virginal while she plays a piece—perhaps by Dowland. Here, M. Hugo introduces as Shakspere's the sonnet by Barnfield from the *Passionate Pilgrim* in which occur the words, "Dowland to thee is dear." While Shakspere sighs for a kiss, the coquette makes advances to others; he loses patience (CXXXIX., CXL.). "Take care," he says; "you are not beautiful enough to be so cruel" (CXXVII., CXXXI., CXXXII.). She persists, until one fine morning she gets the epigram (cxxx.), "My mistress' eyes are nothing like the sun," etc. There is a scene. "You do not love me," she cries. "Cruel," he replies; "how can you say this when I adore your very faults" (cxlix., xxi.). He perceives that the ironical tone succeeds best, and the sonnets that follow are a curious mixture of adorations and sarcasms. "Il semble que Shakespeare veuille se venger sur la femme qu'il aime de l'amour qu'elle lui inspire, tant il l'accable à la fois de tendresses et d'injures" (cxxxvii., cxxxviii., cxlvii., cxlviii.). A laugh on the lips, but a sob in the breast of Shakespeare (cl.). "You ought to be ashamed to love me thus," she says; "you, who have vowed fidelity to another; you break your oath." "Ah," he replies, "it is not you who should reproach me, you who are twice forsworn" (clii.). "Après cette foudroyante réplique, la triste créature semble à bout de résistance. Elle est vaincue. . . . Elle se donne enfin et le xxve. (*i.e.*, cli.) sonnet est . . . le cri de victoire de Shakespeare." The sense of shame (cxxix.) follows. And now he has reason to think that she has beguiled his friend (cxxxiii., cxxxiv.); yet he does not possess any absolute proof that his suspicion is well founded (cxliv.). At length his young friend confesses all, weeping. How does Shakespeare take it? "He finds in the infinite tenderness of his heart a sublime denoûment. He forgives" (xxxiii.–xxxv.). As to the woman, he sees her no more. "Yet," he exclaims, "it may be said, I loved her dearly" (xlii.). From henceforth she is dead to him.

Deceived in love, Shakespeare throws himself wildly into friendship. From friendship he seeks the impossible happiness he has elsewhere sought in vain. He looks for a love unchanging, inexhaustible, ideal. He passes from one extreme to another. He will love only a soul (xx.). His great desire is that the marriage of true minds may be eternal; he declares war with time; he would procure for his friend the twofold perpetuity of offspring and of verse. "Ah! c'est que pour Shakespeare la poésie a un caractère auguste et religieux : elle a, comme l'amour, cette faculté mystérieuse d'engendrer. La muse aussi est mère."

Mr. W. H., according to Hugo, is Southampton. Thorpe wishes W. H. "happiness" and "eternity," as Shakspere in the Dedication of *Lucrece* had wished Southampton "long life, still lengthened with happiness." *Venus and Adonis* is only the symbolic formula of the ideas developed in the sonnets urging marriage on his friend. In Sonnet LIII. he writes:—

> *Describe Adonis, and the counterfeit.*
> *Is poorly imitated after you.*

The date is between 1593–1598; the Sonnets were kept private, as Drake says, because Queen Elizabeth was opposed to Southampton's marriage. Thorpe calls Southampton "Mr. W. H.," because it would not be becoming to connect his name openly with the Sonnets. The rival poet is Marlowe.

The Sonnets are arranged by Hugo in the following order:—CXXXV., CXXXVI., CXLIII., CXLV., CXXVIII., Passionate Pilgrim No. 8, CXXXIX., CXL., CXXVII., CXXXI., CXXXII., CXXX., XXI., CXLIX., CXXXVII., CXXXVIII., CXLVII.,

CXLVIII., CXLI., CL., CXLII., CLII.–CLIV., CLI., CXXIX., CXXXIII., CXXXIV., CXLIV., XXXIII.–XXXV., XL.–XLII., XXVI., XXIII., XXV., XX., XXIV., XLVI., XLVII., XXVII., XXX., XXXI., CXXI., XXXVI., LXVI., XXXIX., L., LI., XLVIII., LII., LXXV., LVI., XXVII., XXVIII., LXI., XLIII., XLIV., XLV., XCVII.–XCIX., LIII., CIX.–CXX., LXXVII., CXXII.– CXXV., XCIV.–XCVI., LXIX., LXVII., LXVIII., LXX., XLIX., LXXXVIII.–XCIII., LIII., CIX.–CXX., LXXVII., CXXII.–CXXV., XCIV.–XCVI., LXIX., LXVII., LXVIII., LXX., XLIX., LXXXVIII.– XCIII., LVII., LVIII., LXXVIII., LXXIX., XXXVIII., LXXX., LXXXII.–LXXXVII., XXXII., CXLVI., C.–CIII., CV., LXXVI., CVI., LIX., CXXVI., CIV., I.–XIX., LX., LXXIII., XXXVII., XXII., LXII., LXXI., LXXII., LXXIV., LXXXI., LXIV., LXIII., LXV., LIV., LV., CVIII., CVII.

SAMUEL NEIL.

[Shakespere, a Critical Biography. London, 1863, pp. 104–108. The Sonnets.]

"Begetter" must mean "collector," for no single person can have been the sole cause of all the sonnets ("the onlie begetter"). May not Mr. W. H. be Mr. William Hathaway, born Nov. 30th, 1578, brother-in-law of William Shakspere. To give his brother-in-law a start, Shakspere may have given him the MS. of the Sonnets, telling him to get the most he could out of the book-sellers for them.

"We do not believe in the continuity of the Sonnets; in the *oneness* of their object, *i.e.*, inspirer; or in the entirely autobiographical theory. Many, we believe, were addressed to Anne Hathaway, as bride and wife; several to his daughter [*e.g.*, LXII.]; some to Queen Elizabeth [*e.g.*, LXXXIII.–LXXXVI. and CVI.]; one at least to his son Hamnet [CVIII.]; a few to, or for, noble and beloved friends; and many, we think, are early exercises in the *concetti* then fashionable, or various forms of pleasing ideas. A few do possess a tone of soliloquy, that makes them seem quite autobiographical."

THOMAS KENNY.

[The Life and Genius of Shakespeare. 1864.]

The Sonnets were not only written by Shakespeare in his own character, but they were written by him directly with a view to his own gratification. They exhibit a weak and erring emotional and moral nature—an extravagant impressionability. . . . There is necessarily perhaps in creative imagination, as in all creative power, a feminine element. Mr. Kenny does not attempt to identify Shakspere's friend. For a reply to Mr. Kenny, see Karl Elze's *William Shakespeare*, pp. 494–505.

N. DELIUS.

[Shakespeare-Jahrbuch, I. 1865. Ueber Shakespeare's Sonette, pp. 18–56.]

The Sonnets are poems of the fancy, in which Shakspere treats non-dramatically some of the themes treated in the plays and in *Venus and Adonis*. "Begetter," in Thorpe's dedication, means *procurer*. An analysis of the Sonnets, showing their grouping, and the significance of each group, concludes the article. It seems impossible to Delius that Sonnets I.–CXXVI. can apply to one and the same person.

J. A. HERAUD.

[Shakspere, his Inner Life as intimated in his Works. London, 1865. pp. xiv. 521. 8vo. Appendix A (pp. 484–502). A New View of Shakspere's Sonnets. An Inductive Critique. Reprinted from *Temple Bar*, April, 1862.)]

The Sonnets exhibit both objective and subjective elements; they are poems of Reformation England. Sonnets I.–XVII. are a Protestant declaration against celibacy, under the form of an address to an Ideal Man. The poet then treats of two attributes of Ideal Man (who is bi-sexual), Beauty and Love. This Ideal Man is Shakspere's ideal self; "Man becomes all but the theistic *Logos*." The dark woman is the Bride of the Canticles, " black but comely." The " better angel " of Sonnet CXLIV. is the Reformed Church ; the " worser spirit," the Celibate Church (Catholicism). Love and its rights, the emancipation of the natural appetites within rational limits, is the argument of the Reformation, as projected by Luther, and the argument also of Shakspere's Sonnets.

F. T. PALGRAVE.

[Songs and Sonnets by William Shakespeare. Edited by Francis Turner Palgrave. London, 1865.]

Mr. Palgrave omits two sonnets, omits also the numbering of the Sonnets, and substitutes for numbers graceful titles of his own invention. A few remarks on the style and character of the poems, and a few notes, are added.

" These revelations of the poet's innermost nature appear to teach us less of the man than the tone of mind which we trace, or seem to trace, in *Measure for Measure, Hamlet,* and *The Tempest;* the strange imagery of passion which passes over the magic mirror has no tangible existence before or behind it." No other known or plausible name but Herbert's has been suggested as the *object* of the Sonnets. The Sonnets present a certain sequence or story, and the external facts of the story are obvious enough : but these are of very minor importance. The difficulty remains. We can hardly understand, we cannot enter into the strange series of feelings which they paint; we cannot understand how our great and gentle Shakespeare could have submitted himself to such passions; we have hardly courage to think that he really endured them. Yet reality appears stamped on the Sonnets, not less forcibly than the mythical character upon the autobiography of Dante's early days. The " excessive affection " condemned by Hallam is characteristic of great genius. This, in the sublime language of the *Phædrus,* is that "possession and ecstasy with which the Muses seize on a plastic and pure soul, awakening it and hurrying it forth like a Bacchanal in the ways of song." Friendship blazes into passion; the furnace of love is seven times heated. We cannot bring ourselves, with Hallam, to wish that Shakespeare had never written them; but there is pleasure also in the belief that this phase of feeling was transient, and that the sanity which, not less than ecstasy, is an especial attribute of the great poet, returned to Shakespeare.

E. A. HITCHCOCK.

[Remarks on the Sonnets of Shakespeare ; with the Sonnets. Showing that they belong to the hermetic class of writings, and explaining their general meaning and purpose. By the author of "Remarks on Alchemy" (E. A. Hitchcock). New York, J. Miller, 1865. 258 pp. I2mo.]

The Sonnets present the poet's mind in relation to the spirit of Beauty, the true source of artistic births. This spirit of Beauty has two sides, a masculine, popularly known as *the reason,* Shakespeare's "better angel" of Sonnet CXLIV.; and a feminine, the "woman colour'd ill," *i.e.,* what is popularly known as *the affections.*

E. W. SIEVERS.

[William Shakspeare : Sein Leben und Dichten, pp. 90-115. 1866.]

Sievers accepts the story of friend and mistress as real. The Sonnets are of an early date ; the friend is South-ampton. The relation of the friends is mirrored in that of Proteus and Valentine in *The Two Gentlemen of Verona.* Shakspere's early life and his moral recovery resemble those of his own Prince Henry.

GERALD MASSEY.

[Shakspeare's Sonnets never before interpreted : his private friends identified : together with a recovered likeness of himself. By Gerald Massey. London, 1866. 8vo, pp. 603. A second and enlarged edition, limited to one hundred copies, for subscribers only. 1872.]

Mr. W. H. is Mr. William Herbert (Earl of Pembroke), the only *obtainer* (" begetter ") of the Sonnets for Thorpe.

The Sonnets require rearrangement to become intelligible.

The earliest in date (1592) were addressed by Shakspere to Southampton. In 1593–4 he began to write dramatic sonnets in the character of Southampton concerning his courtship of Elizabeth Vernon; at the same time he continued to address personal sonnets to the Earl. He further wrote dramatic sonnets expressing the feelings of Elizabeth Vernon towards Southampton. Elizabeth Vernon had given Southampton a table-book, in which Shakspere was to write his sonnets. This book, containing autograph sonnets of Shakspere, was given by Southampton to William Herbert. The dark woman series was written by Shakspere for Herbert with reference to Herbert's unrighteous love of Lady Rich. They have in part a satirical intention. Herbert himself wrote a few of the sonnets which pass for Shakspere's.

The following is Mr. Massey's arrangement:—

Personal Sonnets. To the Earl of Southampton (1592), urging marriage. XXVI. (dedication); I.–XVII.

Personal Sonnets. To the Earl of Southampton (1592–3). (*a*) Praising his beauty, XXV. (dedication), XX. LIX., CVI., XVIII., LXII., XXII., LIII., LIV. (*b*) Promising immortality, XXIII. (dedication), XIX., LX., LXIV., LXV., LV.

Personal Sonnets. To the Earl of Southampton (before June, 1593). Of a Rival Poet (Marlowe), LXXVIII.–LXXX., LXXXVI., LXXXV., XXI., LXXXIII., LXXXIV., LXXXII., XXXII. (In LXXVIII. the "alien pen" and the "learned's wing" refer to Nash; heavy ignor-

ance " to Florio; " given grace a double majesty "
to Marlowe.)

Personal Sonnet (1593–4). Shakspere is about to write
on Southampton's courtship, XXXVIII.

Dramatic Sonnets (1593–4). Southampton in love with
Elizabeth Vernon, XXIX.–XXXI., XXXVII.

Personal Sonnets (1594). Shakspere to Southampton,
he having known him for about three years, CIV.,
CXXVI.

Personal Sonnet. Shakspere proposes to write of the
Earl in his absence abroad, XXXIX.

Dramatic Sonnets. The Earl to Mistress Vernon, on and
in his absence abroad, XXXVI. (lovers' parting), L., LI.,
CXIII., CXIV., XXVII., XXVIII., XLIII., LXI., XLVIII.,
XLIV., XLV., LII. (the Earl's journey).

Personal Sonnets (1595). Shakspere of the Earl in his
Absence, XXIV., XLVI., XLVII.

Dramatic Sonnets. Mistress Vernon jealous of her lover
Southampton and her friend Lady Rich, CXLIV. (a
soliloquy); Elizabeth Vernon to the Earl, XXXIII.–
XXXV., XL.–XLII.; Elizabeth Vernon to Lady Rich,
CXXXIII., CXXXIV., XL.

Personal Sonnet. Shakspere on the slander concerning
Southampton, LXX.

Dramatic Sonnets. The Earl to Elizabeth Vernon after
the jealousy, LVI., LXXV.

Dramatic Sonnets Elizabeth Vernon repays the Earl
by a flirtation of her own; he reproaches her, XLIX.,
LXXXVIII., XCI.–XCIII.

Personal Sonnets. Shakspere is sad for the Earl's " harmful deeds," LXVI.–LXIX., XCIV., XCV., LXXVII. [In ed. 1872 Mr. Massey makes Elizabeth Vernon the speaker of this group.]

Dramatic Sonnets (1597–98). A farewell of the Earl to Elizabeth Vernon, LXXXVII., LXXXIX., XC.

Dramatic Sonnets (1598). The Earl to Elizabeth Vernon after his absence, XCVII.–XCIX.

Personal Sonnets (1598–99). Shakspere to the Earl after some time of silence, C.–CIII., LXXVI., CVIII., CV.

Dramatic Sonnets (1598–99). The Earl to Elizabeth Vernon; their reconciliation before marriage, CIX.–CXII., CXXI., CXVII.–CXIX., CXX.

Personal Sonnet. Shakspere on the Earl's marriage, CXVI.

Personal Sonnets (1599–1600). Shakspere to the Earl, chiefly on the subject of his own death, LXXI.–LXXIV., LXIII., LXXXI.

Dramatic Sonnets (1601–1603). Southampton, a prisoner in the Tower, to his Countess, CXXIII.–CXXV.

Personal Sonnet. Shakspere to the Earl in prison, CXV.

Personal Sonnet. Shakspere's greeting to the Earl on his release from the Tower on the accession of King James, CVII.

Dramatic Sonnet. The Earl to Elizabeth Vernon on parting with the Shakspere Sonnet-Album, given to him by her, CXXII.

Dramatic Sonnets (1599–1600). William Herbert's passion for Lady Rich, CXXVII., CXXXII., CXXVIII., CXXXVIII., CXXX., CXXXI., XCVI., CXXXV., CXXXVI., CXLII., CXLIII., LVII., LVIII., CXXXIX., CXL., CXLIX., CXXXVII., CXLVIII., CXLI., CL., CXLVII., CLII., CLI., CXXIX., CXLVI.

Sonnets by Herbert, CXLV, CXXX.

Two detached sonnets, Cupid's brand, CLIII. (by Herbert), CLIV. (by Shakspere).

In the second edition (1872) of Mr. Massey's book he urges that the sonnets written for Herbert were designed to make sport of his passion for Lady Rich, burlesquing the sonnets of "Uncle Sidney," which celebrated the beauty of Lady Rich in her youth.[1]

G. ROSS.

[Studies Biographical and Literary. London (No date. ? 1867). pp. 52–55.]

"These Sonnets are mysterious only to the dull, who expect to find a fact underlying every sentiment, and know not that a young poet loves to soar into a region where sentiment is the only fact. . . . It is in this exaltation of the spirit, this yearning after an unattainable ideal, that the floating demarcations of life-facts become confused and lost—that friendship ripens into love, sentiment into passion, and the abstractions of the intellect into veritable experience. The problem of sex is soluble by the poet alone, and by him only in the trance of his genius. As in heaven there is no marrying nor giving in marriage, so in the poetic elysium there is no sex. . . . The spirit of Plato is 'sphered' more excellently in these sonnets than in any other product of English genius." Many of the sonnets were addressed to Southampton, who is perhaps the W. H. of the dedication.

[1] Mr. Massey's theory is criticized in *The Athenæum*, April 23, 1866, and by Mr. Robert Bell in *The Fortnightly Review*, August 1, 1866.

ARCHBISHOP TRENCH.

[A Household Book of English Poetry. London, 1868.]

" Shakespeare's Sonnets are so heavily laden with meaning, so double-shotted—if one may so speak—with thought, so penetrated and pervaded with a repressed passion, that, packed as all this is into narrowest limits, it sometimes imparts no little obscurity to them." Of Sonnet CXXIX., Archbishop Trench says: " The subject, the bitter delusion of all sinful pleasures, the reaction of a swift remorse which inevitably dogs them, Shakespeare must have most deeply felt, as he has expressed himself upon it most profoundly. I know no picture of this at all so terrible in its truth as in *The Rape of Lucrece*, the description of Tarquin after he has successfully wrought his deed of shame. But this sonnet on the same theme is worthy to stand by its side."

RICHARD SIMPSON.

[An Introduction to the Philosophy of Shakespeare's Sonnets (pp. 82).
London, 1868.]

The Sonnets are in their first intention philosophical, real persons and events may perhaps be used to illustrate the philosophy. Mr. W. H., "the begetter," was some young man of birth and wit, whose arguments and disputations provoked the poet to embody his conception of the "two loves of comfort and despair."

Love, as Plato says, is the passion for begetting or creating in the beautiful; beauty is both physical and metaphysical, and love is that of matter, or that of spirit, or that of both matter and spirit. Love of the mind alone, intellectual love, is called, in the Italian sonnet philosophy, the good dæmon; love of the body alone, the evil dæmon. Shakspere deals with the first in Sonnets I.–CXXVI.; with the second in Sonnets CXXVII.–CLIV. The love depicted in the first series (friendship) is a force ever growing, triumphing over obstacles, and becoming ever purer and brighter; while the love sung in the second series (concupiscence) is bad in its origin, interrupted but not destroyed by fits of remorse, and growing worse and worse with time. The two series of sonnets are correlative, and both arranged on the same principle. According to the Platonic sonneteers, love in its ascent is transformed from imaginative love to ideal love. Each of these divisions separates into three subdivisions. In the first division—*Imaginative love*— love is (i.) born of the eyes, Sonnets I.–XXV.; (ii.) nursed in the fancy through absence, Sonnets XXVI.–XXXVII.; (iii.) generalized in thought, Sonnets XXXVIII.–XLV. Then after the transition to ideal love, sentiment concurs with sense, the heart supersedes the eyes. In this second division— *Ideal love*—(i.) the heart, more truly than the eye, fur- nishes the idea, Sonnets XLVI.–LXV.; (ii.) the idea is purified in the furnace of jealousy, Sonnets LXVI.–XCVI.; and (iii.) at last it is rendered universal and absolute in the reason, Sonnets XCVII.–CXXV. The second series (the Sonnets CXXVII.–CLIV., to the evil dæmon of love, the dark woman) go through a similar *descending* scale—*Imaginative love*— (i.) love through the eyes, Sonnets CXXVII.–CXXX.; (ii.) love transferred from the sight to the fancy, Sonnets CXXXI., CXXXII.; (iii.) the generalization of fancy, CXXXIII.,

CXXXIV. *Ideal love* (i.), the lover's heart identified with his mistress's will, passes a false judgment on her, Sonnets CXXXV.–CXXXVII. ; (ii.) this false judgment triumphs over falsehood, slander, the disillusion of the senses, and jealousy, Sonnets CXXXVIII.–CXLIII. ; (iii.) love growing to despair and hate, with darkened and perverted conscience, Sonnets CXLIV., CLII.

The indications of time in the Sonnets are imaginary ; the indications of jealousy (of the rival poet) are also imaginary. The Sonnets suggest questions about Shakspere's life, but do not answer them.

Mr. Simpson's little book is of much value in illustrating the Renaissance theories respecting love and beauty.

T. D. BUDD.

[Shakespeare's Sonnets, with commentaries. Philadelphia, J. Campbell, 1868. 172 pp. 4to.]

" The author maintains that the Sonnets are addressed to 'the soul materialized, and they are thus applicable to mankind generally, individually, and to the poet in particular.' " [1]

H. VON FRIESEN.

[(i.) Shakespeare-Jahrbuch, iv. 1869. Ueber Shakespeare's Sonette, pp. 94–120. (ii.) Altengland und William Shakespeare. 1874. pp. 324–348.]

The greater number of Sonnets L.–CXXVI. were addressed to a real person, probably the Earl of Southampton ;

---

[1] Catalogue of the Works of William Shakespeare, original and translated, Barton Collection, Boston Public Library. By James Mascarene Hubbard. Boston, 1878. p. 51.

some may have been written as love sonnets for him, some perhaps form fragments of a poetical correspondence. Everything in the Sonnets is not to be taken literally, but they are founded on fact. They do not form a continuous series; nor are we to look for a harmonious interdependence among poems written in various moods and on various occasions. The Sonnets to the dark woman are but half serious in their description of her person and character. The date of the Sonnets lies between 1590 and 1595.

CARL KARPF.

[Τὸ τί ἦν εἶναι. Die Idee Shakespeare's und deren Verwirklichung. Sonnettenerklärung und Analyse des Dramas Hamlet. Hamburg, 1869. pp. 166.]

Sonnets I.–CXXVI. do not relate to any other person than Shakspere; they treat of the genius of the poet, his creative activity, the Divine spirit in his spirit. Sonnets CXXVII.–CLIV. refer to the poet's art-practice and his Muse (the dark woman). The theory differs from Barnstorff's chiefly in the discovery of Aristotelian philosophy in Shakspere's Sonnets.

HENRY BROWN.

[The Sonnets of Shakespeare Solved, and the Mystery of his Friendship, Love, and Rivalry revealed. By Henry Brown. London, 1870.]

Mr. W. H., the young friend spoken of so much in the Sonnets, was William Herbert, Earl of Pembroke. The date, 1598–1604. The Sonnets are in proper order, and form two poems, I.–CXXVI., and CXXVII.–CLIV. The first poem consists of two parts, I.–LXXVII. and LXXVIII.–CXXVI., an interval of twelve months (1601–1602), during which Shakspere ceased to write sonnets separating the two parts. There are three currents of purpose in the sonnets :—

First, they are satires on mistress-sonneting, and upon the sonneteers of Shakspere's day. Drayton, and afterwards Davies, were more directly the subjects of his sportive musings and feignings.

Second, they are autobiographical.

Third, the key which unlocks the heart of the mystery is the conceit of Shakspere's having married his Muse to Herbert by wedlock of verse and mind. They were written at Herbert's request, who thus, wedded to Shakspere's Muse, was their " only begetter."

The rival poet who addressed dedications to Herbert, and of whose "great verse " Shakspere writes ironically, was John Davies, of Hereford. Shakspere alludes ironically to his fame for calligraphy (LXXXIII., LXXXIV., LXXXV.).

The lady of the sonnets, beloved by Herbert, is unknown. Shakspere professes love to her only because she was beloved by his friend, who was one with himself. It was arranged between Herbert and Shakspere that the latter should picture Herbert's love of the dark lady as a satire upon mistress-sonneting, with pointed allusions to Lady Rich, whom Sidney — Pembroke's uncle—had, to the dishonour of the Pembroke family, celebrated in *Astrophel and Stella.*

Mr. Brown divides the first 126 Sonnets into 40 groups ;

the remaining 28 into 17 groups. A prose paraphrase—
often really helpful—of each sonnet is given.

H. W. HUDSON.

[Shakespeare, his Life, Art, and Character. Boston, 1872.
pp. 24–26.]

The Sonnets punning on the name *Will* were addressed
to Anne Hathaway; so also were XCVII.–XCIX.; so also a
third cluster of nine, which includes CX., CXI., CXVII.
" It will take more than has yet appeared to convince me
that when the poet wrote these and other similar lines
his thoughts were travelling anywhere but home to the
bride of his youth and mother of his children."

F. KREYSSIG.

[(i.) Vorlesungen über Shakespeare (2nd ed. 1874. Vol. i. p. 121.) (ii.)
Shakespeare-Fragen. 1871. pp. 62–67. (iii.) Shakespeare's Lyrische
Gedichte und ihre neuesten Bearbeiter, Preussische Jahrbücher.
Bd. xiii. pp. 484–503, xiv. pp. 91–114 (1864).]

Many of the Sonnets (as those concerning love and
jealousy) are personal, deep in feeling, dealing with real
persons and incidents.

Some of the Sonnets are light poetical exercises in the
fashion of the time.

Some deal with moral questions of a general kind,
suggested by Shakspere's real experience.[1]

[1] W. König (*Shakespeare als Dichter, Weltweiser und Christ.* Leipzig,
1873. pp. 234–245) takes a similar view of the Sonnets. I regret that I
have not seen Kreyssig's articles in the *Preussiche Jahrbücher*, which,
I doubt not, are excellent.

R. GRANT WHITE.

[The Works of William Shakespeare. Edited by Richard Grant White. Boston, 1872. Sonnets (in vol. i. pp. 145–237).]

" Begetter" in the Dedication, which is not written in the common phraseology of the period, and is throughout a piece of elaborate quaintness, means *procurer.* Five of the Sonnets—LXXX., CXXXIII., LXXXV., LXXXVI., and CXXI.—were written to be presented to some lady who had verses addressed to her by at least one other person than the supposed writer of these. The first seventeen sonnets may have been written at the request of a doting mother, who wished to persuade a handsome wayward son into an early marriage. "I hazard this conjecture with little confidence."

DR. INGLEBY.

On June 25, 1873, Dr. Ingleby read a paper before the Royal Society of Literature, maintaining that the "onlie begetter" of Thorpe's dedication means *sole author,* and that Mr. W. H. is a misprint for Mr. W. S., *i.e.,* William Shakspere. (This is also the view of Mr. E. A. Brae.)

PROF. MINTO.

[Characteristics of English Poets from Chaucer to Shirley. By William Minto, M.A. (Blackwood and Sons, Edinburgh and London. 1874), pp. 275–292. William Shakespeare—*Sonnets.*]

Sonnets CXXVII.–CLII. are "exercises of skill, undertaken in a spirit of wanton defiance and derision of commonplace." The only sonnet of the series inconsistent with this theory is CXLVI., which is unequivocally serious.

Shakespeare having taken up the relation between a lover
and a courtesan originally in wanton humorous defiance
of somewhat lackadaisical effusions, his dramatic instinct
could not be restrained from pursuing the relationship
farther into more serious aspects.

Sonnets I.–CXXVI. tell of a real friendship; there is a
sequence in them; they treat of consecutive themes.
Mr. W. H. was Shakespeare's friend and patron; a book-
seller would not have dared to divert the poet's promise
of immortality from a person of rank; no blind was in-
tended in the dedication; it pointed to William Herbert.
"Thy *mother's* glass" (3rd Sonnet), a reference to the
Countess of Pembroke, famous for her beauty and talents.
107th Sonnet refers to the death of Elizabeth; 104th to
the three years since Shakespeare first met his friend.
Pembroke came to London in 1598, a youth of eighteen.
Perhaps the "gaudy spring" of Sonnet I. was the acces-
sion of James I. The rival poet was Chapman—"a man
of overpowering enthusiasm, ever eager in magnifying
poetry, and advancing fervent claims to supernatural in-
spiration."[1] His chief patron, Sir F. Walsingham, was
connected with Pembroke, being father-in-law of Sidney,
Pembroke's uncle.

DR. ULRICI.

[Shakspeare's Dramatic Art. Translated from the third edition of the
German (1874), by L. Dora Schmitz. 1876. Vol. i. pp. 206–217.]

Ulrici believes that the Sonnets refer to real persons
and incidents. He strenuously opposes "the vagaries
of Neil and Massey."

[1] The same conclusion was independently arrived at by my friend Mr.
Harold Littledale.

F. G. FLEAY.

[On the Motive of Shakspere's Sonnets (1–125), a Defence of his Morality (*Macmillan's Magazine*, March, 1875).]

The Sonnets I.–CXXV. form a complete poem, written on a single subject. This is indicated by the placing of the six couplets called Sonnet CXXVI. at the end. We have no right to disturb the original arrangement; they were addressed to a youth by Shakspere in his own person.

The "shame" which Shakspere speaks of as attaching to him is the feeling produced by unfavourable critical opinions of his productions. (See Sonnets CXII., LXXII., XCV., LXI.). The "idle hours" of Sonnet LXI. are the "idle hours" of the dedication to *Venus and Adonis*, and the Earl of Southampton was Mr. W. H. The "absence," "journey," "travel," spoken of in the Sonnets is the separation between Southampton and Shakspere, caused by the metaphorical unfaithfulness of the latter to the former in producing, not poems dedicated to him, but only dramas destined for the multitude. Shakspere writes under the allegory of the marriage of poet and patron. The "jade," "horse," or "beast," ridden by Shakspere (Sonnets L., LI.), is Pegasus.[1] Shakspere's "travelling" means "strolling" as a player. The date of the Sonnets is 1593–1596; the Lord Chamberlain's company was (Mr. Fleay believes) strolling during 1594, 1595, 1596. Southampton forsakes Shakspere by accepting dedications from a rival poet, Nash. Shakspere's lameness (Sonnet LXXXIX.) is the lameness of his verses; the "proud full sail of his (Nash's) great verse" (Sonnet

[1] Can anything surpass this?—unless it be Mr. Fleay's later suggestion about the rose and the lily.

LXXXVI.), refers ironically to a prosaic Sonnet by Nash in *Pierce Pennilesse,* accompanying a complaint that Amyntas' (? Southampton's) name is omitted in the Sonnet Catalogue of English heroes appended to Spenser's *Fairy Queen;* for in this paragraph Nash uses the words "full sail." The "affable familiar ghost" (Sonnet LXXXVI.) may be compared with Pierce Pennilesse, p. 80 (Sh. Society's ed.), on spirits "called spies and tale-carriers;" but probably it means only "malicious interpretation." There are so many allusions to Southampton as a rose, that probably the Rose Theatre is alluded to under a figure. The allusions to lilies probably refer to John Lyly. The two poets, Lyly and Nash, are ironically set up in opposition to the "rose" Southampton. The "brand" set on Shakspere's name (Sonnet CXI.) is that set by satire or adverse criticism on his writings.

Shakspere had promised, 1593, to dedicate all his poems to Southampton. On the reopening of the theatres, December, 1593, or 1594, he returned to the stage, "strolling" with the company. Southampton remonstrated; Shakspere wrote these Sonnets (I.–CXXVI.) as a defence of his conduct. The woman of Sonnets XL.–XLII. is Shakspere's Muse.

A short abstract of the contents of the Sonnets I.–CXXVI., as understood by Mr. Fleay, is given.

PROF. KARL ELZE.

[William Shakespeare. Halle, 1876. pp. 369–380 and pp. 493–505.]

"Begetter" in Thorpe's dedication means "procurer" for the publisher. Perhaps Mr. W. H. was, as Neil suggests, Shakspere's brother-in-law, William Hathaway. But Charles Edwards found at Lamport Hall in 1873 a copy of a work, previously unknown, of Southwell, comprising four poems brought together by W. H., and by him put to press with G. Eld, 1606, the printer three years later of Shakspere's Sonnets. It is unlikely that two W. H.s at about the same time were engaged in literary work of this kind. But is it probable that Shakspere's brother-in-law could have added to his agricultural labours this work in literature?

The Sonnets on the subject of friendship are in the taste of the time; their contents are as conventional as their form. The story of the friends of the Sonnets only repeats what was already told by Lilly in his Euphues (*The Anatomy of Wit*); it is ridiculed by Ben Jonson, who despised sonnets, in his *Bartholomew Fair*.

We need not suppose that there is anything of autobiography in these Sonnets. As to the passion for a dark woman—we cannot say. Doubtless Shakspere did not pass through his London experiences without trials of the heart. But these Sonnets may be only a play of fancy to entertain the writer's friends. Prof. Elze replies at length to Kenny.

F. J. FURNIVALL.

[The Leopold Shakspere. Introduction by F. J. Furnivall [the Sonnets, pp. lxiii.–lxiv.]. (London, 1877.)]

The Sonnets are autobiographical. "Begetter" means the person—unknown to us—to whom they were ad-

H

dressed. The rival poet was Chapman. Mr. Furnivall gives the following grouping and analysis of the sonnets.

Group I.   Sonnets I.–CXXVI.

SECTION SONNETS

1   I.–XXVI.   α I.–XVII. Will's beauty, and his duty to marry and beget a son.

β XVIII.–XXVI. Will's beauty, and Shakspere's love for him.

2   XXVII.–XXXII. First absence. Shakspere travelling, and away from Will.

3   XXXIII.–XXXV. Will's sensual fault blamed, repented, and forgiven.

4   XXXVI.–XXXIX. Shakspere has committed a fault that will separate him from Will.

5   XL.–XLII. Will has taken away Shakspere's mistress (see Group 2, § 6, Sonnets CXXXIII.–CXXXVI.).

6   XLIII.–LXI.   α XLIII.–LVI. Second absence. Will absent. Shakspere has a portrait of him.

β LVII., LVIII. The sovereign; slave watching; so made by God.

γ LIX., LX. Will's beauty.

δ LXI. Waking and watching. Shakspere has rivals.

7   LXII.–LXV. Shakspere full of self-love, conquered by Time, which will conquer Will too; yet Shakspere will secure him eternity.

8   LXVI.–LXX. Shakspere (like Hamlet) tired of the world; but not only on public grounds. Will has mixt with bad company; but Shakspere is sure he is pure, and excuses him.

9   LXXI.–LXXIV. Shakspere on his own death, and his

SECTION SONNETS

entire love for his friend. (Compare the death-thoughts in *Hamlet* and *Measure for Measure.*)

10 LXXV.–LXXVII. Shakspere's love, and always writing on one theme, his Will; with the present of a table-book, dial, and pocket looking-glass combined in one.

11 LXXVIII.–XCIII. *a* LXXVIII.–LXXXVI. Shakspere on his rivals in Will's love. (G. Chapman, the rival poet.)

β LXXXVII.–XCIII. Shakspere's farewell to Will: most beautiful in the self-forgetfulness of Shakspere's love.

12 XCIV.–XCVI. Will vicious.

13 XCVII.–XCIX. Third Absence. Will's flower-like beauty and Shakspere's love for him; followed by faults on both sides, and a separation ended by Will's desire, CXX., l. 11.

14 C.–CXXI. *a* C.–CXII. Renewing of love, three years after the first Sonnets (CIV.). Shakspere's love stronger now in its summer than it was in its spring, CII., l. 5; CXIX., ll. 10–12. Note the "hell of time," CXX., l. 6, that Will's unkindness has made Shakspere pass.

β CXIII., CXIV. Fourth Absence. Shakspere sees Will in all nature.

γ CXV.–CXXI. Shakspere describes his love for Will, and justifies himself.

15 CXXII.–CXXVI. Shakspere excuses himself for giving away Will's present of some tables; again describes his love for Will, and warns Will that he too must grow old.

Group II. Sonnets CXXVII.–CLIV.

1 CXXVII. Of his mistress's dark complexion, brows, and eyes. (Cf. Berowne on his dark Rosaline in *Love's Labour's Lost*.)

2 CXXVIII. On her, his music, playing music (the virginals).

3 CXXIX. On her, after enjoying her. He laments his weakness.

4 CXXX. On her, a chaffing description of her. (Cf. Marlowe's *Ignoto* ; *Lingua*, before 1603, in Dodsley, ix. 370 ; and Shirley's *Sisters*: " Were it not fine," etc.

5 CXXXI., CXXXII. Though plain to others, his mistress is fairest to Shakspere's doting heart. But her deeds are black, and her black eyes pity him.

6 CXXXIII.–CXXXVI. She has taken his friend Will from him (cf. XL.–XLII.). He asks her to restore his friend (CXXXIV.), or to take him as part of her (and his) Will (CXXXV.). If she'll but love his name, she'll love him (Shakspere), as his name, too, is Will (CXXXVI.).

7 CXXXVII.–CXLV. Shakspere knows his mistress is not beautiful, and that she's false, but he loves her (CXXXVII.). Each lies to and flatters the other (CXXXVIII.). Still, if she'd only look kindly on him, it'll be enough (CXXXIX.). She must not look too cruelly, or he might despair and go mad, and tell the world that ill of her that it would only too soon believe (CXL.). He loves

her in spite of his senses (CXLI.). She has broken her bed-vow; then let her pity him (CXLII.). She may catch his friend if she will but give him a smile (CXLIII.). He has two lovers, a fair man, and a dark woman who'd corrupt the man (CXLIV., the *Key Sonnet*). She was going to say she hated him; but, seeing his distress, said, not him (CXLV.).

8   CXLVI. (? Misplaced.) A remonstrance with himself, on spending too much, either on dress or outward self-indulgence, and exhorting himself to give it up for inward culture. (The blank for two words in line 2, I fill with "Hemmed with," cf. *Venus and Adonis*, 1022, "Hemm'd with thieves.")

9   CXLVII., CXLVIII. Shakspere's feverish longing drives him mad, his doctor—Reason—being set aside (CXLVII.). Love has obscured his sight (CXLVIII.).

10   CXLIX.–CLII. He gives himself up wholly to his mistress: loves whom she loves, hates whom she hates (CLXIX.). The worst of her deeds he loves better than any other's best (CL.). The more he ought to hate her, the more he loves her. He is content to be her drudge, for he loves her (CLI.). Yet he's forsworn, for he's told lies of her goodness, and she has broken her bed-vows; he has broken twenty oaths (CLII.).

11   CLIII, CLIV. (May be Group III., or Division 2 of Group II.) Two Sonnets lighter in tone. In both Cupid sleeps, has his brand put out in (CLIII.) a fountain (CLIV.), a well which the

brand turns into medical baths. Shakspere comes for cure to each, but finds none. He wants his mistress's eyes for that (CLIII.). Water cools not love (CLIV.).

G. S. CALDWELL.

[Sir Walter Raleigh the Author of Shakspere's Plays and Sonnets. [By G. S. Caldwell.] Melbourne, Stillwell and Knight. 1877. 32 pp.]

" The Sonnets LXXI., LXXII., LXXIII., and LXXIV., to my mind afford proof than which nothing could be stronger of the identification of Raleigh as the author. With most unwavering confidence I advance the proposition that these Sonnets were addressed by Raleigh to his wife, when he was lying under sentence of death, in 1603."

Some of the Sonnets are addressed by Raleigh to Queen Elizabeth : Sonnet XXXVII. is a tribute to Prince Henry.

Raleigh before 1596 had a limp ; in that year he was wounded, and became lame for the rest of his life. (See Sonnets XXXVII. and LXXXIX.)

PROF. GOEDEKE.

[Ueber Sonette Shakespeare's. Von Karl Goedeke (in Deutsche Rundschau. Marz, 1877. pp. 386–409).]

In the first 126 Sonnets 73 use (as an address to the friend) " thou " and " thee ; " 30 use " you ; " 23 have neither " thou " nor " you." Of these 23 add 11 to the " thou " sonnets, we get 84 ; add the remaining 12 to the " you " sonnets, we get 42. Suppose Shakspere wrote

his Sonnets in books or groups of 14 each (14 perhaps
because there are so many lines in a sonnet), then there
are six books of "thou" Sonnets and three books of
"you" Sonnets, in the total 126. But there remain 28
Sonnets (CXXVI.–CLIV.), *i.e.*, two more books of 14 Sonnets
each.

The Sonnets are a miscellaneous gathering written at
various times, addressed to various persons, real and
imaginary, and thrown together in chance-medley dis-
order.   Many of the Sonnets treat of imaginary persons
and incidents similar to some of those in Shakspere's
plays and poems (*e.g.*, the dark woman and Rosaline of
Love's Labour's Lost; the opening sonnets, and *Venus
and Adonis*).   XXXVIII. is addressed to Queen Elizabeth ;
XXIX., XLIV., XLV., XLVIII., L., LI., XCVII., to Shakspere's
wife ; CVIII. to his son Hamnet.

W. M. ROSSETTI.

[Lives of Famous Poets. London, 1877. pp. 50–56.]

Mr. Rossetti accepts the "personal theory" of the
Sonnets ; he inclines to identify the youth rather with
Pembroke than Southampton, noting the fact that Pem-
broke was very like his mother. (See Sonnet III.)

T. A. SPALDING.

[Shakspere's Sonnets. An article in *The Gentleman's Magazine*, March,
1878. 18 pp.]

The main object of the article is to show that the first
hundred and twenty-six sonnets, at any rate, are arranged,

in the Quarto of 1609, in an order that is probably chronological; they were not intended at the time they were written to form a consecutive poem, though many were written at the same time, but were subsequently strung together in the order in which we now possess them.

They fall into three groups. 1st, From familiarity to friendship, Sonnets I.–XXV.; 2nd, Clouds, Sonnets XXVI.–XCVI.; 3rd, Reconciliation, XCVII.–CXXVI.

The first group (I.–XXV.) consists of two sections: I.–XIV., Will's beauty, and his duty to get married; no deep feeling of affection yet; XV.–XXV., if Will won't marry, Shakspere will make him immortal by verse; evidence of deeper affection.

Second group (XXVI.–XCVI.) consists of the following sections: (*a*) XXVI.–XXXII., Shakspere's feelings in grief and absence (XXVI., Prologue; XXXII., Epilogue). (*b*) XXXIII.–XXXVIII., Will's first offence—he holds aloof from his social inferior, the player Shakspere. (*c*) XXXIX., an Absence-sonnet (second absence), between Will's first and second offence. (*d*) XL.–XLII., Will's second offence, robbing Shakspere of his mistress. (*e*) XLIII.–LV., third absence; Shakspere on a journey; neglected by Will. (*f*) LVI.–LVIII., Will and Shakspere near one another, yet they do not meet. (*g*) LIX.–LXV., Shakspere finds relief in his art. (*h*) LXVI.–LXXIV., gloom; world-weariness. (*i*) LXXV.–LXXXVI., Will favours a rival poet. (*j*) LXXXVII.–XCVI., Farewell to Will.

Third group (XCVII.–CXXVI.), Reconciliation; confession of faults; love triumphant.

HERMANN ISAAC.

[Archiv für das Studium der Neueren Sprachen und Literaturen. 1878–79. Zu den Sonnetten Shakspere's (seven articles).]

The first article gives a survey of the critical literature relating to the Sonnets of love and jealousy. Isaac believes that they are concerned with real persons and events. In subsequent articles a detailed criticism is given of the Sonnets in Part I. of Bodenstedt's arrangement, and in the order adopted by Bodenstedt. (See p. 74.)

TENNYSONIANA.

[2nd Edition. 1879.]

Chapter iv., Tennyson and Shakespeare's Sonnets (pp. 55–77), gives a number of parallel passages from the Sonnets, illustrating passages in *In Memoriam.*

ALGERNON C. SWINBURNE.

[Short Notes on English Poets, in *The Fortnightly Review*, December 1, 1880.]

Mr. Swinburne accepts the story of Shakspere's friendship, his love for a mistress, and the wrong done to him by a friend, as true. He speaks of the Sonnets CXXVII.–CLIV. as "incomparably the more important and altogether precious division of the Sonnets." [1]

[1] It is noteworthy that among the Sonnets chosen by Wordsworth as the most eminent for "merits of thought and language," only one comes from the second division of the Sonnets.

DAVID M. MAIN.

[A Treasury of English Sonnets. 1880.]

Mr. Main inclines to Gerald Massey's view, and supposes that the Earl of Pembroke is Thorpe's Mr. W. H. The selected Sonnets in the *Treasury* are well and fully annotated.

WILLIAM THOMSON.

[The Renascence Drama; or, History made Visible. Melbourne, 1880. 359 pp. The Sonnets, pp. 111–133.]

The Sonnets were written by Bacon, in 1600, to be read by William Herbert to the Queen, and thereby win back her regard for her offending truant Essex, when the " lord of my love " lay under his last eclipse. Elizabeth was a black beauty, not literally, but as hostile in mind and will to Essex.

G. TRAVERS SMITH.

The latest theory of 1880 regarding Shakspere's Sonnets was that of Mr. G. Travers Smith, of Tasmania, in the *Victorian Review* for last December, pp. 253–58.

"The secret of the Sonnets, of the one hundred and twenty-six, is simple. They were addressed to his [Shakspere's] son. Not a son by Anne Hathaway, but to an illegitimate one by some other woman—the evidence would go to show by some woman of high rank. . . . Sonnet XXXIII. is conclusive, even if we did not know Shakspere's love of the pun or play on a word :—

> *Even so,* my Sun *one early morn did shine*
> *With all triumphant splendour on my brow."* [1]

E. STENGEL.

[Bilden die Ersten 126 Sonette Shakspere's einen Sonettcyclus, und welche ist die ursprüngliche Reihenfolge derselben? Englische Studien. 34 pp. 1881.]

They were modelled after Daniel's Sonnets; were written after *Venus and Adonis* and perhaps before *Lucrece,* for the Earl of Southampton, in the fashion of the time, to amuse him and his young friends. The true order of I.–CXXVI. is the following: XXVI. (dedication), I., IV., VIII., VII., XI., III., V., VI., II., IX., X., XII., XX., XIV., XIII., XV., XVI., XVII., LIX., CVI., LIII., CV., LIV., CIV., LXXXI., LV., LXIV., XIX., LXIII., LXV., LX., CVII., XVIII., CXXVI., CVIII., LXXVII., CXXII., C., CI., XXXVIII., XXIII., LXXIII., LXXIV., XXXII., XXXIX., LXXVIII., LXXIX., LXXXII., XXI., LXXVI., CIII., LXXXIII., LXXXV., LXXX., LXXXVI., LXXI., LXXII., CII., LXXXIV., LVIII., LVII., LXVII., LXVIII., CXXIII., LXVI., CXVI., CXV., CXXIV., XXV., XXIX., XXX., XXXI., XXXVII., CXXV., XCI., XCII., XCIII., XCIV., LXIX., LXX., XXXIII., XXXIV., XXXV., XCV., XCVI., XL., XLI., XLII., XXXVI., LXXXVII., L., LI., XXVII., XXVIII., XLIII., LXI., LXII., XXII., XXIV., XLVI., XLVII., XLIV., XLV., XCVII., XCVIII., XCIX., XLVIII. (perhaps

---

[1] F. J. Furnivall, *The Academy,* Aug. 27, 1881.

XLIX., LXXXVIII.–XC. better before LXXXVII.), XLIX., LXXXVIII., LXXXIX., XC., CIX., CXVII., CXXI., CXI., CXII., LXXV., LII., CXIII., CXIV., CXVIII., CXIX., CXX., LVI.

An analysis of each Sonnet is given, and an appendix is added—I. Sonnets 34–40 of Daniel's *Delia ;* II. Cynthia, with certain Sonnets, etc. 1595. Sonnets 1–20.

FRITZ KRAUSS.

[Die schwarze Schöne der Shakespeare-Sonette: Jahrbuch der Shakespeare Gesellschaft. Bd. XVI. pp. 144–212. 1881.]

Supports and developes Gerald Massey's theory as modified in his edition of 1872. What is of most value in Krauss's article is a striking series of parallel passages from Sidney and others illustrating the Sonnets.[1]

RICHARD HENRY STODDARD.

[The Sonnet in English Poetry. *Scribner's Monthly.* October, 1881.]

Agrees with Dyce that "the greater number of the Sonnets were composed in an assumed character, and at different times, for the amusement and probably at the suggestion of the author's intimate associates." To the two Sonnets pointed out by Dyce as having an individual application to Shakspere (CX. and CXI.), Mr. Stoddard adds LXXI. and LXXIII. "The Sonnets of Shakspere extend over a considerable period, but most of them were

---

[1] Herr Krauss refers to an article by him on the Sonnets which I have not seen. "Nord und Sud," Feb. 1879.

written, I think, in his early manhood. The conceits with which they abound, and a certain crude richness of diction, wherein maturity and immaturity struggle for mastery, determine their date."

MRS. C. F. ASHMEAD WINDLE.

[Address to the New Shakspere Society of London. Discovery of Lord Verulam's Undoubted Authorship of the "Shakspere" Works. San Francisco, 1881.]

In the "Shakspere" plays, Bacon expresses an ENIGMA under a VEILED ALLEGORY. The key to the running allegory is contained in the mystery of the Sonnets. An "absolute divineness of ideality underlies their mere outward form, as well as a plaintive autobiographical information of the poet's consciousness." Mrs. Windle illustrates her discovery by the play of *Cymbeline*, where Posthumu symbolizes the posthumous fame of Bacon, Cloten (clothing) his living bodily personality, and Morgan (my organ) the Novum *Organum*. Posthumus is the son of Sicilius: now the sonnet-form is of *Sicilian* origin. Sicilius therefore signifies the poetic genius invoked in the sonnets of Bacon as a "lovely boy," and besought to beget "copies" of itself, which should gain an enduring fame. Hence Posthumus represents the posthumous fame promised in the Sonnets. Tenantius, by whom Sicilius "had his titles" of beauty, grace, and honour, was the writer or dweller in the Sonnets, who gained the sur-addition Leonatus, and he, of course, signifies the author of the dramas, Francis Bacon. "I feel," writes Mrs. Windle,

" that my penetration into, and unfolding of the inmost
mind and heart of these plays, is a realization of the
deepest reach of sympathetic intuition of which the
human intellect and soul are capable—only short of that
attained by the immortal dramatist himself."

SONNETS.

TO . THE . ONLIE . BEGETTER . OF .

THESE . INSVING . SONNETS .

M . W. H. ALL . HAPPINESSE .

AND . THAT . ETERNITIE .

PROMISED .

BY .

OVR . EVER-LIVING . POET .

WISHETH .

THE . WELL-WISHING .

ADVENTVRER . IN .

SETTING .

FORTH .

T. T.

I.

From fairest creatures we desire increase,
That thereby beauty's rose might never die,
But as the riper should by time decease,
His tender heir might bear his memory:
But thou, contracted to thine own bright eyes,
Feed'st thy light's flame with self-substantial fuel,
Making a famine where abundance lies,
Thyself thy foe, to thy sweet self too cruel.
Thou that art now the world's fresh ornament
And only herald to the gaudy spring,
Within thine own bud buriest thy content,
And, tender churl, makest waste in niggarding.
    Pity the world, or else this glutton be,
    To eat the world's due, by the grave and thee.

II.

When forty winters shall besiege thy brow
And dig deep trenches in thy beauty's field,
Thy youth's proud livery, so gazed on now,
Will be a tatter'd weed, of small worth held:
Then being ask'd where all thy beauty lies,
Where all the treasure of thy lusty days,
To say, within thine own deep-sunken eyes,
Were an all-eating shame and thriftless praise.
How much more praise deserved thy beauty's use,
If thou couldst answer, "This fair child of mine
Shall sum my count and make my old excuse,"
Proving his beauty by succession thine!
    This were to be new made when thou art old,
    And see thy blood warm when thou feel'st it cold.

III.

Look in thy glass, and tell the face thou viewest
Now is the time that face should form another;
Whose fresh repair if now thou not renewest,
Thou dost beguile the world, unbless some mother.
For where is she so fair whose unear'd womb
Disdains the tillage of thy husbandry?
Or who is he so fond will be the tomb
Of his self-love, to stop posterity?
Thou art thy mother's glass, and she in thee
Calls back the lovely April of her prime;
So thou through windows of thine age shalt see,
Despite of wrinkles, this thy golden time.
    But if thou live, rememb'red not to be,
    Die single, and thine image dies with thee.

IV.

Unthrifty loveliness, why dost thou spend
Upon thyself thy beauty's legacy?
Nature's bequest gives nothing, but doth lend,
And being frank, she lends to those are free:
Then, beauteous niggard, why dost thou abuse
The bounteous largess given thee to give?
Profitless usurer, why dost thou use
So great a sum of sums, yet canst not live?
For having traffic with thyself alone,
Thou of thyself thy sweet self dost deceive:
Then how, when Nature calls thee to be gone,
What acceptable audit canst thou leave?
    Thy unused beauty must be tomb'd with thee,
    Which, used, lives th' executor to be.

V.

Those hours, that with gentle work did frame
The lovely gaze where every eye doth dwell,
Will play the tyrants to the very same
And that unfair which fairly doth excel;
For never-resting time leads summer on
To hideous winter, and confounds him there;
Sap check'd with frost, and lusty leaves quite gone,
Beauty o'ersnow'd and bareness everywhere:
Then, were not summer's distillation left,
A liquid prisoner pent in walls of glass,
Beauty's effect with beauty were bereft,
Nor it, nor no remembrance what it was:
    But flowers distill'd, though they with winter meet,
    Leese but their show; their substance still lives sweet.

VI.

Then let not winter's ragged hand deface
In thee thy summer, ere thou be distill'd:
Make sweet some vial; treasure thou some place
With beauty's treasure, ere it be self-kill'd.
That use is not forbidden usury,
Which happies those that pay the willing loan;
That's for thyself to breed another thee,
Or ten times happier, be it ten for one;
Ten times thyself were happier than thou art,
If ten of thine ten times refigured thee;
Then what could death do, if thou shouldst depart,
Leaving thee living in posterity?
    Be not self-will'd, for thou art much too fair
    To be death's conquest and make worms thine heir.

VII.

Lo, in the Orient when the gracious light
Lifts up his burning head, each under eye
Doth homage to his new-appearing sight,
Serving with looks his sacred majesty;
And having climb'd the steep-up heavenly hill,
Resembling strong youth in his middle age,
Yet mortal looks adore his beauty still,
Attending on his golden pilgrimage;
But when from highmost pitch, with weary car,
Like feeble age, he reeleth from the day,
The eyes, 'fore duteous, now converted are
From his low tract, and look another way:
    So thou, thyself outgoing in thy noon,
    Unlook'd on diest, unless thou get a son.

VIII.

Music to hear, why hear'st thou music sadly?
Sweets with sweets war not, joy delights in joy:
Why lovest thou that which thou receivest not gladly,
Or else receivest with pleasure thine annoy?
If the true concord of well-tuned sounds,
By unions married, do offend thine ear,
They do but sweetly chide thee, who confounds
In singleness the parts that thou shouldst bear.
Mark how one string, sweet husband to another,
Strikes each in each by mutual ordering;
Resembling sire and child and happy mother,
Who, all in one, one pleasing note do sing:
    Whose speechless song, being many, seeming one,
    Sings this to thee: " Thou single wilt prove none."

IX.

Is it for fear to wet a widow's eye
That thou consumest thyself in single life?
Ah! if thou issueless shalt hap to die,
The world will wail thee, like a makeless wife;
The world will be thy widow, and still weep
That thou no form of thee hast left behind,
When every private widow well may keep
By children's eyes her husband's shape in mind.
Look, what an unthrift in the world doth spend
Shifts but his place, for still the world enjoys it;
But beauty's waste hath in the world an end,
And, kept unused, the user so destroys it.
  No love toward others in that bosom sits
    That on himself such murderous shame commits.

X.

For shame! deny that thou bear'st love to any,
Who for thyself art so unprovident.
Grant, if thou wilt, thou art beloved of many,
But that thou none lovest is most evident;
For thou art so possess'd with murderous hate
That 'gainst thyself thou stick'st not to conspire,
Seeking that beauteous roof to ruinate
Which to repair should be thy chief desire.
O, change thy thought, that I may change my mind!
Shall hate be fairer lodged than gentle love?
Be, as thy presence is, gracious and kind,
Or to thyself at least kind-hearted prove:
  Make thee another self, for love of me,
    That beauty still may live in thine or thee.

XI.

As fast as thou shalt wane, so fast thou grow'st
In one of thine, from that which thou departest;
And that fresh blood which youngly thou bestow'st
Thou mayst call thine when thou from youth convertest.
Herein lives wisdom, beauty and increase;
Without this, folly, age and cold decay:
If all were minded so, the times should cease
And threescore year would make the world away.
Let those whom Nature hath not made for store,
Harsh, featureless and rude, barrenly perish:
Look, whom she best endow'd she gave the more;
Which bounteous gift thou shouldst in bounty cherish:
   She carved thee for her seal, and meant thereby
   Thou shouldst print more, nor let that copy die.

XII.

When I do count the clock that tells the time,
And see the brave day sunk in hideous night;
When I behold the violet past prime,
And sable curls all silver'd o'er with white;
When lofty trees I see barren of leaves,
Which erst from heat did canopy the herd,
And summer's green all girded up in sheaves,
Borne on the bier with white and bristly beard,
Then of thy beauty do I question make,
That thou among the wastes of time must go,
Since sweets and beauties do themselves forsake
And die as fast as they see others grow;
   And nothing 'gainst Time's scythe can make defence
   Save breed, to brave him when he takes thee hence.

XIII.

O, that you were yourself! but, love, you are
No longer yours than you yourself here live :
Against this coming end you should prepare,
And your sweet semblance to some other give ;
So should that beauty which you hold in lease
Find no determination ; then you were
Yourself again, after yourself's decease,
When your sweet issue your sweet form should bear.
Who lets so fair a house fall to decay,
Which husbandry in honour might uphold
Against the stormy gusts of winter's day
And barren rage of death's eternal cold?
    O, none but unthrifts ! Dear my love, you know
    You had a father : let your son say so.

XIV.

Not from the stars do I my judgement pluck ;
And yet methinks I have astronomy,
But not to tell of good or evil luck,
Of plagues, of dearths, or seasons' quality ;
Nor can I fortune to brief minutes tell,
Pointing to each his thunder, rain and wind,
Or say with princes if it shall go well,
By oft predict that I in heaven find :
But from thine eyes my knowledge I derive,
And, constant stars, in them I read such art
As " Truth and beauty shall together thrive,
If from thyself to store thou wouldst convert ; "
    Or else of thee this I prognosticate :
    " Thy end is truth's and beauty's doom and date."

XV.

When I consider every thing that grows
Holds in perfection but a little moment,
That this huge stage presenteth nought but shows
Whereon the stars in secret influence comment;
When I perceive that men as plants increase,
Cheered and check'd even by the selfsame sky,
Vaunt in their youthful sap, at height decrease,
And wear their brave state out of memory;
Then the conceit of this inconstant stay
Sets you most rich in youth before my sight,
Where wasteful Time debateth with Decay,
To change your day of youth to sullied night;
    And all in war with Time for love of you,
    As he takes from you, I engraft you new.

XVI.

But wherefore do not you a mightier way
Make war upon this bloody tyrant, Time?
And fortify yourself in your decay
With means more blessed than my barren rime?
Now stand you on the top of happy hours,
And many maiden gardens, yet unset,
With virtuous wish would bear your living flowers
Much liker than your painted counterfeit:
So should the lines of life that life repair,
Which this, Time's pencil, or my pupil pen,
Neither in inward worth nor outward fair,
Can make you live yourself in eyes of men.
    To give away yourself keeps yourself still;
    And you must live, drawn by your own sweet skill.

XVII.

Who will believe my verse in time to come,
If it were fill'd with your most high deserts?
Though yet, heaven knows, it is but as a tomb
Which hides your life and shows not half your parts.
If I could write the beauty of your eyes
And in fresh numbers number all your graces,
The age to come would say " This poet lies;
Such heavenly touches ne'er touch'd earthly faces."
So should my papers, yellowed with their age,
Be scorn'd, like old men of less truth than tongue,
And your true rights be term'd a poet's rage
And stretched metre of an antique song:
   But were some child of yours alive that time,
   You should live twice, in it and in my rime.

XVIII.

Shall I compare thee to a summer's day?
Thou art more lovely and more temperate:
Rough winds do shake the darling buds of May,
And summer's lease hath all too short a date:
Sometime too hot the eye of heaven shines,
And often is his gold complexion dimm'd;
And every fair from fair sometime declines,
By chance or nature's changing course untrimm'd:
But thy eternal summer shall not fade,
Nor lose possession of that fair thou owest,
Nor shall death brag thou wander'st in his shade,
When in eternal lines to time thou grow'st;
   So long as men can breathe, or eyes can see,
   So long lives this, and this gives life to thee.

XIX.

Devouring Time, blunt thou the lion's paws,
And make the earth devour her own sweet brood;
Pluck the keen teeth from the fierce tiger's jaws,
And burn the long-lived phœnix in her blood;
Make glad and sorry seasons as thou fleets,
And do whate'er thou wilt, swift-footed Time,
To the wide world and all her fading sweets;
But I forbid thee one most heinous crime:
O, carve not with thy hours my love's fair brow,
Nor draw no lines there with thine antique pen;
Him in thy course untainted do allow
For beauty's pattern to succeeding men.
   Yet do thy worst, old Time: despite thy wrong,
   My love shall in my verse ever live young.

XX.

A woman's face with Nature's own hand painted
Hast thou, the master-mistress of my passion;
A woman's gentle heart, but not acquainted
With shifting change, as is false women's fashion;
An eye more bright than theirs, less false in rolling,
Gilding the object whereupon it gazeth;
A man in hue all hues in his controlling,
Which steals men's eyes and women's souls amazeth.
And for a woman wert thou first created;
Till Nature, as she wrought thee, fell a-doting,
And by addition me of thee defeated,
By adding one thing to my purpose nothing.
   But since she prick'd thee out for women's pleasure,
   Mine be thy love, and thy love's use their treasure.

XXI.

So is it not with me as with that Muse
Stirr'd by a painted beauty to his verse,
Who heaven itself for ornament doth use
And every fair with his fair doth rehearse,
Making a couplement of proud compare,
With sun and moon, with earth and sea's rich·gems,
With April's first-born flowers, and all things rare
That heaven's air in this huge rondure hems.
O, let me, true in love, but truly write,
And then believe me, my love is as fair
As any mother's child, though not so bright
As those gold candles fix'd in heaven's air :
    Let them say more that like of hear-say well ;
    I will not praise that purpose not to sell.

XXII.

My glass shall not persuade me I am old,
So long as youth and thou are of one date ;
But when in thee time's furrows I behold,
Then look I death my days should expiate.
For all that beauty that doth cover thee
Is but the seemly raiment of my heart,
Which in thy breast doth live, as thine in me :
How can I then be elder than thou art ?
O, therefore, love, be of thyself so wary
As I, not for myself, but for thee will ;
Bearing thy heart, which I will keep so chary
As tender nurse her babe from faring ill.
    Presume not on thy heart when mine is slain ;
    Thou gavest me thine, not to give back again.

XXIII.

As an unperfect actor on the stage,
Who with his fear is put besides his part,
Or some fierce thing replete with too much rage,
Whose strength's abundance weakens his own heart;
So I, for fear of trust, forget to say
The perfect ceremony of love's rite,
And in mine own love's strength seem to decay,
O'ercharged with burthen of mine own love's might.
O, let my books be then the eloquence
And dumb presagers of my speaking breast,
Who plead for love, and look for recompense,
More than that tongue that more hath more express'd.
   O, learn to read what silent love hath writ:
   To hear with eyes belongs to love's fine wit.

XXIV.

Mine eye hath play'd the painter and hath stell'd
Thy beauty's form in table of my heart;
My body is the frame wherein 'tis held,
And perspective it is best painter's art.
For through the painter must you see his skill,
To find where your true image pictured lies,
Which in my bosom's shop is hanging still,
That hath his windows glazed with thine eyes.
Now see what good turns eyes for eyes have done:
Mine eyes have drawn thy shape, and thine for me
Are windows to my breast, where-through the sun
Delights to peep, to gaze therein on thee;
   Yet eyes this cunning want to grace their art,
   They draw but what they see, know not the heart.

XXV.

Let those who are in favour with their stars
Of public honour and proud titles boast,
Whilst I, whom fortune of such triumph bars,
Unlook'd for joy in that I honour most.
Great princes' favourites their fair leaves spread
But as the marigold at the sun's eye,
And in themselves their pride lies buried,
For at a frown they in their glory die.
The painful warrior famoused for fight,
After a thousand victories once foil'd,
Is from the book of honour razed quite,
And all the rest forgot for which he toil'd:
    Then happy I, that love and am beloved
    Where I may not remove nor be removed.

XXVI.

Lord of my love, to whom in vassalage
Thy merit hath my duty strongly knit,
To thee I send this written ambassage,
To witness duty, not to show my wit:
Duty so great, which wit so poor as mine
May make seem bare, in wanting words to show it,
But that I hope some good conceit of thine
In thy soul's thought, all naked, will bestow it;
Till whatsoever star that guides my moving
Points on me graciously with fair aspect,
And puts apparel on my tatter'd loving,
To show me worthy of thy sweet respect:
    Then may I dare to boast how I do love thee;
    Till then not show my head where thou mayst prove me.

XXVII.

Weary with toil, I haste me to my bed,
The dear repose for limbs with travel tired;
But then begins a journey in my head
To work my mind, when body's work's expired:
For then my thoughts, from far where I abide,
Intend a zealous pilgrimage to thee,
And keep my drooping eyelids open wide,
Looking on darkness which the blind do see:
Save that my soul's imaginary sight
Presents thy shadow to my sightless view,
Which, like a jewel hung in ghastly night,
Makes black night beauteous and her old face new.
   Lo, thus, by day my limbs, by night my mind,
   For thee, and for myself no quiet find.

XXVIII.

How can I then return in happy plight,
That am debarr'd the benefit of rest?
When day's oppression is not eased by night,
But day by night, and night by day, oppress'd;
And each, though enemies to either's reign,
Do in consent shake hands to torture me,
The one by toil, the other to complain
How far I toil, still farther off from thee?
I tell the day, to please him, thou art bright
And dost him grace when clouds do blot the heaven:
So flatter I the swart-complexion'd night;
When sparkling stars twire not thou gild'st the even.
   But day doth daily draw my sorrows longer,
    And night doth nightly make grief's length seem
      stronger.

XXIX.

When, in disgrace with fortune and men's eyes,
I all alone beweep my outcast state,
And trouble deaf heaven with my bootless cries,
And look upon myself, and curse my fate,
Wishing me like to one more rich in hope,
Featured like him, like him with friends possess'd,
Desiring this man's art, and that man's scope,
With what I most enjoy contented least;
Yet in these thoughts myself almost despising,
Haply I think on thee, and then my state,
Like to the lark at break of day arising
From sullen earth, sings hymns at heaven's gate:
    For thy sweet love rememb'red such wealth brings
    That then I scorn to change my state with kings.

XXX.

When to the sessions of sweet silent thought
I summon up remembrance of things past,
I sigh the lack of many a thing I sought,
And with old woes new wail my dear time's waste:
Then can I drown an eye, unused to flow,
For precious friends hid in death's dateless night,
And weep afresh love's long since cancell'd woe,
And moan the expense of many a vanish'd sight:
Then can I grieve at grievances foregone,
And heavily from woe to woe tell o'er
The sad account of fore-bemoaned moan,
Which I new pay as if not paid before.
    But if the while I think on thee, dear friend,
    All losses are restored and sorrows end.

XXXI.

Thy bosom is endeared with all hearts,
Which I by lacking have supposed dead;
And there reigns Love, and all Love's loving parts,
And all those friends which I thought buried.
How many a holy and obsequious tear
Hath dear religious love stol'n from mine eye,
As interest of the dead, which now appear
But things removed that hidden in thee lie!
Thou art the grave where buried love doth live,
Hung with the trophies of my lovers gone,
Who all their parts of me to thee did give;
That due of many now is thine alone:
  Their images I loved I view in thee,
  And thou, all they, hast all the all of me.

XXXII.

If thou survive my well-contented day,
When that churl Death my bones with dust shall cover,
And shalt by fortune once more re-survey
These poor rude lines of thy deceased lover,
Compare them with the bettering of the time,
And though they be outstripp'd by every pen,
Reserve them for my love, not for their rime,
Exceeded by the height of happier men.
O, then vouchsafe me but this loving thought:
" Had my friend's Muse grown with this growing age,
A dearer birth than this his love had brought,
To march in ranks of better equipage:
  But since he died, and poets better prove,
  Theirs for their style I'll read, his for his love."

XXXIII.

Full many a glorious morning have I seen
Flatter the mountain tops with sovereign eye,
Kissing with golden face the meadows green,
Gilding pale streams with heavenly alchemy;
Anon permit the basest clouds to ride
With ugly rack on his celestial face,
And from the forlorn world his visage hide,
Stealing unseen to west with this disgrace:
Even so my sun one early morn did shine
With all-triumphant splendour on my brow;
But, out, alack! he was but one hour mine,
The region cloud hath mask'd him from me now.
   Yet him for this my love no whit disdaineth;
    Suns of the world may stain when heaven's sun
      staineth.

XXXIV.

Why didst thou promise such a beauteous day,
And make me travel forth without my cloak,
To let base clouds o'ertake me in my way,
Hiding thy bravery in their rotten smoke?
'Tis not enough that through the cloud thou break,
To dry the rain on my storm-beaten face,
For no man well of such a salve can speak
That heals the wound and cures not the disgrace:
Nor can thy shame give physic to my grief;
Though thou repent, yet I have still the loss:
The offender's sorrow lends but weak relief
To him that bears the strong offence's cross.
   Ah, but those tears are pearl which thy love sheds,
   And they are rich and ransom all ill deeds.

K

XXXV.

No more be grieved at that which thou hast done :
Roses have thorns, and silver fountains mud ;
Clouds and eclipses stain both moon and sun,
And loathsome canker lives in sweetest bud.
All men make faults, and even I in this,
Authorizing thy trespass with compare,
Myself corrupting, salving thy amiss,
Excusing thy sins more than thy sins are ;
For to thy sensual fault I bring in sense—
Thy adverse party is thy advocate—
And 'gainst myself a lawful plea commence :
Such civil war is in my love and hate,
    That I an accessary needs must be
    To that sweet thief which sourly robs from me.

XXXVI.

Let me confess that we two must be twain,
Although our undivided loves are one :
So shall those blots that do with me remain,
Without thy help, by me be borne alone.
In our two loves there is but one respect,
Though in our lives a separable spite,
Which, though it alter not love's sole effect,
Yet doth it steal sweet hours from love's delight.
I may not evermore acknowledge thee,
Lest my bewailed guilt should do thee shame,
Nor thou with public kindness honour me,
Unless thou take that honour from thy name :
    But do not so ; I love thee in such sort
    As, thou being mine, mine is thy good report.

XXXVII.

As a decrepit father takes delight
To see his active child do deeds of youth,
So I, made lame by fortune's dearest spite,
Take all my comfort of thy worth and truth;
For whether beauty, birth, or wealth, or wit,
Or any of these all, or all, or more,
Entitled in thy parts do crowned sit,
I make my love engrafted to this store :
So then I am not lame, poor, nor despised,
Whilst that this shadow doth such substance give
That I in thy abundance am sufficed
And by a part of all thy glory live.
   Look, what is best, that best I wish in thee :
   This wish I have ; then ten times happy me !

XXXVIII.

How can my Muse want subject to invent,
While thou dost breathe, that pour'st into my verse
Thine own sweet argument, too excellent
For every vulgar paper to rehearse ?
O, give thyself the thanks, if aught in me
Worthy perusal stand against thy sight ;
For who's so dumb that cannot write to thee,
When thou thyself dost give invention light ?
Be thou the tenth Muse, ten times more in worth
Than those old nine which rimers invocate ;
And he that calls on thee, let him bring forth
Eternal numbers to outlive long date.
   If my slight Muse do please these curious days,
   The pain be mine, but thine shall be the praise.

XXXIX.

O, how thy worth with manners may I sing,
When thou art all the better part of me?
What can mine own praise to mine own self bring?
And what is't but mine own when I praise thee?
Even for this let us divided live,
And our dear love lose name of single one,
That by this separation I may give
That due to thee which thou deservest alone.
O absence, what a torment wouldst thou prove,
Were it not thy sour leisure gave sweet leave
To entertain the time with thoughts of love,
Which time and thoughts so sweetly doth deceive,
   And that thou teachest how to make one twain,
   By praising him here who doth hence remain!

XL.

Take all my loves, my love, yea, take them all;
What hast thou then more than thou hadst before?
No love, my love, that thou mayst true love call;
All mine was thine before thou hadst this more.
Then if for my love thou my love receivest,
I cannot blame thee for my love thou usest;
But yet be blamed, if thou thyself deceivest
By wilful taste of what thyself refusest.
I do forgive thy robbery, gentle thief,
Although thou steal thee all my poverty;
And yet love knows it is a greater grief
To bear love's wrong than hate's known injury.
   Lascivious grace, in whom all ill well shows,
   Kill me with spites; yet we must not be foes.

XLI.

Those pretty wrongs that liberty commits,
When I am sometime absent from thy heart,
Thy beauty and thy years full well befits,
For still temptation follows where thou art.
Gentle thou art, and therefore to be won,
Beauteous thou art, therefore to be assailed;
And when a woman woos, what woman's son
Will sourly leave her till she have prevailed?
Ay me! but yet thou mightst my seat forbear,
And chide thy beauty and thy straying youth,
Who lead thee in their riot even there
Where thou art forced to break a twofold truth,—
 Hers, by thy beauty tempting her to thee,
 Thine, by thy beauty being false to me.

XLII.

That thou hast her, it is not all my grief,
And yet it may be said I loved her dearly;
That she hath thee, is of my wailing chief,
A loss in love that touches me more nearly.
Loving offenders, thus I will excuse ye:
Thou dost love her, because thou know'st I love her;
And for my sake even so doth she abuse me,
Suffering my friend for my sake to approve her.
If I lose thee, my loss is my love's gain,
And losing her, my friend hath found that loss;
Both find each other, and I lose both twain,
And both for my sake lay on me this cross:
 But here's the joy; my friend and I are one;
 Sweet flattery! then she loves but me alone.

XLIII.

When most I wink, then do mine eyes best see,
For all the day they view things unrespected;
But when I sleep, in dreams they look on thee,
And, darkly bright, are bright in dark directed.
Then thou, whose shadow shadows doth make bright,
How would thy shadow's form form happy show
To the clear day with thy much clearer light,
When to unseeing eyes thy shade shines so!
How would, I say, mine eyes be blessed made
By looking on thee in the living day,
When in dead night thy fair imperfect shade
Through heavy sleep on sightless eyes doth stay!
    All days are nights to see till I see thee,
      And nights bright days when dreams do show thee
        me.

XLIV.

If the dull substance of my flesh were thought,
Injurious distance should not stop my way;
For then, despite of space, I would be brought,
From limits far remote, where thou dost stay.
No matter then although my foot did stand
Upon the farthest earth removed from thee;
For nimble thought can jump both sea and land,
As soon as think the place where he would be.
But, ah, thought kills me that I am not thought,
To leap large lengths of miles when thou art gone,
But that, so much of earth and water wrought,
I must attend time's leisure with my moan;
    Receiving nought by elements so slow
    But heavy tears, badges of either's woe.

XLV.

The other two, slight air and purging fire,
Are both with thee, wherever I abide ;
The first my thought, the other my desire,
These present-absent with swift motion slide ;
For when these quicker elements are gone
In tender embassy of love to thee,
My life, being made of four, with two alone
Sinks down to death, oppress'd with melancholy ;
Until life's composition be recured
By those swift messengers return'd from thee,
Who even but now come back again, assured
Of thy fair health, recounting it to me :
    This told, I joy ; but then no longer glad,
    I send them back again, and straight grow sad.

XLVI.

Mine eye and heart are at a mortal war,
How to divide the conquest of thy sight ;
Mine eye my heart thy picture's sight would bar,
My heart mine eye the freedom of that right.
My heart doth plead that thou in him dost lie,
A closet never pierced with crystal eyes,
But the defendant doth that plea deny,
And says in him thy fair appearance lies.
To 'cide this title is impannelled
A quest of thoughts, all tenants to the heart ;
And by their verdict is determined
The clear eye's moiety and the dear heart's part :
    As thus ; mine eye's due is thine outward part,
    And my heart's right thine inward love of heart.

XLVII.

Betwixt mine eye and heart a league is took,
And each doth good turns now unto the other :
When that mine eye is famish'd for a look,
Or heart in love with sighs himself doth smother,
With my love's picture then my eye doth feast,
And to the painted banquet bids my heart ;
Another time mine eye is my heart's guest,
And in his thoughts of love doth share a part :
So, either by thy picture or my love,
Thyself away art present still with me ;
For thou not farther than my thoughts canst move,
And I am still with them and they with thee ;
   Or, if they sleep, thy picture in my sight
   Awakes my heart to heart's and eye's delight.

XLVIII.

How careful was I, when I took my way,
Each trifle under truest bars to thrust,
That to my use it might unused stay
From hands of falsehood, in sure wards of trust !
But thou, to whom my jewels trifles are,
Most worthy comfort, now my greatest grief,
Thou, best of dearest and mine only care,
Art left the prey of every vulgar thief.
Thee have I not lock'd up in any chest,
Save where thou art not, though I feel thou art,
Within the gentle closure of my breast,
From whence at pleasure thou mayst come and part ;
   And even thence thou wilt be stol'n, I fear,
   For truth proves thievish for a prize so dear.

XLIX.

Against that time, if ever that time come,
When I shall see thee frown on my defects,
When as thy love hath cast his utmost sum,
Call'd to that audit by advised respects ;
Against that time when thou shalt strangely pass,
And scarcely greet me with that sun, thine eye,
When love, converted from the thing it was,
Shall reasons find of settled gravity ;
Against that time do I ensconce me here
Within the knowledge of mine own desert,
And this my hand against myself uprear,
To guard the lawful reasons on thy part :
    To leave poor me thou hast the strength of laws,
    Since why to love I can allege no cause.

L.

How heavy do I journey on the way,
When what I seek, my weary travel's end,
Doth teach that ease and that repose to say,
" Thus far the miles are measured from thy friend ! "
The beast that bears me, tired with my woe,
Plods dully on, to bear that weight in me,
As if by some instinct the wretch did know
His rider loved not speed, being made from thee :
The bloody spur cannot provoke him on
That sometimes anger thrusts into his hide,
Which heavily he answers with a groan
More sharp to me than spurring to his side ;
    For that same groan doth put this in my mind :
    My grief lies onward, and my joy behind.

LI.

Thus can my love excuse the slow offence
Of my dull bearer when from thee I speed :
From where thou art why should I haste me thence ?
Till I return, of posting is no need.
O, what excuse will my poor beast then find,
When swift extremity can seem but slow ?
Then should I spur, though mounted on the wind,
In winged speed no motion shall I know :
Then can no horse with my desire keep pace ;
Therefore desire, of perfect'st love being made,
Shall neigh, no dull flesh in his fiery race ;
But love, for love, thus shall excuse my jade,—
   " Since from thee going he went wilful-slow,
    Towards thee I'll run and give him leave to go."

LII.

So am I as the rich, whose blessed key
Can bring him to his sweet up-locked treasure,
The which he will not every hour survey,
For blunting the fine point of seldom pleasure.
Therefore are feasts so solemn and so rare,
Since, seldom coming, in the long year set,
Like stones of worth they thinly placed are,
Or captain jewels in the carcanet.
So is the time that keeps you as my chest,
Or as the wardrobe which the robe doth hide,
To make some special instant special blest,
By new unfolding his imprison'd pride.
   Blessed are you, whose worthiness gives scope,
    Being had, to triumph ; being lack'd, to hope.

LIII.

What is your substance, whereof are you made,
That millions of strange shadows on you tend?
Since every one hath, every one, one shade,
And you, but one, can every shadow lend.
Describe Adonis, and the counterfeit
Is poorly imitated after you;
On Helen's cheek all art of beauty set,
And you in Grecian tires are painted new:
Speak of the spring and foison of the year,
The one doth shadow of your beauty show,
The other as your bounty doth appear;
And you in every blessed shape we know.
    In all external grace you have some part,
    But you like none, none you, for constant heart.

LIV.

O, how much more doth beauty beauteous seem
By that sweet ornament which truth doth give!
The rose looks fair, but fairer we it deem
For that sweet odour which doth in it live.
The canker-blooms have full as deep a dye
As the perfumed tincture of the roses,
Hang on such thorns, and play as wantonly
When summer's breath their masked buds discloses:
But, for their virtue only is their show,
They live unwoo'd and unrespected fade;
Die to themselves. Sweet roses do not so;
Of their sweet deaths are sweetest odours made:
    And so of you, beauteous and lovely youth,
    When that shall vade, by verse distils your truth.

LV.

Not marble, nor the gilded monuments
Of princes, shall outlive this powerful rime;
But you shall shine more bright in these contents
Than unswept stone, besmear'd with sluttish time.
When wasteful war shall statues overturn,
And broils root out the work of masonry,
Nor Mars his sword nor war's quick fire shall burn
The living record of your memory.
'Gainst death and all-oblivious enmity
Shall you pace forth; your praise shall still find room
Even in the eyes of all posterity
That wear this world out to the ending doom.
   So, till the judgement that yourself arise,
    You live in this, and dwell in lovers' eyes.

LVI.

Sweet love, renew thy force; be it not said
Thy edge should blunter be than appetite,
Which but to-day by feeding is allay'd,
To-morrow sharp'ned in his former might:
So, love, be thou; although to-day thou fill
Thy hungry eyes even till they wink with fullness,
To-morrow see again, and do not kill
The spirit of love with a perpetual dullness.
Let this sad interim like the ocean be
Which parts the shore, where two contracted new
Come daily to the banks, that, when they see
Return of love, more blest may be the view;
   Or call it winter, which, being full of care,
    Makes summer's welcome thrice more wish'd, more
      rare.

LVII.

Being your slave, what should I do but tend
Upon the hours and times of your desire?
I have no precious time at all to spend,
Nor services to do, till you require.
Nor dare I chide the world-without-end hour
Whilst I, my sovereign, watch the clock for you,
Nor think the bitterness of absence sour
When you have bid your servant once adieu ;
Nor dare I question with my jealous thought
Where you may be, or your affairs suppose,
But, like a sad slave, stay and think of nought
Save, where you are how happy you make those.
   So true a fool is love that in your will,
    Though you do any thing, he thinks no ill.

LVIII.

That god forbid that made me first your slave,
I should in thought control your times of pleasure,
Or at your hand the account of hours to crave,
Being your vassal, bound to stay your leisure !
O, let me suffer, being at your beck,
The imprison'd absence of your liberty ;
And patience, tame to sufferance, bide each check,
Without accusing you of injury.
Be where you list, your charter is so strong
That you yourself may privilege your time
To what you will; to you it doth belong·
Yourself to pardon of self-doing crime.
   I am to wait, though waiting so be hell,
    Not blame your pleasure, be it ill or well.

LIX.

If there be nothing new, but that which is
Hath been before, how are our brains beguiled,
Which, labouring for invention, bear amiss
The second burthen of a former child!
O, that record could with a backward look,
Even of five hundred courses of the sun,
Show me your image in some antique book,
Since mind at first in character was done!
That I might see what the old world could say
To this composed wonder of your frame;
Whether we are mended, or whe'r better they,
Or whether revolution be the same.
    O, sure I am, the wits of former days
    To subjects worse have given admiring praise.

LX.

Like as the waves make towards the pebbled shore,
So do our minutes hasten to their end;
Each changing place with that which goes before,
In sequent toil all forwards do contend.
Nativity, once in the main of light,
Crawls to maturity, wherewith being crown'd,
Crooked eclipses 'gainst his glory fight,
And Time that gave doth now his gift confound.
Time doth transfix the flourish set on youth
And delves the parallels in beauty's brow,
Feeds on the rarities of nature's truth,
And nothing stands but for his scythe to mow:
    And yet to times in hope my verse shall stand,
    Praising thy worth, despite his cruel hand.

LXI.

Is it thy will thy image should keep open
My heavy eyelids to the weary night?
Dost thou desire my slumbers should be broken,
While shadows like to thee do mock my sight?
Is it thy spirit that thou send'st from thee
So far from home into my deeds to pry,
To find out shames and idle hours in me,
The scope and tenour of thy jealousy?
O, no! thy love, though much, is not so great:
It is my love that keeps mine eye awake;
Mine own true love that doth my rest defeat,
To play the watchman ever for thy sake:
   For thee watch I whilst thou dost wake elsewhere,
   From me far off, with others all too near.

LXII.

Sin of self-love possesseth all mine eye
And all my soul and all my every part;
And for this sin there is no remedy,
It is so grounded inward in my heart.
Methinks no face so gracious is as mine,
No shape so true, no truth of such account;
And for myself mine own worth do define,
As I all other in all worths surmount.
But when my glass shows me myself indeed,
Beated and chopp'd with tann'd antiquity,
Mine own self-love quite contrary I read;
Self so self-loving were iniquity.
   'Tis thee, myself, that for myself I praise,
   Painting my age with beauty of thy days.

LXIII.

Against my love shall be, as I am now,
With Time's injurious hand crush'd and o'erworn;
When hours have drain'd his blood and fill'd his brow
With lines and wrinkles; when his youthful morn
Hath travell'd on to age's steepy night;
And all those beauties whereof now he's king
Are vanishing or vanish'd out of sight,
Stealing away the treasure of his spring;
For such a time do I now fortify
Against confounding age's cruel knife,
That he shall never cut from memory
My sweet love's beauty, though my lover's life:
  His beauty shall in these black lines be seen,
  And they shall live, and he in them still green.

LXIV.

When I have seen by Time's fell hand defaced
The rich-proud cost of outworn buried age;
When sometime lofty towers I see down-razed,
And brass eternal slave to mortal rage;
When I have seen the hungry ocean gain
Advantage on the kingdom of the shore,
And the firm soil win of the watery main,
Increasing store with loss and loss with store;
When I have seen such interchange of state,
Or state itself confounded to decay;
Ruin hath taught me thus to ruminate,
That Time will come and take my love away.
  This thought is as a death, which cannot choose
  But weep to have that which it fears to lose.

LXV.

Since brass, nor stone, nor earth, nor boundless sea,
But sad mortality o'ersways their power,
How with this rage shall beauty hold a plea,
Whose action is no stronger than a flower?
O, how shall summer's honey breath hold out
Against the wreckful siege of battering days,
When rocks impregnable are not so stout,
Nor gates of steel so strong, but Time decays?
O fearful meditation! where, alack,
Shall Time's best jewel from Time's chest lie hid?
Or what strong hand can hold his swift foot back?
Or who his spoil of beauty can forbid?
   O, none, unless this miracle have might,
    That in black ink my love may still shine bright.

LXVI.

Tired with all these, for restful death I cry,
As, to behold desert a beggar born,
And needy nothing trimm'd in jollity,
And purest faith unhappily forsworn,
And gilded honour shamefully misplaced,
And maiden virtue rudely strumpeted,
And right perfection wrongfully disgraced,
And strength by limping sway disabled,
And art made tongue-tied by authority,
And folly, doctor-like, controlling skill,
And simple truth miscall'd simplicity,
And captive good attending captain ill:
   Tired with all these, from these would I be gone,
    Save that, to die, I leave my love alone.

L

LXVII.

Ah, wherefore with infection should he live
And with his presence grace impiety,
That sin by him advantage should achieve
And lace itself with his society?
Why should false painting imitate his cheek,
And steal dead seeing of his living hue?
Why should poor beauty indirectly seek
Roses of shadow, since his rose is true?
Why should he live, now Nature bankrupt is,
Beggar'd of blood to blush through lively veins?
For she hath no exchequer now but his,
And, proud of many, lives upon his gains.
    O, him she stores, to show what wealth she had
    In days long since, before these last so bad.

LXVIII.

Thus is his cheek the map of days outworn,
When beauty lived and died as flowers do now,
Before these bastard signs of fair were born,
Or durst inhabit on a living brow;
Before the golden tresses of the dead,
The right of sepulchres, were shorn away,
To live a second life on second head;
Ere beauty's dead fleece made another gay:
In him those holy antique hours are seen,
Without all ornament, itself and true,
Making no summer of another's green,
Robbing no old to dress his beauty new;
    And him as for a map doth Nature store,
    To show false Art what beauty was of yore.

LXIX.

Those parts of thee that the world's eye doth view
Want nothing that the thought of hearts can mend;
All tongues, the voice of souls, give thee that due,
Uttering bare truth, even so as foes commend.
Thy outward thus with outward praise is crown'd;
But those same tongues, that give thee so thine own,
In other accents do this praise confound
By seeing farther than the eye hath shown.
They look into the beauty of thy mind,
And that, in guess, they measure by thy deeds;
Then, churls, their thoughts, although their eyes were
    kind,
To thy fair flower add the rank smell of weeds:
  But why thy odour matcheth not thy show,
  The soil is this, that thou dost common grow.

LXX.

That thou art blamed shall not be thy defect,
For slander's mark was ever yet the fair;
The ornament of beauty is suspect,
A crow that flies in heaven's sweetest air.
So thou be good, slander doth but approve
Thy worth the greater, being woo'd of time;
For canker vice the sweetest buds doth love,
And thou present'st a pure, unstained prime.
Thou hast pass'd by the ambush of young days,
Either not assail'd, or victor being charged;
Yet this thy praise cannot be so thy praise,
To tie up envy evermore enlarged:
  If some suspect of ill mask'd not thy show,
  Then thou alone kingdoms of hearts shouldst owe.

LXXI.

No longer mourn for me when I am dead
Than you shall hear the surly sullen bell
Give warning to the world that I am fled
From this vile world, with vilest worms to dwell:
Nay, if you read this line, remember not
The hand that writ it; for I love you so,
That I in your sweet thoughts would be forgot,
If thinking on me then should make you woe.
O, if, I say, you look upon this verse
When I perhaps compounded am with clay,
Do not so much as my poor name rehearse,
But let your love even with my life decay;
    Lest the wise world should look into your moan,
    And mock you with me after I am gone.

LXXII.

O, lest the world should task you to recite
What merit lived in me, that you should love
After my death, dear love, forget me quite,
For you in me can nothing worthy prove;
Unless you would devise some virtuous lie,
To do more for me than mine own desert,
And hang more praise upon deceased I
Than niggard truth would willingly impart:
O, lest your true love may seem false in this,
That you for love speak well of me untrue,
My name be buried where my body is,
And live no more to shame nor me nor you.
    For I am shamed by that which I bring forth,
    And so should you, to love things nothing worth.

LXXIII.

That time of year thou mayst in me behold
When yellow leaves, or none, or few, do hang
Upon those boughs which shake against the cold,
Bare ruin'd choirs, where late the sweet birds sang.
In me thou see'st the twilight of such day
As after sunset fadeth in the west;
Which by and by black night doth take away,
Death's second self, that seals up all in rest.
In me thou see'st the glowing of such fire,
That on the ashes of his youth doth lie,
As the death-bed whereon it must expire,
Consumed with that which it was nourish'd by.
   This thou perceivest, which makes thy love more
      strong,
   To love that well which thou must leave ere long.

LXXIV.

But be contented: when that fell arrest
Without all bail shall carry me away,
My life hath in this line some interest,
Which for memorial still with thee shall stay.
When thou reviewest this, thou dost review
The very part was consecrate to thee:
The earth can have but earth, which is his due;
My spirit is thine, the better part of me:
So then thou hast but lost the dregs of life,
The prey of worms, my body being dead;
The coward conquest of a wretch's knife,
Too base of thee to be remembered.
   The worth of that is that which it contains,
   And that is this, and this with thee remains.

LXXV.

So are you to my thoughts as food to life,
Or as sweet-season'd showers are to the ground;
And for the peace of you I hold such strife
As 'twixt a miser and his wealth is found;
Now proud as an enjoyer, and anon
Doubting the filching age will steal his treasure;
Now counting best to be with you alone,
Then better'd that the world may see my pleasure:
Sometime, all full with feasting on your sight,
And by and by clean starved for a look;
Possessing or pursuing no delight,
Save what is had or must from you be took.
  Thus do I pine and surfeit day by day,
   Or gluttoning on all, or all away.

LXXVI.

Why is my verse so barren of new pride,
So far from variation or quick change?
Why with the time do I not glance aside
To new-found methods and to compounds strange?
Why write I still all one, ever the same,
And keep invention in a noted weed,
That every word doth almost tell my name,
Showing their birth and where they did proceed?
O, know, sweet love, I always write of you,
And you and love are still my argument;
So all my best is dressing old words new,
Spending again what is already spent:
  For as the sun is daily new and old,
   So is my love still telling what is told.

LXXVII.

Thy glass will show thee how thy beauties wear,
Thy dial how thy precious minutes waste;
The vacant leaves thy mind's imprint will bear,
And of this book this learning mayst thou taste.
The wrinkles which thy glass will truly show
Of mouthed graves will give thee memory;
Thou by thy dial's shady stealth mayst know
Time's thievish progress to eternity.
Look, what thy memory cannot contain
Commit to these waste blanks, and thou shalt find
Those children nursed, deliver'd from thy brain,
To take a new acquaintance of thy mind.
   These offices, so oft as thou wilt look,
    Shall profit thee and much enrich thy book.

LXXVIII.

So oft have I invoked thee for my Muse
And found such fair assistance in my verse
As every alien pen hath got my use
And under thee their poesy disperse.
Thine eyes, that taught the dumb on high to sing
And heavy ignorance aloft to fly,
Have added feathers to the learned's wing
And given grace a double majesty.
Yet be most proud of that which I compile,
Whose influence is thine and born of thee:
In others' works thou dost but mend the style,
And arts with thy sweet graces graced be;
   But thou art all my art, and dost advance
    As high as learning my rude ignorance.

LXXIX.

Whilst I alone did call upon thy aid,
My verse alone had all thy gentle grace ;
But now my gracious numbers are decay'd,
And my sick Muse doth give another place.
I grant, sweet love, thy lovely argument
Deserves the travail of a worthier pen ;
Yet what of thee thy poet doth invent
He robs thee of, and pays it thee again.
He lends thee virtue, and he stole that word
From thy behaviour; beauty doth he give,
And found it in thy cheek; he can afford
No praise to thee but what in thee doth live.
    Then thank him not for that which he doth say,
    Since what he owes thee thou thyself dost pay.

LXXX.

O, how I faint when I of you do write,
Knowing a better spirit doth use your name,
And in the praise thereof spends all his might,
To make me tongue-tied, speaking of your fame !
But since your worth, wide as the ocean is,
The humble as the proudest sail doth bear,
My saucy bark, inferior far to his,
On your broad main doth wilfully appear.
Your shallowest help will hold me up afloat,
Whilst he upon your soundless deep doth ride,
Or, being wreck'd, I am a worthless boat,
He of tall building and of goodly pride :
    Then if he thrive and I be cast away,
    The worst was this ; my love was my decay.

LXXXI.

Or I shall live your epitaph to make,
Or you survive when I in earth am rotten;
From hence your memory death cannot take,
Although in me each part will be forgotten.
Your name from hence immortal life shall have,
Though I, once gone, to all the world must die:
The earth can yield me but a common grave,
When you entombed in men's eyes shall lie.
Your monument shall be my gentle verse,
Which eyes not yet created shall o'er-read;
And tongues to be your being shall rehearse,
When all the breathers of this world are dead;
   You still shall live—such virtue hath my pen—
   Where breath most breathes, even in the mouths of
   men.

LXXXII.

I grant thou wert not married to my Muse,
And therefore mayst without attaint o'erlook
The dedicated words which writers use
Of their fair subject, blessing every book.
Thou art as fair in knowledge as in hue,
Finding thy worth a limit past my praise;
And therefore art enforced to seek anew
Some fresher stamp of the time-bettering days.
And do so, love; yet when they have devised
What strained touches rhetoric can lend,
Thou truly fair wert truly sympathised
In true plain words by thy true-telling friend;
   And their gross painting might be better used
   Where cheeks need blood; in thee it is abused.

LXXXIII.

I never saw that you did painting need,
And therefore to your fair no painting set;
I found, or thought I found, you did exceed
The barren tender of a poet's debt:
And therefore have I slept in your report,
That you yourself, being extant, well might show
How far a modern quill doth come too short,
Speaking of worth, what worth in you doth grow.
This silence for my sin you did impute,
Which shall be most my glory, being dumb;
For I impair not beauty being mute,
When others would give life and bring a tomb.
   There lives more life in one of your fair eyes
   Than both your poets can in praise devise.

LXXXIV.

Who is it that says most? which can say more
Than this rich praise, that you alone are you?
In whose confine immured is the store
Which should example where your equal grew.
Lean penury within that pen doth dwell
That to his subject lends not some small glory;
But he that writes of you, if he can tell
That you are you, so dignifies his story,
Let him but copy what in you is writ,
Not making worse what nature made so clear,
And such a counterpart shall fame his wit,
Making his style admired everywhere.
   You to your beauteous blessings add a curse,
   Being fond on praise, which makes your praises
      worse.

LXXXV.

My tongue-tied Muse in manners holds her still,
While comments of your praise, richly compiled,
Reserve their character with golden quill,
And precious phrase by all the Muses filed.
I think good thoughts, whilst other write good words,
And, like unlettered clerk, still cry " Amen "
To every hymn that able spirit affords,
In polish'd form of well-refined pen.
Hearing you praised, I say, " 'Tis so, 'tis true,"
And to the most of praise add something more ;
But that is in my thought, whose love to you,
Though words come hindmost, holds his rank before.
   Then others for the breath of words respect,
   Me from my dumb thoughts, speaking in effect.

LXXXVI.

Was it the proud full sail of his great verse,
Bound for the prize of all too precious you,
That did my ripe thoughts in my brain inhearse,
Making their tomb the womb wherein they grew?
Was it his spirit, by spirits taught to write
Above a mortal pitch, that struck me dead ?
No, neither he, nor his compeers by night
Giving him aid, my verse astonished.
He, nor that affable familiar ghost
Which nightly gulls him with intelligence,
As victors, of my silence cannot boast ;
I was not sick of any fear from thence :
   But when your countenance fill'd up his line,
   Then lack'd I matter ; that enfeebled mine.

LXXXVII.

Farewell! thou art too dear for my possessing,
And like enough thou know'st thy estimate:
The charter of thy worth gives thee releasing;
My bonds in thee are all determinate.
For how do I hold thee but by thy granting?
And for that riches where is my deserving?
The cause of this fair gift in me is wanting,
And so my patent back again is swerving.
Thyself thou gavest, thy own worth then not knowing,
Or me, to whom thou gavest it, else mistaking;
So thy great gift, upon misprision growing,
Comes home again, on better judgement making.
    Thus have I had thee, as a dream doth flatter,
    In sleep a king, but waking no such matter.

LXXXVIII.

When thou shalt be disposed to set me light,
And place my merit in the eye of scorn,
Upon thy side against myself I'll fight,
And prove thee virtuous, though thou art forsworn.
With mine own weakness being best acquainted,
Upon thy part I can set down a story
Of faults conceal'd, wherein I am attainted;
That thou in losing me shalt win much glory:
And I by this will be a gainer too;
For bending all my loving thoughts on thee,
The injuries that to myself I do,
Doing thee vantage, double-vantage me.
    Such is my love, to thee I so belong,
    That for thy right myself will bear all wrong.

LXXXIX.

Say that thou didst forsake me for some fault,
And I will comment upon that offence:
Speak of my lameness, and I straight will halt,
Against thy reasons making no defence.
Thou canst not, love, disgrace me half so ill,
To set a form upon desired change,
As I'll myself disgrace; knowing thy will,
I will acquaintance strangle and look strange;
Be absent from thy walks; and in my tongue
Thy sweet beloved name no more shall dwell,
Lest I, too much profane, should do it wrong,
And haply of our old acquaintance tell.
  For thee, against myself I'll vow debate,
  For I must ne'er love him whom thou dost hate.

XC.

Then hate me when thou wilt; if ever, now;
Now, while the world is bent my deeds to cross,
Join with the spite of fortune, make me bow,
And do not drop in for an after-loss:
Ah, do not, when my heart hath 'scaped this sorrow,
Come in the rearward of a conquer'd woe;
Give not a windy night a rainy morrow,
To linger out a purposed overthrow.
If thou wilt leave me, do not leave me last,
When other petty griefs have done their spite,
But in the onset come: so shall I taste
At first the very worst of fortune's might;
  And other strains of woe, which now seem woe,
  Compared with loss of thee will not seem so.

XCI.

Some glory in their birth, some in their skill,
Some in their wealth, some in their body's force;
Some in their garments, though new-fangled ill;
Some in their hawks and hounds, some in their horse;
And every humour hath his adjunct pleasure,
Wherein it finds a joy above the rest:
But these particulars are not my measure;
All these I better in one general best.
Thy love is better than high birth to me,
Richer than wealth, prouder than garments' cost,
Of more delight than hawks or horses be;
And having thee, of all men's pride I boast:
    Wretched in this alone, that thou mayst take
    All this away and me most wretched make.

XCII.

But do thy worst to steal thyself away,
For term of life thou art assured mine;
And life no longer than thy love will stay,
For it depends upon that love of thine.
Then need I not to fear the worst of wrongs,
When in the least of them my life hath end.
I see a better state to me belongs
Than that which on thy humour doth depend:
Thou canst not vex me with inconstant mind,
Since that my life on thy revolt doth lie.
O, what a happy title do I find,
Happy to have thy love, happy to die!
    But what's so blessed-fair that fears no blot?
    Thou mayst be false, and yet I know it not.

XCIII.

So shall I live, supposing thou art true,
Like a deceived husband; so love's face
May still seem love to me, though alter'd new;
Thy looks with me, thy heart in other place:
For there can live no hatred in thine eye,
Therefore in that I cannot know thy change.
In many's looks the false heart's history
Is writ in moods and frowns and wrinkles strange,
But heaven in thy creation did decree
That in thy face sweet love should ever dwell;
Whate'er thy thoughts or thy heart's workings be,
Thy looks should nothing thence but sweetness tell.
   How like Eve's apple doth thy beauty grow,
   If thy sweet virtue answer not thy show!

XCIV.

They that have power to hurt and will do none,
That do not do the thing they most do show,
Who, moving others, are themselves as stone,
Unmoved, cold, and to temptation slow;
They rightly do inherit heaven's graces
And husband nature's riches from expense;
They are the lords and owners of their faces,
Others but stewards of their excellence.
The summer's flower is to the summer sweet,
Though to itself it only live and die,
But if that flower with base infection meet,
The basest weed outbraves his dignity:
   For sweetest things turn sourest by their deeds;
   Lilies that fester smell far worse than weeds.

XCV.

How sweet and lovely dost thou make the shame
Which, like a canker in the fragrant rose,
Doth spot the beauty of thy budding name !
O, in what sweets dost thou thy sins inclose !
That tongue that tells the story of thy days,
Making lascivious comments on thy sport,
Cannot dispraise but in a kind of praise;
Naming thy name blesses an ill report.
O, what a mansion have those vices got
Which for their habitation chose out thee,
Where beauty's veil doth cover every blot
And all things turn to fair that eyes can see !
   Take heed, dear heart, of this large privilege;
   The hardest knife ill-used doth lose his edge.

XCVI.

Some say, thy fault is youth, some wantonness;
Some say, thy grace is youth and gentle sport;
Both grace and faults are loved of more and less:
Thou makest faults graces that to thee resort.
As on the finger of a throned queen
The basest jewel will be well esteem'd,
So are those errors that in thee are seen
To truths translated and for true things deem'd.
How many lambs might the stern wolf betray,
If like a lamb he could his looks translate !
How many gazers mightst thou lead away,
If thou wouldst use the strength of all thy state !
   But do not so; I love thee in such sort,
   As thou being mine, mine is thy good report.

XCVII.

How like a winter hath my absence been
From thee, the pleasure of the fleeting year!
What freezings have I felt, what dark days seen!
What old December's bareness everywhere!
And yet this time removed was summer's time;
The teeming autumn, big with rich increase,
Bearing the wanton burthen of the prime,
Like widow'd wombs after their lords' decease:
Yet this abundant issue seem'd to me
But hope of orphans and unfather'd fruit;
For summer and his pleasures wait on thee,
And, thou away, the very birds are mute:
   Or, if they sing, 'tis with so dull a cheer
   That leaves look pale, dreading the winter's near.

XCVIII.

From you have I been absent in the spring,
When proud-pied April, dress'd in all his trim,
Hath put a spirit of youth in everything,
That heavy Saturn laugh'd and leap'd with him.
Yet nor the lays of birds, nor the sweet smell
Of different flowers in odour and in hue,
Could make me any summer's story tell,
Or from their proud lap pluck them where they grew:
Nor did I wonder at the lily's white,
Nor praise the deep vermilion in the rose;
They were but sweet, but figures of delight,
Drawn after you, you pattern of all those.
   Yet seem'd it winter still, and, you away,
   As with your shadow I with these did play.

M

XCIX.

The forward violet thus did I chide :
Sweet thief, whence didst thou steal thy sweet that smells,
If not from my love's breath ? The purple pride
Which on thy soft cheek for complexion dwells
In my love's veins thou hast too grossly dyed.
The lily I condemned for thy hand,
And buds of marjoram had stol'n thy hair ;
The roses fearfully on thorns did stand,
One blushing shame, another white despair ;
A third, nor red nor white, had stol'n of both,
And to his robbery had annex'd thy breath ;
But, for his theft, in pride of all his growth
A vengeful canker eat him up to death.
   More flowers I noted, yet I none could see
   But sweet or colour it had stol'n from thee.

C.

Where art thou, Muse, that thou forget'st so long
To speak of that which gives thee all thy might ?
Spend'st thou thy fury on some worthless song,
Darkening thy power to lend base subjects light ?
Return, forgetful Muse, and straight redeem
In gentle numbers time so idly spent ;
Sing to the ear that doth thy lays esteem
And gives thy pen both skill and argument.
Rise, resty Muse, my love's sweet face survey,
If Time have any wrinkle graven there ;
If any, be a satire to decay,
And make Time's spoils despised everywhere.
   Give my love fame faster than Time wastes life ;
   So thou prevent'st his scythe and crooked knife.

CI.

O truant Muse, what shall be thy amends
For thy neglect of truth in beauty dyed?
Both truth and beauty on my love depends;
So dost thou too, and therein dignified.
Make answer, Muse: wilt thou not haply say,
" Truth needs no colour, with his colour fix'd;
Beauty no pencil, beauty's truth to lay;
But best is best, if never intermix'd "?
Because he needs no praise, wilt thou be dumb?
Excuse not silence so; for 't lies in thee
To make him much outlive a gilded tomb
And to be praised of ages yet to be.
 Then do thy office, Muse; I teach thee how
 To make him seem long hence as he shows now.

CII.

My love is strengthen'd, though more weak in seeming;
I love not less, though less the show appear:
That love is merchandized whose rich esteeming
The owner's tongue doth publish everywhere.
Our love was new, and then but in the spring,
When I was wont to greet it with my lays;
As Philomel in summer's front doth sing,
And stops her pipe in growth of riper days:
Not that the summer is less pleasant now
Than when her mournful hymns did hush the night,
But that wild music burthens every bough,
And sweets grown common lose their dear delight.
 Therefore, like her, I sometime hold my tongue,
 Because I would not dull you with my song.

CIII.

Alack, what poverty my Muse brings forth,
That having such a scope to show her pride,
The argument, all bare, is of more worth
Than when it hath my added praise beside !
O, blame me not, if I no more can write !
Look in your glass, and there appears a face
That over-goes my blunt invention quite,
Dulling my lines and doing me disgrace.
Were it not sinful then, striving to mend,
To mar the subject that before was well?
For to no other pass my verses tend
Than of your graces and your gifts to tell;
　　And more, much more, than in my verse can sit,
　　Your own glass shows you when you look in it,

CIV.

To me, fair friend, you never can be old,
For as you were when first your eye I eyed,
Such seems your beauty still.   Three winters cold
Have from the forests shook three summers' pride,
Three beauteous springs to yellow autumn turn'd
In process of the seasons have I seen,
Three April perfumes in three hot Junes burn'd,
Since first I saw you fresh, which yet are green.
Ah, yet doth beauty, like a dial-hand,
Steal from his figure, and no pace perceived;
So your sweet hue, which methinks still doth stand,
Hath motion, and mine eye may be deceived :
　　For fear of which, hear this, thou age unbred :
　　Ere you were born was beauty's summer dead.

CV.

Let not my love be call'd idolatry,
Nor my beloved as an idol show,
Since all alike my songs and praises be
To one, of one, still such, and ever so.
Kind is my love to-day, to-morrow kind,
Still constant in a wondrous excellence ;
Therefore my verse, to constancy confined,
One thing expressing, leaves out difference.
" Fair, kind, and true," is all my argument,
" Fair, kind, and true," varying to other words;
And in this change is my invention spent,
Three themes in one, which wondrous scope affords.
   "Fair, kind, and true," have often lived alone,
    Which three till now never kept seat in one.

CVI.

When in the chronicle of wasted time
I see descriptions of the fairest wights,
And beauty making beautiful old rime
In praise of ladies dead and lovely knights,
Then, in the blazon of sweet beauty's best,
Of hand, of foot, of lip, of eye, of brow,
I see their antique pen would have express'd
Even such a beauty as you master now.
So all their praises are but prophecies
Of this our time, all you prefiguring ;
And, for they look'd but with divining eyes,
They had not skill enough your worth to sing :
   For we, which now behold these present days,
    Have eyes to wonder, but lack tongues to praise.

CVII.

Not mine own fears, nor the prophetic soul
Of the wide world dreaming on things to come,
Can yet the lease of my true love control,
Supposed as forfeit to a confined doom.
The mortal moon hath her eclipse endured,
And the sad augurs mock their own presage;
Incertainties now crown themselves assured,
And peace proclaims olives of endless age.
Now with the drops of this most balmy time
My love looks fresh, and Death to me subscribes,
Since, spite of him, I'll live in this poor rime,
While he insults o'er dull and speechless tribes:
    And thou in this shalt find thy monument,
    When tyrants' crests and tombs of brass are spent.

CVIII.

What's in the brain, that ink may character,
Which hath not figured to thee my true spirit?
What's new to speak, what new to register,
That may express my love, or thy dear merit?
Nothing, sweet boy; but yet, like prayers divine,
I must each day say o'er the very same;
Counting no old thing old, thou mine, I thine,
Even as when first I hallow'd thy fair name.
So that eternal love in love's fresh case
Weighs not the dust and injury of age,
Nor gives to necessary wrinkles place,
But makes antiquity for aye his page;
    Finding the first conceit of love there bred,
    Where time and outward form would show it dead.

CIX.

O, never say that I was false of heart,
Though absence seem'd my flame to qualify.
As easy might I from myself depart
As from my soul, which in thy breast doth lie:
That is my home of love: if I have ranged,
Like him that travels, I return again;
Just to the time, not with the time exchanged,
So that myself bring water for my stain.
Never believe, though in my nature reign'd
All frailties that besiege all kinds of blood.
That it could so preposterously be stain'd,
To leave for nothing all thy sum of good;
   For nothing this wide universe I call,
   Save thou, my rose; in it thou art my all.

CX.

Alas, 'tis true I have gone here and there,
And made myself a motley to the view,
Gored mine own thoughts, sold cheap what is most dear,
Made old offences of affections new;   •
Most true it is that I have look'd on truth
Askance and strangely; but, by all above,
These blenches gave my heart another youth,
And worse essays proved thee my best of love.
Now all is done, have what shall have no end:
Mine appetite I never more will grind
On newer proof, to try an older friend,
A god in love, to whom I am confined.
   Then give me welcome, next my heaven the best,
   Even to thy pure and most most loving breast.

CXI.

O, for my sake do you with Fortune chide,
The guilty goddess of my harmful deeds,
That did not better for my life provide
Than public means which public manners breeds.
Thence comes it that my name receives a brand,
And almost thence my nature is subdued
To what it works in, like the dyer's hand :
Pity me then and wish I were renew'd ;
Whilst, like a willing patient, I will drink
Potions of eisel, 'gainst my strong infection ;
No bitterness that I will bitter think,
Nor double penance, to correct correction.
    Pity me then, dear friend, and I assure ye
    Even that your pity is enough to cure me.

CXII.

Your love and pity doth the impression fill
Which vulgar scandal stamp'd upon my brow ;
For what care I who calls me well or ill,
So you o'er-green my bad, my good allow ?
You are my all the world, and I must strive
To know my shames and praises from your tongue ;
None else to me, nor I to none alive,
That my steel'd sense or changes right or wrong.
In so profound abysm I throw all care
Of others' voices, that my adder's sense
To critic and to flatterer stopped are.
Mark how with my neglect I do dispense :
    You are so strongly in my purpose bred
    That all the world besides methinks they're dead.

CXIII.

Since I left you mine eye is in my mind,
And that which governs me to go about
Doth part his function and is partly blind,
Seems seeing, but effectually is out;
For it no form delivers to the heart
Of bird, of flower, or shape, which it doth latch:
Of his quick objects hath the mind no part,
Nor his own vision holds what it doth catch;
For if it see the rudest or gentlest sight,
The most sweet favour or deformed'st creature,
The mountain or the sea, the day or night,
The crow or dove, it shapes them to your feature:
    Incapable of more, replete with you,
    My most true mind thus maketh mine untrue.

CXIV.

Or whether doth my mind, being crown'd with you,
Drink up the monarch's plague, this flattery?
Or whether shall I say, mine eye saith true,
And that your love taught it this alchemy,
To make of monsters and things indigest
Such cherubins as your sweet self resemble, .
Creating every bad a perfect best,
As fast as objects to his beams assemble?
O, 'tis the first; 'tis flattery in my seeing,
And my great mind most kingly drinks it up:
Mine eye well knows what with his gust is 'greeing,
And to his palate doth prepare the cup:
    If it be poison'd, 'tis the lesser sin
    That mine eye loves it and doth first begin.

CXV.

Those lines that I before have writ do lie,
Even those that said I could not love you dearer :
Yet then my judgement knew no reason why
My most full flame should afterwards burn clearer.
But reckoning Time, whose million'd accidents
Creep in 'twixt vows, and change decrees of kings,
Tan sacred beauty, blunt the sharp'st intents,
Divert strong minds to the course of altering things ;
Alas, why, fearing of Time's tyranny,
Might I not then say "Now I love you best,"
When I was certain o'er incertainty,
Crowning the present, doubting of the rest?
  Love is a babe ; then might I not say so,
  To give full growth to that which still doth grow?

CXVI.

Let me not to the marriage of true minds
Admit impediments.   Love is not love
Which alters when it alteration finds,
Or bends with the remover to remove :
O, no ! it is an ever-fixed mark,
That looks on tempests and is never shaken ;
It is the star to every wandering bark,
Whose worth's unknown, although his height be taken.
Love's not Time's fool, though rosy lips and cheeks
Within his bending sickle's compass come ;
Love alters not with his brief hours and weeks,
But bears it out even to the edge of doom.
  If this be error and upon me proved,
  I never writ, nor no man ever loved.

CXVII.

Accuse me thus: that I have scanted all
Wherein I should your great deserts repay,
Forgot upon your dearest love to call,
Whereto all bonds do tie me day by day;
That I have frequent been with unknown minds,
And given to time your own dear-purchased right;
That I have hoisted sail to all the winds
Which should transport me farthest from your sight.
Book both my wilfulness and errors down,
And on just proof surmise accumulate;
Bring me within the level of your frown,
But shoot not at me in your waken'd hate;
    Since my appeal says I did not strive to prove
    The constancy and virtue of your love.

CXVIII.

Like as, to make our appetites more keen,
With eager compounds we our palate urge;
As, to prevent our maladies unseen,
We sicken to shun sickness when we purge;
Even so, being full of your ne'er-cloying sweetness,
To bitter sauces did I frame my feeding;
And sick of welfare found a kind of meetness
To be diseased, ere that there was true needing.
Thus policy in love, to anticipate
The ills that were not, grew to faults assured,
And brought to medicine a healthful state,
Which, rank of goodness, would by ill be cured:
    But thence I learn, and find the lesson true,
    Drugs poison him that so fell sick of you.

CXIX.

What potions have I drunk of Siren tears,
Distill'd from limbecks foul as hell within,
Applying fears to hopes and hopes to fears,
Still losing when I saw myself to win!
What wretched errors hath my heart committed,
Whilst it hath thought itself so blessed never!
How have mine eyes out of their spheres been fitted,
In the distraction of this madding fever!
O benefit of ill! now I find true
That better is by evil still made better;
And ruin'd love, when it is built anew,
Grows fairer than at first, more strong, far greater.
    So I return rebuked to my content,
    And gain by ills thrice more than I have spent.

CXX.

That you were once unkind befriends me now,
And for that sorrow which I then did feel
Needs must I under my transgression bow,
Unless my nerves were brass or hammer'd steel.
For if you were by my unkindness shaken,
As I by yours, you've pass'd a hell of time;
And I, a tyrant, have no leisure taken
To weigh how once I suffer'd in your crime.
O, that our night of woe might have remember'd
My deepest sense, how hard true sorrow hits,
And soon to you, as you to me, then tender'd
The humble salve which wounded bosoms fits!
    But that your trespass now becomes a fee;
    Mine ransoms yours, and yours must ransom me.

CXXI.

'Tis better to be vile than vile esteem'd,
When not to be receives reproach of being;
And the just pleasure lost, which is so deem'd
Not by our feeling, but by others' seeing:
For why should others' false adulterate eyes
Give salutation to my sportive blood?
Or on my frailties why are frailer spies,
Which in their wills count bad what I think good?
No, I am that I am, and they that level
At my abuses reckon up their own:
I may be straight, though they themselves be bevel;
By their rank thoughts my deeds must not be shown;
   Unless this general evil they maintain,
   All men are bad and in their badness reign.

CXXII.

Thy gift, thy tables, are within my brain
Full character'd with lasting memory,
Which shall above that idle rank remain,
Beyond all date, even to eternity:
Or, at the least, so long as brain and heart
Have faculty by nature to subsist;
Till each to razed oblivion yield his part
Of thee, thy record never can be miss'd.
That poor retention could not so much hold,
Nor need I tallies thy dear love to score;
Therefore to give them from me was I bold,
To trust those tables that receive thee more:
   To keep an adjunct to remember thee
   Were to import forgetfulness in me.

CXXIII.

No, Time, thou shalt not boast that I do change:
Thy pyramids built up with newer might
To me are nothing novel, nothing strange;
They are but dressings of a former sight.
Our dates are brief, and therefore we admire
What thou dost foist upon us that is old;
And rather make them born to our desire
Than think that we before have heard them told.
Thy registers and thee I both defy,
Not wondering at the present nor the past,
For thy records and what we see doth lie,
Made more or less by thy continual haste.
    This I do vow, and this shall ever be,
    I will be true, despite thy scythe and thee.

CXXIV.

If my dear love were but the child of state,
It might for Fortune's bastard be unfather'd,
As subject to Time's love or to Time's hate,
Weeds among weeds, or flowers with flowers gather'd.
No, it was builded far from accident;
It suffers not in smiling pomp, nor falls
Under the blow of thralled discontent,
Whereto th' inviting time our fashion calls:
It fears not policy, that heretic,
Which works on leases of short number'd hours,
But all alone stands hugely politic,
That it nor grows with heat nor drowns with showers.
    To this I witness call the fools of time,
    Which die for goodness, who have lived for crime.

CXXV.

Were 't aught to me I bore the canopy,
With my extern the outward honouring,
Or laid great bases for eternity,
Which prove more short than waste or ruining?
Have I not seen dwellers on form and favour
Lose all, and more, by paying too much rent,
For compound sweet foregoing simple savour,
Pitiful thrivers, in their gazing spent?
No, let me be obsequious in thy heart,
And take thou my oblation, poor but free,
Which is not mix'd with seconds, knows no art
But mutual render, only me for thee.
 Hence, thou suborn'd informer! a true soul
 When most impeach'd stands least in thy control.

CXXVI.

O thou, my lovely boy, who in thy power
Dost hold Time's fickle glass, his sickle, hour;
Who hast by waning grown, and therein show'st
Thy lovers withering as thy sweet self grow'st;
If Nature, sovereign mistress over wrack,
As thou goest onwards, still will pluck thee back,
She keeps thee to this purpose, that her skill
May time disgrace and wretched minutes kill.
Yet fear her, O thou minion of her pleasure!
She may detain, but not still keep, her treasure:
Her audit, though delay'd, answer'd must be,
And her quietus is to render thee.

CXXVII.

In the old age black was not counted fair,
Or if it were, it bore not beauty's name;
But now is black beauty's successive heir,
And beauty slander'd with a bastard shame:
For since each hand hath put on nature's power,
Fairing the foul with art's false borrow'd face,
Sweet beauty hath no name, no holy bower,
But is profaned, if not lives in disgrace.
Therefore my mistress' eyes are raven black,
Her eyes so suited, and they mourners seem
At such who, not born fair, no beauty lack,
Slandering creation with a false esteem:
    Yet so they mourn, becoming of their woe,
    That every tongue says beauty should look so.

CXXVIII.

How oft, when thou, my music, music play'st
Upon that blessed wood whose motion sounds
With thy sweet fingers, when thou gently sway'st
The wiry concord that mine ear confounds,
Do I envy those jacks that nimble leap
To kiss the tender inward of thy hand,
Whilst my poor lips, which should that harvest reap,
At the wood's boldness by thee blushing stand!
To be so tickled, they would change their state
And situation with those dancing chips,
O'er whom thy fingers walk with gentle gait,
Making dead wood more blest than living lips.
    Since saucy jacks so happy are in this,
    Give them thy fingers, me thy lips to kiss.

CXXIX.

The expense of spirit in a waste of shame
Is lust in action; and till action, lust
Is perjured, murderous, bloody, full of blame,
Savage, extreme, rude, cruel, not to trust;
Enjoy'd no sooner but despised straight;
Past reason hunted; and no sooner had,
Past reason hated, as a swallow'd bait,
On purpose laid to make the taker mad:
Mad in pursuit, and in possession so;
Had, having, and in quest to have, extreme;
A bliss in proof, and proved, a very woe;
Before, a joy proposed; behind, a dream.
   All this the world well knows; yet none knows well
   To shun the heaven that leads men to this hell.

CXXX.

My mistress' eyes are nothing like the sun;
Coral is far more red than her lips' red:
If snow be white, why then her breasts are dun;
If hairs be wires, black wires grow on her head.
I have seen roses damask'd, red and white,
But no such roses see I in her cheeks;
And in some perfumes is there more delight
Than in the breath that from my mistress reeks.
I love to hear her speak, yet well I know
That music hath a far more pleasing sound:
I grant I never saw a goddess go,
My mistress, when she walks, treads on the ground:
   And yet, by heaven, I think my love as rare
   As any she belied with false compare.

CXXXI.

Thou art as tyrannous, so as thou art,
As those whose beauties proudly make them cruel ;
For well thou know'st to my dear doting heart
Thou art the fairest and most precious jewel.
Yet, in good faith, some say that thee behold,
Thy face hath not the power to make love groan :
To say they err I dare not be so bold,
Although I swear it to myself alone.
And to be sure that is not false I swear,
A thousand groans, but thinking on thy face,
One on another's neck, do witness bear
Thy black is fairest in my judgement's place.
    In nothing art thou black save in thy deeds,
    And thence this slander, as I think, proceeds.

CXXXII.

Thine eyes I love, and they, as pitying me,
Knowing thy heart torments me with disdain,
Have put on black and loving mourners be,
Looking with pretty ruth upon my pain.
And truly not the morning sun of heaven
Better becomes the gray cheeks of the east,
Nor that full star that ushers in the even
Doth half that glory to the sober west,
As those two mourning eyes become thy face :
O, let it then as well beseem thy heart
To mourn for me, since mourning doth thee grace,
And suit thy pity like in every part.
    Then will I swear beauty herself is black,
    And all they foul that thy complexion lack.

CXXXIII.

Beshrew that heart that makes my heart to groan
For that deep wound it gives my friend and me!
Is 't not enough to torture me alone,
But slave to slavery my sweet'st friend must be?
Me from myself thy cruel eye hath taken,
And my next self thou harder hast engross'd:
Of him, myself, and thee, I am forsaken;
A torment thrice threefold thus to be cross'd.
Prison my heart in thy steel bosom's ward,
But then my friend's heart let my poor heart bail;
Whoe'er keeps me, let my heart be his guard;
Thou canst not then use rigour in my gaol:
   And yet thou wilt; for I, being pent in thee,
   Perforce am thine, and all that is in me.

CXXXIV.

So, now I have confess'd that he is thine,
And I myself am mortgaged to thy will,
Myself I'll forfeit, so that other mine
Thou wilt restore, to be my comfort still:
But thou wilt not, nor he will not be free,
For thou art covetous and he is kind;
He learn'd but surety-like to write for me,
Under that bond that him as fast doth bind.
The statute of thy beauty thou wilt take,
Thou usurer, that put'st forth all to use,
And sue a friend came debtor for my sake;
So him I lose through my unkind abuse.
   Him have I lost; thou hast both him and me:
   He pays the whole, and yet am I not free.

CXXXV.

Whoever hath her wish, thou hast thy *Will*,
And *Will* to boot, and *Will* in overplus;
More than enough am I that vex thee still,
To thy sweet will making addition thus.
Wilt thou, whose will is large and spacious,
Not once vouchsafe to hide my will in thine?
Shall will in others seem right gracious,
And in my will no fair acceptance shine?
The sea, all water, yet receives rain still,
And in abundance addeth to his store;
So thou, being rich in *Will*, add to thy *Will*
One will of mine, to make thy large *Will* more.
    Let no unkind, no fair beseechers kill;
    Think all but one, and me in that one *Will*.

CXXXVI.

If thy soul check thee that I come so near,
Swear to thy blind soul that I was thy *Will*,
And will, thy soul knows, is admitted there;
Thus far for love, my love-suit, sweet, fulfil.
Will will fulfil the treasure of thy love,
Ay, fill it full with wills, and my will one.
In things of great receipt with ease we prove
Among a number one is reckon'd none:
Then in the number let me pass untold,
Though in thy store's account I one must be;
For nothing hold me, so it please thee hold
That nothing me, a something sweet to thee:
    Make but my name thy love, and love that still,
    And then thou lovest me, for my name is *Will*.

CXXXVII.

Thou blind fool, Love, what dost thou to mine eyes,
That they behold, and see not what they see?
They know what beauty is, see where it lies,
Yet what the best is take the worst to be.
If eyes, corrupt by over-partial looks,
Be anchor'd in the bay where all men ride,
Why of eyes' falsehood hast thou forged hooks,
Whereto the judgement of my heart is tied?
Why should my heart think that a several plot
Which my heart knows the wide world's common place?
Or mine eyes seeing this, say this is not,
To put fair truth upon so foul a face?
    In things right true my heart and eyes have err'd,
    And to this false plague are they now transferr'd.

CXXXVIII.

When my love swears that she is made of truth,
I do believe her, though I know she lies,
That she might think me some untutor'd youth,
Unlearned in the world's false subtleties.
Thus vainly thinking that she thinks me young,
Although she knows my days are past the best,
Simply I credit her false-speaking tongue:
On both sides thus is simple truth supprest.
But wherefore says she not she is unjust?
And wherefore say not I that I am old?
O, love's best habit is in seeming trust,
And age in love loves not to have years told:
    Therefore I lie with her, and she with me,
    And in our faults by lies we flatter'd be.

CXXXIX.

O, call not me to justify the wrong
That thy unkindness lays upon my heart;
Wound me not with thine eye, but with thy tongue;
Use power with power, and slay me not by art.
Tell me thou lovest elsewhere; but in my sight,
Dear heart, forbear to glance thine eye aside:
What need'st thou wound with cunning, when thy might
Is more than my o'erpress'd defence can bide?
Let me excuse thee: ah, my love well knows
Her pretty looks have been mine enemies;
And therefore from my face she turns my foes,
That they elsewhere might dart their injuries:
    Yet do not so; but since I am near slain,
    Kill me outright with looks, and rid my pain.

CXL.

Be wise as thou art cruel; do not press
My tongue-tied patience with too much disdain;
Lest sorrow lend me words, and words express
The manner of my pity-wanting pain.
If I might teach thee wit, better it were,
Though not to love, yet, love, to tell me so;
As testy sick men, when their deaths be near,
No news but health from their physicians know;
For, if I should despair, I should grow mad,
And in my madness might speak ill of thee:
Now this ill-wresting world is grown so bad,
Mad slanderers by mad ears believed be.
    That I may not be so, nor thou belied,
    Bear thine eyes straight, though thy proud heart go
        wide.

CXLI.

In faith, I do not love thee with mine eyes,
For they in thee a thousand errors note;
But 'tis my heart that loves what they despise,
Who, in despite of view, is pleased to dote;
Nor are mine ears with thy tongue's tune delighted;
Nor tender feeling, to base touches prone,
Nor taste, nor smell, desire to be invited
To any sensual feast with thee alone;
But my five wits nor my five senses can
Dissuade one foolish heart from serving thee,
Who leaves unsway'd the likeness of a man,
Thy proud heart's slave and vassal wretch to be:
   Only my plague thus far I count my gain,
   That she that makes me sin awards me pain.

CXLII.

Love is my sin, and thy dear virtue hate,
Hate of my sin, grounded on sinful loving:
O, but with mine compare thou thine own state,
And thou shalt find its merits not reproving;
Or, if it do, not from those lips of thine,
That have profaned their scarlet ornaments
And seal'd false bonds of love as oft as mine,
Robb'd others' beds' revenues of their rents.
Be it lawful I love thee, as thou lovest those
Whom thine eyes woo as mine importune thee:
Root pity in thy heart, that, when it grows,
Thy pity may deserve to pitied be.
   If thou dost seek to have what thou dost hide,
   By self-example mayst thou be denied!

CXLIII.

Lo, as a careful housewife runs to catch
One of her feather'd creatures broke away,
Sets down her babe, and makes all swift despatch
In pursuit of the thing she would have stay;
Whilst her neglected child holds her in chase,
Cries to catch her whose busy care is bent
To follow that which flies before her face,
Not prizing her poor infant's discontent:
So runn'st thou after that which flies from thee,
Whilst I thy babe chase thee afar behind;
But if thou catch thy hope, turn back to me,
And play the mother's part, kiss me, be kind:
   So will I pray that thou mayst have thy *Will*,
   If thou turn back and my loud crying still.

CXLIV.

Two loves I have of comfort and despair,
Which like two spirits do suggest me still:
The better angel is a man right fair,
The worser spirit a woman colour'd ill.
To win me soon to hell, my female evil
Tempteth my better angel from my side,
And would corrupt my saint to be a devil,
Wooing his purity with her foul pride.
And whether that my angel be turn'd fiend
Suspect I may, yet not directly tell;
But being both from me, both to each friend,
I guess one angel in another's hell:
   Yet this shall I ne'er know, but live in doubt,
   Till my bad angel fire my good one out.

CXLV.

Those lips that Love's own hand did make
Breathed forth the sound that said " I hate,"
To me that languish'd for her sake :
But when she saw my woeful state,
Straight in her heart did mercy come,
Chiding that tongue that ever sweet
Was used in giving gentle doom ;
And taught it thus anew to greet ;
" I hate " she alter'd with an end,
That follow'd it as gentle day
Doth follow night, who, like a fiend,
From heaven to hell is flown away ;
   " I hate " from hate away she threw,
   And saved my life, saying—" Not you."

CXLVI.

Poor soul, the centre of my sinful earth,
[Press'd by] these rebel powers that thee array,
Why dost thou pine within and suffer dearth,
Painting thy outward walls so costly gay?
Why so large cost, having so short a lease,
Dost thou upon thy fading mansion spend ?
Shall worms, inheritors of this excess,
Eat up thy charge?   Is this thy body's end ?
Then, soul, live thou upon thy servant's loss,
And let that pine to aggravate thy store ;
Buy terms divine in selling hours of dross ;
Within be fed, without be rich no more :
   So shalt thou feed on Death, that feeds on men,
   And Death once dead, there's no more dying then.

CXLVII.

My love is as a fever, longing still
For that which longer nurseth the disease;
Feeding on that which doth preserve the ill,
The uncertain sickly appetite to please.
My reason, the physician to my love,
Angry that his prescriptions are not kept,
Hath left me, and I desperate now approve
Desire is death, which physic did except.
Past cure I am, now reason is past care,
And frantic-mad with evermore unrest;
My thoughts and my discourse as madmen's are,
At random from the truth, vainly express'd;
  For I have sworn thee fair, and thought thee bright,
  Who art as black as hell, as dark as night.

CXLVIII.

O me, what eyes hath Love put in my head,
Which have no correspondence with true sight!
Or, if they have, where is my judgement fled,
That censures falsely what they see aright?
If that be fair whereon my false eyes dote,
What means the world to say it is not so?
If it be not, then love doth well denote
Love's eye is not so true as all men's: no,
How can it? O, how can Love's eye be true,
That is so vex'd with watching and with tears?
No marvel then, though I mistake my view;
The sun itself sees not till heaven clears.
  O cunning Love! with tears thou keep'st me blind,
  Lest eyes well-seeing thy foul faults should find.

CXLIX.

Canst thou, O cruel! say I love thee not,
When I against myself with thee partake?
Do I not think on thee, when I forgot
Am of myself, all tyrant, for thy sake?
Who hateth thee that I do call my friend?
On whom frown'st thou that I do fawn upon?
Nay, if thou lour'st on me, do I not spend
Revenge upon myself with present moan?
What merit do I in myself respect,
That is so proud thy service to despise,
When all my best doth worship thy defect,
Commanded by the motion of thine eyes?
   But, love, hate on, for now I know thy mind;
   Those that can see thou lovest, and I am blind.

CL.

O, from what power hast thou this powerful might
With insufficiency my heart to sway?
To make me give the lie to my true sight,
And swear that brightness doth not grace the day?
Whence hast thou this becoming of things ill,
That in the very refuse of thy deeds
There is such strength and warrantise of skill,
That, in my mind, thy worst all best exceeds?
Who taught thee how to make me love thee more,
The more I hear and see just cause of hate?
O, though I love what others do abhor,
With others thou shouldst not abhor my state:
   If thy unworthiness raised love in me,
   More worthy I to be beloved of thee.

CLI.

Love is too young to know what conscience is;
Yet who knows not conscience is born of love?
Then, gentle cheater, urge not my amiss,
Lest guilty of my faults thy sweet self prove:
For, thou betraying me, I do betray
My nobler part to my gross body's treason;
My soul doth tell my body that he may
Triumph in love; flesh stays no farther reason,
But rising at thy name doth point out thee
As his triumphant prize.   Proud of this pride,
He is contented thy poor drudge to be,
To stand in thy affairs, fall by thy side.
   No want of conscience hold it that I call
   Her " love " for whose dear love I rise and fall.

CLII.

In loving thee thou know'st I am forsworn,
But thou art twice forsworn, to me love swearing;
In act thy bed-vow broke, and new faith torn,
In vowing new hate after new love bearing.
But why of two oaths' breach do I accuse thee,
When I break twenty?   I am perjured most;
For all my vows are oaths but to misuse thee,
And all my honest faith in thee is lost:
For I have sworn deep oaths of thy deep kindness,
Oaths of thy love, thy truth, thy constancy;
And, to enlighten thee, gave eyes to blindness,
Or made them swear against the thing they see;
   For I have sworn thee fair; more perjured I,
   To swear against the truth so foul a lie!

CLIII.

Cupid laid by his brand and fell asleep :
A maid of Dian's this advantage found,
And his love-kindling fire did quickly steep
In a cold valley-fountain of that ground ;
Which borrow'd from this holy fire of Love
A dateless lively heat, ʀtill to endure,
And grew a seething bath, which yet men prove
Against strange maladies a sovereign cure.
But at my mistress' eye Love's brand new-fired,
The boy for trial needs would touch my breast ;
I, sick withal, the help of bath desired,
And thither hied, a sad distemper'd guest,
 But found no cure : the bath for my help lies
 Where Cupid got new fire, my mistress' eyes.

CLIV.

The little Love-god lying once asleep
Laid by his side his heart-inflaming brand,
Whilst many nymphs that vow'd chaste life to keep
Came tripping by ; but in her maiden hand
The fairest votary took up that fire
Which many legions of true hearts had warm'd ;
And so the general of hot desire
Was sleeping by a virgin hand disarm'd.
This brand she quenched in a cool well by,
Which from Love's fire took heat perpetual,
Growing a bath and healthful remedy
For men diseased ; but I, my mistress' thrall,
 Came there for cure, and this by that I prove,
 Love's fire heats water, water cools not love.

NOTES.

I. The theme of this and other early sonnets is similarly treated in *Venus and Adonis*, ll. 162–174:—

Torches are made to light, jewels to wear,
Dainties to taste, fresh beauty for the use,
Herbs for their smell, and sappy plants to bear :
Things growing to themselves are growth's abuse :
 Seeds spring from seeds and beauty breedeth beauty ;
 Thou wast begot ; to get it is thy duty.

Upon the earth's increase why shouldst thou feed,
Unless the earth with thy increase be fed ?
By law of nature thou art bound to breed,
That thine may live when thou thyself art dead :
 And so, in spite of death, thou dost survive,
 In that thy likeness still is left alive.

Herr Krauss *(Shakespeare-Jahrbuch*, 1881) cites, as a parallel to the arguments in favour of marriage in these sonnets, the versified dialogue between Geron and Histor at the close of Sidney's *Arcadia*, lib. iii.

6. *Self-substantial fuel*, fuel of the substance of the flame itself.

12. *Makest waste in niggarding.* Compare *Romeo and Juliet*, Act I. sc. 1, l. 223 :—

BEN. *Then she hath sworn that she will still live chaste?*
ROM. *She hath, and* in that sparing makes huge waste.

13, 14. Pity the world, or else be a glutton devouring the world's due, by means of the grave (which will swallow your beauty—compare Sonnet LXXVII. 6, and note), and of yourself, who refuse to beget offspring. Compare *All's Well*, Act I. sc. 1, Parolles speaking, "Virginity . . . consumes itself to the very paring, and so dies with feeding his own stomach." Steevens proposed "*be thy* grave and thee," *i.e.*, be at once thyself and thy grave.

II. Perhaps in anticipating a time when his friend's child may represent that friend's lost beauty and the warm blood of youth (l. 14), Shakspere pictures the son as of like years with Shakspere's friend when the sonnet was written. If the friend were now about twenty, in twenty years more, when he should be forty, his son might be twenty. Shakspere fixes on so early an age as forty because, had he said fifty, it might have allowed time for his friend's son to pass beyond the point of youthful perfection to which Shakspere's friend has now attained, and this is forbidden by the idea of the sonnet.

Perhaps the forty years are counted from the *present age* of the young friend, bringing him thus to about sixty years of age.

It has, however, been shown by Prof. Elze (*Shakespeare-Jahrbuch*, Bd. xi. pp. 288–294) that Elizabethan writers often use *four, forty,* and *forty thousand* to express an indefinite number. The usage is also common in German. Krauss cites from Sidney's *Arcadia* two examples of "forty winters."

In Sonnet I. the Friend is " contracted to his own bright eyes ; " such a marriage is fruitless, and at forty the eyes will be " deep-sunken." The " glutton" of I. reappears here in the phrase " all-eating shame; " the " makest waste " of I. reappears in the " thriftless praise " of II. Hazlitt reads *whole excuse.*

8. *Thriftless praise,* unprofitable praise. " What *thriftless* sighs shall poor Olivia breathe ! " *Twelfth Night,* Act II. sc. 2, l. 40.

11. *Shall sum my count and make my old excuse,* shall complete my account, and serve as the excuse of my oldness.

III. A proof by example of the truth set forth in II. Here is a parent finding in a child the excuse for age and wrinkles. But here that parent is the mother. Were the father of Shakspere's friend living, it would have been natural to mention him ; XIII. 14 " you had a father " confirms our impression that he was dead.

There are two kinds of mirrors—first, that of glass ; secondly, a child who reflects his parent's beauty.

5. *Unear'd,* unploughed. Compare the Dedication of *Venus and Adonis,* " I shall . . . never after *ear* so barren a land, for fear it yield me still so bad a harvest."

5, 6. Compare *Measure for Measure,* Act I. sc. 4, ll. 43, 44 :—

> *Her plenteous womb*
> *Expresseth his full tilth and husbandry.*

O

7, 8. Compare *Venus and Adonis*, ll. 757–761 :—

> *What is thy body but a swallowing grave*
> *Seeming to bury that posterity,*
> *Which by the rights of time thou needs must have,*
> *If thou destroy them not in dark obscurity ?*

9, 10. Compare *Lucrece*, ll. 1758, 1759 (old Lucretius addressing his dead daughter) :—

> *Poor broken glass, I often did behold*
> *In thy sweet semblance my old age new-born.*

11. Compare *A Lover's Complaint*, l. 14 :—

> *Some beauty peep'd through lattice of sear'd age.*

12. *Golden time.* So *King Richard III.*, Act I. sc. 2, l. 248, " the *golden prime* of this sweet prince."

13. *If thou live.* Capell suggests *love*.

IV. In Sonnet III. Shakspere has viewed his friend as an inheritor of beauty from his mother; this legacy of beauty is now regarded as the bequest of nature. The ideas of unthriftiness (l. 1) and niggardliness (l. 5) are derived from Sonnets I., II.; the "audit" (l. 12) is another form of the "sum my count" of II. 11. The new idea introduced in this sonnet is that of usury, which reappears in VI. 5, 6.

3. So *Measure for Measure*, Act I. sc. 1, ll. 36–41. Shakspere imagines Nature, as a thrifty goddess, lending, but, like a strict creditor, exacting thanks and interest.

> *Spirits are not finely touch'd*
> *But to·fine issues, nor Nature never lends*

> *The smallest scruple of her excellence*
> *But, like a thrifty goddess, she determines*
> *Herself the glory of a creditor,*
> *Both thanks and use.*

Compare with this sonnet the arguments put into the
mouth of Comus by Milton: *Comus*, 679–684:—

> *Why should you be so cruel to yourself*
> *And to those dainty limbs which Nature lent*
> *For gentle usage, and soft delicacy?*
> *But you invert the covenants of her trust,*
> *And harshly deal like an ill-borrower*
> *With that which you received on other terms;*

and ll. 720–727 :—

> *If all the world*
> *Should in a pet of temperance feed on pulse,*
> *Drink the clear stream, and nothing wear but frieze,*
> *The All-giver would be unthanked, would be unpraised,*
> *Not half his riches known, and yet despised;*
> *And we would serve him as a grudging master,*
> *As a penurious niggard of his wealth,*
> *And live like Nature's bastards, not her sons.*

4. *Free*, liberal.

8. *Live*, subsist. With all your usury you have not
a livelihood, for trafficking only with yourself, you put
a cheat upon yourself, and win nothing by such usury.

14. *Th' executor.* Malone reads "thy executor."

V. In Sonnets v., vi., youth and age are compared to
the seasons of the year: in vii. they are compared
to morning and evening, the seasons of the day.

1. *Hours*, a dissyllable, as in *The Tempest*, Act v. l. 4. " On the sixth *hour;* at which time my lord."

2. *Gaze*, object gazed at, as in *Macbeth*, Act v. sc. 8, l. 24. " Live to be the show and *gaze* o' the time."

4. *Unfair*, deprive of beauty; not elsewhere used by Shakspere, but in Sonnet CXXVII. we find, " Fairing the foul with art's false borrow'd face."

9. *Summer's distillation*, perfumes made from flowers. Compare Sonnet LIV. and *A Midsummer Night's Dream*. Act I. sc. 1, ll. 76, 77 :—

> *Earthlier happy is the rose distill'd,*
> *Than that which withering on the virgin thorn*
> *Grows, lives and dies in single blessedness.*

14. *Leese*, lose. In the Authorized Version of the Bible, 1 Kings xviii. 5, this word occurred, " that we *leese* not all the beasts ; " it has been changed to " lose " in modern editions.

VI. This sonnet carries on the thoughts of IV. and V. —the distilling of perfume from V., and the interest paid on money lent from IV.

5. *Use*, interest, as in *Much Ado*, Act II. sc. 1, l. 288 : " Indeed, my lord, he lent it me awhile; and I gave him *use* for it, a double heart for his single one." Compare with this sonnet the solicitation of Adonis by Venus, ll. 767, 768.

> *Foul cankering rust the hidden treasure frets,*
> *But gold that's put to use more gold begets.*

And *Merchant of Venice*, Act I. sc 3, ll. 70–97. Shylock,

to justify his usury, compares his gold and silver to Laban's ewes and rams, which Jacob caused to breed parti-coloured lambs :—

ANTONIO.—*Was this inserted to make interest good,*
  Or is your gold and silver ewes and rams?
SHYLOCK.—*I cannot tell ; I make it breed as fast.*

The mediæval theologians argued against requiring interest on money, on the ground that "all money is sterile by nature," an absurdity of Aristotle. "The Greek word for interest (τόκος, from τίκτω, I beget) was probably connected with this delusion." "In England money-lending was first formally permitted under Henry VIII." Lecky, *Hist. of Rationalism in Europe*, chap. vi. note.

13. *Self-will'd.* Delius conjectures, "self-kill'd."

VII. After imagery drawn from summer and winter, Shakspere finds new imagery in morning and evening.

3. *Each under eye.* Compare *The Winter's Tale*, Act iv. sc. 2, l. 40, I have eyes under my service."

5. *Steep-up heavenly.* Mr. W. J. Craig suggests that Shakspere may have written "steep up-heavenly."

7, 8. Compare *Romeo and Juliet*, Act I. sc. 1, ll. 125, 126 :—

  Madam, an hour before the worshipp'd sun
  Peer'd forth the golden window of the east.

10. *He reeleth from the day.* Compare *Romeo and Juliet*, Act II. sc. 3, l. 3 :—

  Flecked darkness like a drunkard reels
  From forth day's path.

Chapman writes in *The Shadow of Night : Hymnus in Cynthiam* :—

> *Time's motion being like the reeling sun's.*

11, 12. Compare *Timon of Athens,* Act I. sc. 2, l. 150 :—

> *Men shut their doors against a setting sun.*

13. *Thyself outgoing in thy noon,* passing beyond your zenith.

VIII. In the Additional MS. 15,226, British Museum, is a copy, written in James I.'s reign, of this Sonnet.

1. Thou, whom to hear is music, why, etc. Compare Jessica in *The Merchant of Venice,* Act V. sc. 1, l. 69, " I am never merry when I hear sweet music."

8. *Bear.* Staunton proposes *share.*

13, 14. Perhaps there is an allusion to the old proverbial expression that one is no number. Compare Sonnet CXXXVI., " Among a number one is reckon'd none ; " and *Romeo and Juliet,* Act I. sc. 2, ll. 31, 32 :—

> *Of many mine being one*
> *May stand in number, though in reckoning none.*

The conceit in the last two lines of the sonnet seems to be that since many make but one, one will prove also less than itself, that is, will prove none.

IX. The thought of married happiness in VIII.—husband, child, and mother united in joy—suggests its opposite, the grief of a weeping widow. " Thou single

wilt prove none " of VIII. 14, is carried on in "consum'st
thyself in single life " of IX. 2.

4. *Makeless,* companionless.

> *Th' Elfe, therewith astownd,*
> *Upstarted lightly from his looser Make.*
> > Spenser, *Faerie Queene,* Bk. I. c. vii. st. 7.

12. *User.* Sewell has *us'rer.*

X. The "murderous shame " of IX. 14 reappears in the
"For shame!" and "murderous hate " of X. In IX.
Shakspere denies that his friend loves any one ; he carries
on the thought in the opening of X., and this leads up to
his friend's love of Shakspere, which is first mentioned
in this sonnet.

7, 8. Seeking to bring to ruin that house (*i.e.,* family)
which it ought to be your chief care to repair. These
lines confirm the conjecture that the father of Shakspere's
friend was dead. See Sonnet XIII. 9–14. Compare
3 *King Henry VI.,* Act v. sc. 1, ll. 83, 84 :—

> *I will not ruinate my father's house,*
> *Who gave his blood to lime the stones together;*

and *The Two Gentlemen of Verona,* Act v. sc. 4, ll. 7–11 :—

> *O thou that dost inhabit in my breast,*
> *Leave not the mansion so long tenantless,*
> *Lest, growing ruinous, the building fall*
> *And leave no memory of what it was!*
> *Repair me with thy presence, Silvia.*

9. *O change,* etc. O be willing to marry and beget

children, that I may cease to think you a being devoid
of love.

XI. The first five lines enlarge on the thought (x. 14)
of beauty living " *in thine ;* " showing how the beauty of
a child may be called *thine.*

2. *Departest,* leavest. " Ere I depart his house," *King
Lear,* Act III. sc. 5, l. 1.

4. *Convertest,* dost alter, or turn away. Compare Son-
net XIV. 12 :—

> *If from thyself to store thou wouldst convert.*

7. *The times,* the generations of men.

9. *Store,* " *i.e.,* to be preserved for *use.*"—MALONE.
" Increase of men, fertility, population." — SCHMIDT.
Compare *Othello,* Act IV. sc. 3, ll. 84–86 :—

> DES. *I do not think there is any such woman.*
>
> EMIL. *Yes, a dozen ; and as many to the vantage as*
> *would* store *the world they played for.*

11. To whom she gave much, she gave more. Sewell,
Malone, Staunton, Delius, read " gave *thee* more."

14. *Nor let that copy die.* Here " copy " means the
original from which the impression is taken. In *Twelfth
Night,* Act I. sc. 5, l. 261, it means the transcript impres-
sion taken from an original :—

> *Lady, you are the cruell'st she alive,*
> *If you will lead these graces to the grave*
> *And leave the world no* copy.

See also *Macbeth,* Act III. sc. 2, l. 38.

XII. This sonnet seems to be a gathering into one of
v., vi., vii. Lines 1, 2, like vii., speak of the decay and
loss of the brightness and beauty of the *day;* lines 3–8,
like v., vii., of the loss of the sweets and beauties of the
year.

3. *Violet past prime.* Compare *Hamlet,* Act I. sc. 3,
l. 7, "A violet in the youth of primy nature."

4. *Sable curls all silver'd.* The Quarto, 1609, reads "or
silver'd." An anonymous critic suggests "*o'er-silver'd*
with white." Compare *Hamlet,* Act I. sc. 2, l. 242 (Ho-
ratio, of the ghost's beard) :—

> *It was as I have seen it in his life,*
> *A sable silver'd.*

8. Compare *A Midsummer Night's Dream,* Act II. sc. 1,
l. 95 :—
> *The green corn*
> *Hath rotted ere his youth attain'd a beard.*

9. *Question make,* consider.

XIII. Shakspere imagines his friend in XII. 14 borne
away by Time. It is only while he lives here that he is
his own, XIII. 1, 2. Note "you" instead of "thee," and
the address "my love" for the first time.

1. *Yourself.* This seems to mean *your own.* So in the
Argument of Daniel's "Letter of Octavia," Antony could
not "dispose of himself, being not himself," *i.e.,* not his
own, but Cleopatra's.

5. So Daniel, *Delia,* XLVII. :—

> *in* beauty's lease *expired appears*
> *The date of age, the calends of our death.*

6. "*Determination* in legal language means end."—
MALONE.

9–13. The same thought of thriftless waste which
appears in Sonnets I., IV.

14. *You had a father.* Compare *All's Well that Ends
Well*, Act I. sc. 1, ll. 19, 20, "This young gentlewoman
had a father,—O, that 'had!' how sad a passage 'tis!"
The father of Shakspere's friend was probably dead.
Shakspere looks forward to the time when his friend
also shall be dead (l. 12), and wishes that a son may then
be living to say, as Shakspere's friend says now, "I had a
father."

XIV. In XIII. Shakspere predicts stormy winter (the
"seasons' quality" of XIV. 4) and the cold of death; he
now explains what his astrology is, and at the close of
the sonnet repeats his melancholy prediction.

1, 2. So Sidney, *Arcadia*, Book III. "O sweet Philo-
clea, . . . thy heavenly face is my astronomy." *Astrophel
and Stella* (ed. 1591), Sonnet XXVI. :—

> *Though dusty wits dare scorn astrology*
>
> .　　　　　.　　　　　.
>
> *[I] oft forejudge my after-following race
> By only those two stars in Stella's face.*

So Daniel, *Delia*, Sonnet XXX. (on Delia's eyes):—

> *Stars are they sure, whose motions rule desires;
> And calm and tempest follow their aspects.*

6. *Pointing.* "Write 'Pointing, *i.e.*, appointing; or at

least so understand the word. *Tarquin and Lucrece,* Stanza CXXVI. :—

> *Whoever plots the sin, thou* [Opportunity] *point'st the season.*"—W. S. WALKER.

8. *Oft predict,* frequent prognostication. Sewell (ed. 2) reads "By aught predict," *i.e.,* by anything predicted.

9, 10. Compare *Love's Labour's Lost,* Act IV. sc. 3, ll. 350–353 :—

> *From women's eyes this doctrine I derive :*
> *They sparkle still the right Promethean fire ;*
> *They are the books, the arts, the academes,*
> · *That show, contain, and nourish all the world.*

10–14. I introduce the inverted commas before *truth* after *convert,* before *Thy* and after *date.*

10. *Read such art,* gather by reading such truths of science as the following.

12. *Store.* See note on XI. 9.

Convert, rhyming here with "art ; " so in Daniel, *Delia,* Sonnet XI., "convert" rhymes with "heart."

XV. Introduces Verse as an antagonist of Time. The stars in XIV., determining weather, plagues, dearths, and fortune of princes, reappear in xv. 4, commenting in secret influence on the shows of this world.

3. *Stage.* Malone reads *state.* But the word *present* like *show* is theatrical, and confirms the text of the Quarto. Compare *Antony and Cleopatra,* Act III. sc. 13, ll. 29–31 :—

> *Yes, like enough, high-battled Cæsar will*
> *Unstate his happiness, and be* staged *to the* show,
> *Against a sworder.*

4. *Conceit,* conception, imagination.

11. *Debateth with Decay,* holds a discussion with Decay, or combats along with Decay. *Debate* is used frequently by Shakspere in each of these senses.

XVI. The gardening image " engraft," in xv. 14, suggests the thought of " maiden gardens " and " living flowers " of this sonnet.

7. *Bear your living flowers;* " bear you," Lintott, Gildon, Malone, and others; but " your living flowers " stands over against " your painted counterfeit."

8. *Counterfeit,* portrait. *Timon of Athens,* Act v. sc. 1, ll. 83, 84 (to the Painter), "Thou draw'st a counterfeit best in all Athens."

9. *Lines of life, i.e.,* children. The unusual expression is selected because it suits the imagery of the sonnet, lines applying to (1) Lineage, (2) delineation with a pencil, a portrait, (3) lines of verse as in xviii. 12. Lines of life are living lines, living poems and pictures, children.

10. *This, Time's pencil.* The Quarto reads " this (Times pensel or my pupill pen)." G. Massey conjectures " this time's pencil," adding :—" What Shakspeare says is, that the best painter, the master-pencil of the time, or his own pen of a learner, will alike fail to draw the Earl's lines of life as he himself can do it, by his own sweet skill. This pencil of the time may have been Mirevelt's; he

painted the Earl [of Southampton's] portrait in early manhood."—*Shakspere's Sonnets and his Private Friends*, pp. 115, 116 (note). Prof. Stengel proposes " With this, Time's pencil, for my pupil pen," etc. Are we to understand the line as meaning " Which this pencil of Time or .this my pupil pen ? " and is Time here conceived as a limner who has painted the youth so fair, but whose work cannot last for future generations ? In xix. " Devouring Time" is transformed into a scribe; may not "tyrant Time" be transformed here into a painter ? In xx. it is Nature who paints the face of the beautiful youth. This masterpiece of twenty years can endure neither as painted by Time's pencil, nor as represented by Shakspere's unskilful, pupil pen. Is the " painted counterfeit" of l. 8 Shakspere's portrayal in his verse? Compare liii. l. 5.

11. *Fair*, beauty.

XVII. In xvi. Shakspere has said that his "pupil pen " cannot make his friend live to future ages. He now carries on this thought; his verse, although not showing half his friend's excellences, will not be believed in times to come.

12. Keats prefixed this line as motto to his *Endymion;* " stretched metre " means overstrained poetry.

13, 14. If a child were alive his beauty would verify the descriptions in Shakspere's verse, and so the friend would possess a twofold life, in his child and in his poet's rhyme.

XVIII. Shakspere takes heart, expects immortality for his verse, and so immortality for his friend as surviving in it. He therefore gives expression fearlessly to the " poet's rage."

3. *May*, a summer month ; we must remember that May in Shakspere's time ran on to within a few days of our mid June. Compare *Cymbeline*, Act I. sc. 3, l. 36 :—

> *And like the tyrannous breathing of the north*
> *Shakes all our buds from growing.*

5. *Eye of heaven.* So *King Richard II.*, Act III. sc. 2, l. 37, " the searching eye of heaven."

10. *That fair thou owest*, that beauty thou possessest.

11, 12. This anticipation of immortality for their verse was a commonplace with the Sonnet-writers of the time of Elizabeth. See Spenser, *Amoretti*, Sonnets 27, 69, 75 ; Drayton, *Idea*, Sonnets 6, 44 ; Daniel, *Delia*, Sonnet 39.

XIX. Shakspere, confident of the immortality of his friend in verse, defies Time.

1. *Devouring Time.* So *Love's Labour's Lost*, Act I. sc. 1, l. 4, " Cormorant devouring Time." S. Walker conjectures *destroying*.

5. *Fleets.* The Quarto has *fleet'st*. I follow Dyce, believing that Shakspere cared more for his rhyme than his grammar, at a time when grammatical freedom was great. Compare *confounds*, Sonnet VIII. 7.

XX. A flight of praise ; his friend the ideal of human beauty, " beauty's pattern " (XIX. 12), and as such owning the attributes of male and female beauty.

1. *A woman's face,* but not, as women's faces are, painted by art.

2. *Master-mistress of my passion,* who sways my love with united charms of man and woman. Mr. H. C. Hart suggests to me that *passion* may be used in the old sense of *love-poem,* frequent in Watson.

5. *Less false in rolling.* Compare Spenser, *Faerie Queene,* Bk. III. c. i. s. 41 :—

> Her wanton eyes (*ill signes of womanhed*)
> Did roll too lightly.

8. In the Quarto, "A man in hew all *Hews* in his controwling." The italics and capital letter suggested to Tyrwhitt that more is meant here than meets the eye, that the Sonnets may have been addressed to some one named Hews or Hughes, and that Mr. W. H. may be Mr. William Hughes. But the following words have also capital letters and are in italics :—Rose I. 2 ; Audit IV. 12 ; Statues LV. 5 ; Intrim LVI. 9 ; Alien LXXVIII. 3 ; Satire C. 11 ; Autumne CIV. 5 ; Abisme CXII. 9 ; Alcumie CXIV. 4 ; Syren CXIX. 1 ; Heriticke CXXIV. 9 ; Informer CXXV. 13 ; Audite CXXVI. 11 ; Quietus CXXVI. 12. The word " hue " was used by Elizabethan writers not only in the sense of *complexion,* but also in that of *shape, form.* The following are instances :—

> Her snowy substance melted as with heat,
> Ne of that goodly hew remained ought,
> But th' empty Girdle which about her waist was wrought.
> > *Faerie Queene,* Bk. V. c. iii. s. 24.

In *Faerie Queene,* Bk. V. c. ix. ss. 17, 18, Talus tries

to seize Malengin, who transforms himself into a fox, a bush, a bird, a stone, and then a hedgehog :—

> *Then gan it* [the hedgehog] *run away incontinent,*
> *Being returned to his former* hew.

Nash's *Pierce Pennilesse,* pp. 82, 83 (Shakespeare Society's Reprint). " The spirits of the water have slow bodies, resembling birds and women, of which kinde the Naiades and Nereides are much celebrated amongst poets. Nevertheless, however they are restrayned to their severall similitudes, it is certain that all of them desire no forme or figure so much as the likenesse of a man, and doo thinke themselves in heaven when they are infeoft in that *hue.*" The meaning of lines 7, 8 in this sonnet then may be, " A man in form and appearance, having the mastery over all forms in that of his, which steals," etc. If one were to amuse oneself with fancied discoveries, why not insist on the fact that this mysterious *Hews* contains the initials of both W. H. and W. S. With the phrase " controlling hues " compare Sonnet cvi. 8 :—

> *Even such a* beauty *as you* master *now.*

11. *Defeated,* defrauded, disappointed. So *A Midsummer Night's Dream,* Act iv. sc. 1, ll. 153–155 :—

> *They would have stolen away ; they would, Demetrius,*
> *Thereby to have defeated you and me,*
> *You of your wife and me of my consent.*

XXI. The first line of xx. suggests this sonnet. The face of Shakspere's friend is painted by Nature alone, and so too there is no false painting, no poetical hyperbole in the description. As containing examples of such extravagant comparisons, amorous fancies, far-fetched conceits of sonnet-writers as Shakspere here speaks of, Mr. Main (*Treasury of English Sonnets*, p. 283) cites Spenser's *Amoretti*, 9 and 64; Daniel's *Delia*, 19; Barnes's *Parthenophil and Parthenophe*, Sonnet 48. Compare also Griffin's *Fidessa*, Sonnet XXXIX., and Constable's *Diana* (1594), the sixth Decade, Sonnet I. "True love," says Charles Lamb (*Essays of Elia; Some Sonnets of Sir Philip Sidney*), "thinks no labour to send out Thoughts upon the vast and more than Indian voyages, to bring home rich pearls, outlandish wealth, gums, jewels, spicery, to sacrifice in self-depreciating similitudes as shadows of true amiabilities in the Beloved."

On the other hand, Elizabethan sonnet-writers protest against using "new-found tropes" and "strange similes," as Sidney, in *Astrophel and Stella*, III. :—

> *Let dainty wits cry on the Sisters nine*, etc.

So Shakspere's Berowne, in *Love's Labour's Lost*, Act v. sc. 2, ll. 405–413.

5. *Making a couplement of proud compare*, joining in proud comparisons. It is worth noting that the word often printed *compliment* in Spenser's *Prothalamion*, St. 6, ought to be *couplement*.

8. *Rondure*, circle, as in *King John*, Act II. sc. 1, l. 259, "the *roundure* of your old-faced walls." Staunton proposes "vault" in place of "air" in this line.

12. *Gold candles.* Compare "These blessed candles of the night," *The Merchant of Venice*, Act v. l. 220; also

Romeo and Juliet, Act III. sc. 5, l. 9 ; *Macbeth,* Act II. sc. 1, l. 5.

13. *That like of hearsay well.* " To like of " meaning " to like " is frequent in Shakspere. Schmidt's explanation is " that fall in love with what has been praised by others ; " but does it not rather mean " that like to be buzzed about by talk " ?

14. Compare *Love's Labour's Lost,* Act IV. sc. 3, ll. 239, 240 :—

> *Fie, painted rhetoric! O, she needs it not :*
> *To things of sale a seller's praise belongs.*

XXII. The praise of his friend's beauty suggests by contrast Shakspere's own face marred by time. He comforts himself by claiming his friend's beauty as his own. Lines 11–14 give the first hint of possible wrong committed by the youth against friendship.

4. *Expiate,* bring to an end. So *King Richard* III., Act III. sc. 3, l. 23 :—

> *Make haste : the hour of death is* expiate

(changed in the second Folio to " now expired "). In Chapman's *Byron's Conspiracie* an old courtier says he is

> *A poor and* expiate *humour of the court.*

Steevens conjectures in this sonnet *expirate,* which R. Grant White introduces into the text.

9–12. Compare Sidney's poem in *Arcadia,* p. 344 (ed. 1613) :—

> *My true love hath my heart, and I have his,* etc.

And *Love's Labour's Lost*, Act v. sc. 2, l. 826 :—

> *Hence ever then my heart is in thy breast.*

10. *As I*, etc., as I will be wary of myself for thy sake, not my own.

XXIII. The sincerity and silent love of his verses: returning to the thought of XXI.

1, 2. So *Coriolanus*, Act v. sc. 3, ll. 40–42 :—

> *Like a dull actor now,*
> *I have forgot my part, and I am out,*
> *Even to a full disgrace.*

5. *For fear of trust*, fearing to trust myself. Schmidt explains " doubting of being trusted," but the comparison is to an imperfect actor, who dare not trust himself. Observe the construction of the first eight lines; 5, 6 refer to 1, 2; 7, 8 to 3, 4. Staunton proposes for " fear or trust," *i.e.*, through timidity or too much confidence.

9. *Books.* Sewell and Malone's friend C. [Capell probably] would read "O, let my *looks*," etc. But the Quarto text may be right; so l. 13 :—

> *O learn to* read *what silent love hath* writ.

The books of which Shakspere speaks are probably the manuscript books in which he writes his sonnets, sending them, when a group has been written or a book filled, to his friend. In support of *looks* H. Isaac cites Spenser, *Amoretti*, 43 :—

> *Yet I my heart with silence secretly*
> *Will teach to speak, and my just cause to plead ;*
> *And eke my eies, with meek humility,*
> *Love-learned letters to her eyes to read.*

Compare also Sonnet XCIII.; *Love's Labour's Lost*, IV. 2, 113; *Midsummer Night's Dream*, II. 2, 121 ; *Winter's Tale*, IV. 4, 172; *Romeo and Juliet*, I. 3, 86.

12. *More than,* etc., more than that tongue (the tongue of another person than Shakspere) which hath more fully expressed more ardours of love, or more of your perfections.

XXIV. Suggested by the thought, XXII. 6, of Shakspere's heart being lodged in his friend's breast, and by the conceit of XXIII. 14. There eyes are able to hear through love's fine wit; here eyes do other singular things, play the painter.

1. *Stell'd,* fixed: *steeld,* Quarto. Compare *Lucrece,* 1444:—

> *To find a face where all distress is* stell'd.

2. *Table,* that on which a picture is painted. Compare *All's Well that Ends Well,* Act I. sc. 1, ll. 104–106 :—

> *To sit and draw*
> *His arched brows, his hawking eye, his curls,*
> *In our* heart's table.

4. *Perspective.* Schmidt explains perspective here in the same sense in which he supposes it is used in *King Richard II.,* Act II. sc. 2, l. 18, a glass cut in such a manner as to produce an optical deception when looked through. "Perspective" certainly meant a cunning

picture, which seen directly seemed in confusion, and seen obliquely became an intelligible composition. But here does it not simply mean that a painter's highest art is to produce the illusion of distance, one thing seeming to lie behind another? You must look *through* the painter (my eye or myself) to see your picture, the product of his skill, which lies within him (in my heart).

The stage conceits in this sonnet are paralleled in Constable: *Diana* (1594), Sonnet 5 (p. 4, ed. Hazlitt):—

> *Thine eye, the glasse where I behold my heart,*
> *Mine eye, the window through the which thine eye*
> *May see my heart, and there thyselfe espy*
> *In bloody colours how thou painted art.*

Compare also Watson's *The Teares of Fancie* (1593), Sonnets 45, 46 (Thomas Watson, Poems, ed. Arber, p. 201):—

> *My Mistres seeing her faire counterfet*
> *So sweetlie framed in my bleeding brest*
>
> .   .   .   .   .   .
>
> *But it so fast was fixed to my heart,* etc.

Compare *Love's Labour's Lost*, Act v. sc. 1, l. 848:—

> *Behold the window of my heart, mine eye.*

5. Prof. Stengel changes *you* and *your* in ll. 4, 5, to *thou, thy*. But may not *you* and *your* be used indefinitely, not with reference to the person addressed, but to what is of common application, as in "Your marriage comes by destiny," *All's Well that Ends Well*, I. iii. 66.

XXV. In this sonnet Shakspere makes his first complaint against Fortune, against his low condition. He is about to undertake a journey on some needful business of his own, and rejoices to think that at least in one place he has a fixed abode, in his friend's heart.

> *Then happy I, that love and am beloved,*
> *Where I may not remove nor be removed.*

Thoughts of the cruelty of Fortune reappear and become predominant in XXIX.–XXXI.

Prof. Hales ("From Stratford to London," *Cornhill Magazine*, January, 1877) suggests that the journeys spoken of in the Sonnets may have been to Shakspere's Stratford home.

4. *Unlook'd for.* Staunton proposes " Unhonour'd."

5. *Great princes' favourites*, etc. Compare *Much Ado about Nothing*, Act III. sc. 1, ll. 8–10 :—

> *Honeysuckles, ripen'd by the sun,*
> *Forbid the sun to enter, like favourites*
> *Made proud by princes.*

Prof. Hales thinks that Essex or Raleigh may have furnished the suggestion of the simile.

6. *The marigold.* Compare Constable, *Diana*, Sonnet 9 :—

> *The marigold abroad his leaves doth spread*
> *Because the sun's and her power are the same ;*

and *Lucrece*, l. 397.

There are three plants which claim to be the old Marigold: 1. The marsh marigold; this does not open and close its flowers with the sun. 2. The corn marigold; there is no proof that this was called marigold in Shakspere's day. 3. The garden marigold, or Ruddes (calendula officinalis); it turns its flowers to the sun, and follows his guidance in their opening and shutting. The old name is goldes; it was the Heliotrope, Solsequium, or Turnesol of our forefathers. (Condensed from "Marigold," in Ellacombe's *Plant Lore and Garden Craft of Shakespeare.*)

9. *Famoused for fight.* The Quarto reads *for worth.* The emendation is due to Theobald, who "likewise proposed if *worth* was retained to read *razèd forth.*"— MALONE. Capell suggested *for might.*

XXVI. In xxv. Shakspere is in disfavour with his stars, and unwillingly—as I suppose—about to undertake some needful journey. He now sends this written embassage to his friend (perhaps it is the *Envoy* to the preceding group of sonnets), and dares to anticipate a time when the "star that guides his *moving*," now unfavourable, may point on him graciously with fair aspect (l. 10).

Drake writes (*Shakspeare and his Times,* vol. ii. p. 63):— "Perhaps one of the most striking proofs of this position [that the Sonnets are addressed to the Earl of Southampton] is the hitherto unnoticed fact that the language of the *Dedication to the Rape of Lucrece* and that of part of the *twenty-sixth sonnet* are almost precisely the same. The *Dedication* runs thus:—The *love* I dedicate to your Lordship is without end. . . . The warrant I have of your honourable disposition, not the worth of my untutored lines, makes it assured of acceptance. What I have is yours, what I have to do is yours; being part of all I have devoted yours. Were my worth greater, my duty would show greater." C. [Capell ?] had previously noted the parallel.

1, 2. Compare *Macbeth*, Act III. sc. 1, ll. 15–18 :—

> *Let your highness*
> *Command upon me ; to the which my duties*
> *Are with a most indissoluble tie*
> *For ever knit.*

8. *Bestow it*, lodge it. As in *The Tempest*, Act. v. l. 299 :—

> *Hence, and bestow your luggage where you found it.*

Shakspere says, I hope some happy idea of yours will convey my duty—even naked as it is—into your soul's thought.

12. *Thy sweet respect*, regard, consideration. The Quarto reads *their* for *thy*, an error which occurs several times.

13, 14. The rhyme has an echo of Daniel's *Delia*, x. (1594) :—

> *Once let her know! sh'hath done enough to prove me,*
> *And let her pity, if she cannot love me.*

XXVII. Written on a journey, which removes Shakspere farther and farther from his friend.

1. "We can see that it was not without knowledge Shakspere made Autolycus sing :—

> *A merry heart goes all the way;*
> *Your sad heart tires in a mile-a."*
>
> J. W. HALES.

3. Modern editors put a comma after " head," perhaps rightly. But may not the construction be " a journey in my head begins to work my mind " ?

6. *Intend,* bend, pursue: used frequently of travel. " If he should *intend* this voyage toward my wife," *The Merry Wives of Windsor,* Act II. sc. 1, 1. 188. " Cæsar through Syria *intends* his journey," *Antony and Cleopatra,* Act V. sc. 1, 1. 200.

10. *Thy.* The Quarto reads *their.* See XXVI. 12.

11, 12. Compare *Romeo and Juliet,* Act, I. sc. 5, ll. 47, 48 :—

> *It seems she hangs upon the cheek of night,*
> *Like a rich jewel in an Ethiope's ear.*

13, 14. By day my limbs find no quiet for myself, *i.e.,* on account of business of my own ; by night my mind finds no quiet for thee, *i.e.,* on your account, thinking of you.

XXVIII. A continuation of Sonnet XXVII.

9. Cambridge editors and Furness read, " I tell the day, to please him thou art bright."

12. *Twire,* peep. Compare Ben Jonson, *Sad Shepherd,* Act II. sc. 1 :—

> *Which maids will* twire *at, tween their fingers, thus.*

Beaumont and Fletcher, *Woman Pleas'd,* Act IV. sc. 1 :—

> *I saw the wench that* twir'd *and twinkled at thee*
> *The other day.*

Marston : *Antonio and Mellida,* Act IV. (Works, vol. i. p. 52, ed. Halliwell), " I sawe a thing stirre under a hedge, and I peep't, and I spyed a thing, and I peer'd and I *tweerd* underneath."

Malone conjectured in this sonnet "twirl not;" Steevens, "twirk not;" Massey, "tire not," in the sense of *attire.*

12. *Gild'st.* The Quarto reads "guil'st."

13, 14. Dyce and others read " And night doth nightly make grief's *strength* seem stronger," which possibly is right. The meaning of the Quarto text must be: Each day's journey draws out my sorrows to a greater length; but this process of drawing-out does not weaken my sorrows, for my night-thoughts come to make my sorrows as strong as before, nay stronger. It might be supposed that my grief if long were light, but this is not so; it grows in length indeed each day, but also to this length is added strength each night. C. [Capell?] suggested to Malone "draw my sorrows stronger . . . length seem longer."

XXIX. These are the night-thoughts referred to in the last line of XXVIII.; hence a special appropriateness in the image of the lark rising at break of day.

8. *With what I most enjoy contented least.* The preceding line makes it not improbable that Shakspere is here speaking of his own poems.

12. *Sings hymns at heaven's gate.* Compare *Cymbeline,* Act II. sc. 3, ll. 21, 22 :—

> *Hark, hark! the lark at heaven's gate sings,*
> *And Phœbus 'gins arise.*

Lyly, *Campaspe*, Act v. sc. 1 :—

> *How at heaven's gates she [the lark] claps her wings,*
> *The morne not waking till she sings.*

XXX. Sonnet XXIX. was occupied with thoughts of *present* wants and troubles ; XXX. tells of thoughts of past griefs and losses.

1, 2. Compare *Othello*, Act III. sc. 3, ll. 138–141 :—

> *Who has a breast so pure,*
> *But some uncleanly apprehensions*
> *Keep leets and law-days, and in session sit*
> *With meditations lawful.*

6. *Dateless*, endless, as in Sonnet CLIII., "a dateless, lively heat, still to endure."

8. *Moan the expense.* Schmidt explains *expense* as loss ; but does not "moan the expense" mean *pay my account of moans for?* The words are explained by what follows :—

> *Tell o'er*
> *The sad account of fore-bemoaned moan*
> *Which I new pay as if not paid before.*

Malone has a long note idly attempting to show that *sight* is used for *sigh.*

10. *Tell o'er*, count over.

XXXI. Continues the subject of XXX.—Shakspere's friend compensates all losses in the past.

5. *Obsequious*, funereal, as in *Hamlet*, Act I. sc. 2, l. 92, "To do *obsequious* sorrow."

6. *Dear religious love.* In *A Lover's Complaint*, the beautiful youth pleads to his love that all earlier hearts which had paid homage to him now yield themselves through him to her service (a thought similar to that of this sonnet). One of these fair admirers was a nun, a sister sanctified, but (l. 250) :—

> Religious love *put out Religion's eye.*

8. *In thee lie.* The Quarto reads " in there lie."

10. *Hung with the trophies of my lovers gone.* Compare from the same passage of *A Lover's Complaint* (l. 218) :—

> *Lo, all these trophies of affections hot*
> . . . . .
> *. . . must your oblations be.*

XXXII. From the thought of dead friends of whom he is the survivor, Shakspere passes to the thought of his own death, and his friend as the survivor. This sonnet reads like an *Envoy.*

4. *Lover,* commonly used by Elizabethan writers generally for *one who loves* another, without reference to the special passion of love between man and woman. In *Coriolanus*, Act v. sc. 2, l. 13, Menenius says :—

> *I tell thee, fellow,*
> *Thy general is my* lover.

" Ben Jonson concludes one of his letters to Dr. Donne by telling him that he is his " ever true *lover* ," and Drayton, in a letter to Mr. Drummond of Hawthornden, informs him that Mr. Joseph Davies is *in love* with him."— MALONE.

5, 6. May we infer from these lines (and 10) that Shakspere had a sense of the wonderful progress of poetry in the time of Elizabeth?

7. *Reserve*, preserve. So *Pericles*, Act IV. sc. 1, l. 40, " *Reserve* that excellent complexion." Daniel, *Delia* Sonnet 41.:—

> *Thou may'st in after ages live esteem'd,*
> *Unbury'd in these lines*, reserv'd *in pureness.*

XXXIII. A new group seems to begin with this sonnet. It introduces the wrongs done to Shakspere by his friend.

4. Compare *King John*, Act III. sc. 1, ll. 77–80 :—

> *The glorious sun*
> *Stays in his course and plays the alchemist,*
> *Turning with splendour of his precious eye*
> *The meagre cloddy earth to glittering gold.*

6. *Rack*, a mass of vapoury clouds. *Hamlet*, Act II. sc. 2, ll. 505, 506 :—

> *But, as we often see, against some storm*
> *A silence in the heaven, the* rack *stand still.*

" The winds in the upper region, which move the clouds above (which we call the *rack*)," Bacon, *Sylva Sylvarum*, sec. 115, p. 32, ed. 1658 (quoted by Dyce, *Glossary*, under *rack*). Compare with 5, 6, 1 *King Henry IV.*, Act I. sc. 2, ll. 221–227 :—

> *Herein will I imitate the* sun,
> *Who doth* permit *the* base *contagious* clouds

To smother up his beauty from the world,
That when he please again to be himself,
Being wanted, he may be more wonder'd at,
By breaking through the foul and ugly *mists*
Of vapours that did seem to strangle him.

8. *To west.* Steevens proposes *to rest.*

12. *The region cloud.* Compare *Hamlet*, Act II. sc. 2, l. 606, "the *region* kites." Region, "originally a division of the sky marked out by the Roman augurs. In later times the atmosphere was divided into three regions, upper, middle, and lower. By Shakespeare the word is used to denote the air generally."—Clarendon Press *Hamlet.*

14. *Stain,* used in the transitive and intransitive senses for *dim.* Watson, *Teares of Fancie*, Sonnet 55, says of the sun and the moon, "his beauty *stains* her brightness." Faithlessness in friendship is spoken of in the same way as a *stain* in Sonnet CIX. 11, 12.

XXXIV. Carries on the idea and metaphor of XXXIII.

4. *Rotten smoke.* We find *smoke* meaning vapour in 1 *King Henry VI.*, Act II. sc. 2, l. 27. Compare *Coriolanus*, Act III. sc. 3, l. 121, "reek o' the rotten fens."

12. *Cross.* The Quarto reads *losse.* The forty-second sonnet confirms the emendation, and explains what this cross and this loss were :—

Losing her [his mistress], *my friend hath found that loss;*
Both find each other, and I lose both twain,
And both for my sake lay on me this cross.

See also Sonnet CXXXIII., addressed to his lady, in which Shakspere speaks of himself as " crossed " by her robbery of his friend's heart; and Sonnet CXXXIV. 1. 13, " Him have I *lost*."

XXXV. The " tears " of XXXIV. suggest the opening. Moved to pity, Shakspere will find guilt in himself rather than in his friend.

5, 6. *And even I,* etc., and even I am faulty in this, that I find precedents for your misdeed by comparisons with roses, fountains, sun, and moon.

7. *Salving thy amiss.* Shakspere's friend offers a salve, XXXIV.: see also CXX. 12; here Shakspere in his turn tries to " salve " his friend's wrong-doing.

8. The word *thy* in this line is twice printed *their* in the Quarto. Steevens explains the line thus: " Making the excuse more than proportioned to the offence." Staunton proposes "more than thy sins *bear*," *i.e.,* I bear more sins than thine.

9. *In sense.* Malone proposed *incense.* Sense here means reason, judgment, discretion. If we receive the present text, " thy adverse party " (1. 10) must mean Shakspere. But may we read :—

For to thy sensual fault I bring in sense, [*i.e.,* judgment, reason]
Thy adverse party, as *thy advocate.*

Sense—against which he has offended—brought in *as* his advocate ?

14. *Sweet thief,* etc. Compare Sonnet XL. :—

I do forgive thy robbery, gentle thief.

XXXVI. According to the announcement made in
xxxv., Shakspere proceeds to make himself out the guilty
party.

1. *We two must be twain.* So *Troilus and Cressida*, Act
III. sc. 1, l. 110, "She'll none of him; they two are twain."

5. *Respect,* regard, as in *Coriolanus*, Act III. sc. 3,
l. 112:—

> *I do* love
> *My country's good with a* respect *more tender,*
> *More holy and profound than my own life.*

6. *Separable spite.* "A cruel fate, that *spitefully sepa-*
rates us from each other. *Separable* for *separating.*"—
MALONE.

9. *Evermore.* "Perhaps *ever more.*"—W. S. WALKER.

10. *My bewailed guilt.* Explained by Spalding and
others as "the blots that remain with Shakspere on
account of his profession" as an actor. But perhaps the
passage means: "I may not claim you as a friend, lest
my relation to the dark woman—now a matter of grief—
should convict you of faithlessness in friendship."

12. *That honour, i.e.,* the honour which you give me.

13, 14. These lines are repeated in Sonnet XCVI.

XXXVII. Continues the thought of XXXVI. 13, 14.

3. *I, made lame.* Compare Sonnet LXXXIX. :—

> *Speak of my lameness and I straight will halt.*

Shakspere uses "to lame" in the sense of "disable."
Here the *worth* and *truth* of his friend are set over against
the lameness of Shakspere; the lameness then is meta-
phorical; a disability to join in the joyous movement of

life, as his friend does. Capell and others conjectured that Shakspere was literally lame. Mr. Swinburne, in his mocking "Report of the Proceedings, etc., of the Newest Shakespeare Society," introduces Mr. E. reading a paper on "The Lameness of Shakespeare—was it moral or physical?" Mr. E. assumes at once that the infirmity was physical. "Then arose the question—In which leg?" Perhaps it is best so to dismiss the subject—with a jest.

3. *Dearest*, chief, strongest; as in *Hamlet*, Act I. sc. 2, l. 182 :—

> *Would I had met my* dearest *foe in heaven.*

7. *Entitled in thy parts do crowned sit.* The Quarto reads "*their* parts;" but the misprint *their* for *thy* happens several times. Schmidt accepts the Quarto text and explains, "*i.e.*, or more excellences, having a just claim to the first place as their due. Blundering M. Edd. *e. in thy parts*." "*Entitled* means, I think, ennobled."—MALONE. "Perhaps."—DYCE. Perhaps it means "having a title in, having a claim upon," as in *Lucrece*, 57 :—

> *But beauty, in that white* [the paleness of Lucrece] *intituled,*
> *From Venus' doves doth challenge that fair field.*

XXXVIII. The same thought as that of the two preceding sonnets: "The pain be mine, but thine shall be the praise." In XXXVII. 14, Shakspere is "ten times happy" in his friend's happiness and glory; he also is ten times happy in the inspiration he receives from his

friend who is " the tenth Muse, ten times more in worth "
than the old nine Muses.

Prof. Stengel notices that " argument," " subject,"
" light," are also found together in Sonnet C.

XXXIX. In XXXVIII. Shakspere spoke of his friend's
worth as ten times that of the nine Muses, but in XXXVII.
he had spoken of his friend as the better part of himself.
He now asks how he can with modesty sing the worth
of his own better part. Thereupon he returns to the
thought of XXXVI., " we two must be twain ; " and now,
not only are the two lives to be divided, but " our dear
love "—undivided in XXXVI.—must " lose name of single
one."

19. *Doth.* The Quarto has " dost."

13, 14. Absence teaches how to make of the absent
beloved two persons, one, absent in reality, the other,
present to imagination.

XL. In XXXIX. Shakspere desires that his love and his
friend's may be separated, in order that he may give his
friend what otherwise he must give also to himself.
Now, separated, he gives his beloved all his loves, yet
knows that, before the gift, all his was his friend's by
right. Our love " losing name of single one " (XXXIX. 6)
suggests the manifold loves, mine and thine.

5. Then if for love of me thou receivest her whom I
love.

6. *For,* because : I cannot blame thee for using my
love, *i.e.,* her whom I love.

7, 8. The Quarto has " this selfe " for thyself. Yet you

are to blame if you deceive yourself by an unlawful union while you refuse loyal wedlock.

11. *And yet love knows it*, etc. Printed by many editors, " And yet, love knows, it."

XLI. The thought of XL. 13, "Lascivious grace, in whom all ill well shows," is carried out in this sonnet.

1. *Pretty wrongs.* Bell and Palgrave read *petty*.

5, 6. Compare 1 *King Henry VI.*, Act v. sc. 3, ll. 77, 78 :—

> *She's beautiful, and therefore to be woo'd ;*
> *She is a woman, therefore to be won.*

8. *Till she have prevail'd.* The Quarto has " till *he*," which may be right.

9. *Thou mightst my seat forbear.* Malone reads " Thou mightst, my sweet, forbear ; " but "seat" is right, and the meaning is explained by *Othello*, Act II. sc. 1, l. 304, (Iago jealous of Othello) :—

> *I do suspect the lusty Moor*
> *Hath leap'd into my* seat.

Dr. Ingleby adds, as a parallel, *Lucrece*, 412, 413 :—

> *Who [Tarquin], like a foul usurper, went about*
> *From this fair throne to heave the owner out.*

XLII. In XLI. 13, 14, Shakspere declares that he loves both friend and mistress ; he now goes on to say that the loss of his friend is the greater of the two.

10, 12. The " loss " and " cross " of these lines are spoken of in XXXIV.

11. *Both twain.* This is found also in *Love's Labour's Lost*, Act v. sc. 2, l. 459 :—

PRINCESS. *What, will you have me, or your pearl again?*
BIRON. *Neither of either ; I remit* both twain.

XLIII. Does this begin a new group of Sonnets ?

1. *Wink,* to close the eyes, not necessarily for a moment, but as in sleep. Compare *Cymbeline,* Act II. sc. 3, ll. 25, 26 :—

> *And* winking *Mary-buds begin*
> *To ope their golden eyes.*

2. *Unrespected,* unregarded.

4. *And darkly,* etc. And illumined, although closed, are clearly directed in the darkness. It is strange that no one of the officious emenders has proposed " *right* in dark directed."

5. *Whose shadow shadows,* etc. Whose image makes bright the shades of night.

6. *Shadow's form,* the form which casts thy shadow.

11. *Thy.* The Quarto has *their.*

13, 14. *All days are nights to see,* etc. Malone proposed " nights to *me.*" Steevens, defending the Quarto text, explains it, " All days *are gloomy to behold, i.e., look* like nights." Mr. Lettsom proposed :—

> *All days are nights to* me *till thee* I see,
> *And nights bright days when dreams do show* me thee

" To *see* till I *see* thee," is probably right in this sonnet, which has a more than common fancy for doubling a word in the same line, as in lines 4, 5, 6.

XLIV. In XLIII. he obtains sight of his friend in dreams; XLIV. expresses the longing of the waking hours to come into his friend's presence by some preternatural means.

4. *Where thou dost stay.* I would be brought where (*i.e.*, to where) thou dost stay.

9. *Thought kills me.* Perhaps "thought" here means melancholy contemplation, as in *Julius Cæsar*, Act II. sc. 1, l. 187, "Take *thought* and die for Cæsar."

10. *So much of earth and water wrought.* So large a proportion of earth and water having entered into my composition. *Twelfth Night*, Act II. sc. 3, l. 10. "Does not our life consist of the four elements?" Compare *Julius Cæsar*, Act V. sc. 5, l. 73:—

> The elements
> So mixed in him that Nature might stand up,
> And say to all the world, "This was a man."

Antony and Cleopatra, Act V. sc. 2, l. 292:—

> I am air and fire; my other elements
> I give to baser life.

And *King Henry V.*, Act III. sc. 7, l. 22, "He is pure air and fire; and the dull elements of earth and water never appear in him, but only in patient stillness," etc.

XLV. Sonnet XLIV. tells of the duller elements of earth and water; this sonnet, of the elements of air and fire.

9. *Recured*, restored to wholeness and soundness. *Venus*

and Adonis, l. 465. *King Richard III.*, Act III. sc. 7, l. 130.

12. *Thy fair health.* The Quarto has *their* for *thy*.

XLVI. As XLIV. and XLV. are a pair of companion sonnets, so are XLVI. and XLVII. The theme of the first pair is the opposition of the four elements in the person of the poet; the theme of the second is the opposition of the heart and the eye, *i.e.*, of love and the senses.

3. *Thy picture's sight.* The Quarto has *their*; so also in lines 8, 13, 14.

10. *A quest of thoughts.* An inquest or jury. *King Richard III.*, Act I. sc. 4, l. 189 :—

> *What lawful quest have given their verdict up*
> *Unto the frowning judge?*

12. *Moiety*, portion.

XLVII. Companion sonnet to the last.

3. *Famished for a look.* Compare Sonnet LXXV. 10. So *Comedy of Errors*, Act II. sc. 1, l. 88 :—

> *Whilst I at home starve for a merry look.*

10. *Art present.* The Quarto has *are*.

11, 12. *Not.* Quarto *nor*. The same thought which appears in XLV.

Compare with these sonnets—XLVI. and XLVII.—Sonnets 19, 20, of Watson's *Teare of Fancie*, 1593 (Watson's Poems, ed. Arber, p. 188) :—

> *My hart impos'd this penance on mine eies,*
> *(Eies the first causers of my harts lamenting :)*

That they should weepe till loue and fancie dies,
Fond love the last cause of my harts repenting.
Mine eies upon my hart inflict this paine
(Bold hart that dard to harbour thoughts of loue)
That it should loue and purchase fell disdaine,
A grieuous penance which my hart doth proue,
Mine eies did weepe as hart had them imposed,
My hart did pine as eies had it constrained, etc.

Sonnet 20 continues the same :—

My hart accus'd mine eies and was offended,

. . . . .

Hart said that loue did enter at the eies,
And from the eies descended to the hart ;
Eies said that in the hart did sparkes arise, etc.

Compare also *Diana* (ed. 1584), Sixth Decade, Sonnet 7
(Arber's *English Garner*, vol. ii. p. 254) ; and Drayton,
Idea, 33.

XLVIII.   Line 6 of xLVI., in which Shakspere speaks
of keeping his friend in the closet of his breast :—

A closet never pierced with crystal eyes,

suggests xLVIII.; see lines 9–12.   I have said he is safe
in my breast ; yet ah ! I feel he is not.

5. I locked up my trifles, much more my jewels ; but
my jewels are trifles compared with you.

11. *Gentle closure of my breast.*   So *Venus and Adonis,*
l. 782, "the quiet closure of my breast."

14. Does not this refer to the woman, who has sworn

love (CLII. l. 2), and whose truth to Shakspere (spoken of in XLI. 13) now proves thievish? Compare *Venus and Adonis*, l. 724, "Rich preys make true men thieves."

XLIX. Continues the sad strain with which XLVIII. closes. Notice the construction of the sonnet, each of the three quatrains beginning with the same words, "Against that time;" so also LXIV., three quatrains beginning with the words "When I have seen." So Daniel's Sonnet beginning "If this be love," repeated in the first line of each quatrain.

3. *Cast his utmost sum*, closed his account and cast up the sum total.

4. *Advis'd respects*, deliberate, well-considered reasons. So *King John*, Act IV. sc. 2, l. 214:—

> *Perchance it frowns*
> *More upon humour than* advised respects.

8. *Reasons*, *i.e.*, for its conversion from the thing it was.

9. *Ensconce*, " protect or cover as with a *sconce* or fort." —DYCE.

10. *Desert.* Quarto, *desart*, rhyming with *part*.

L. This sonnet and the next are a pair, as XLIV., XLV. are, and XLVI., XLVII. The journey, l. 1, is that spoken of in XLVIII. l. 1.

5. *Beast.* Still used for *horse* in parts of Ireland.

6. *Dully.* The Quarto has *duly*, but compare LI. 2, " my *dull* bearer," and l. 11, " no *dull* flesh."

LI. Companion to L.

6. *Swift extremity*, the extreme of swiftness. So *Macbeth*, Act I. sc. 4, l. 17 :—

Swiftest *wing of recompence is* slow.

7. *Mounted on the wind.* So 2 *King Henry IV.* Induction, l. 4, "Making the *wind my post-horse.*" Compare *Cymbeline*, Act III. sc. 4, l. 38 ; *Macbeth*, Act I. sc. 7, ll. 21–23.

10. *Perfect'st.* The Quarto has *perfects.*

11. Malone and other editors print :—

Shall neigh (no dull flesh) in, etc.

I.e., Desire shall neigh, being no dull flesh, etc. But does it not mean Desire, which is all love, shall neigh, there being no dull flesh to cumber him as he rushes forward in his fiery race ? Compare the neighing stallion of Adonis, *Venus and Adonis*, ll. 300–312. Mr. Massey takes "neigh" as a transitive verb governing "flesh," "Shall neigh to no dull flesh," an explanation on which surely no comment is needful.

14. *Go,* move step by step, walk, as in *The Tempest*, Act III. sc. 2, l. 22 :—

STEPHANO. *We'll not run, Monsieur Monster.*
TRINCULO. *Nor* go *neither.*

Two Gentlemen of Verona, Act III. sc. 1, l. 388, "Thou must run to him, for thou hast stayed so long that *going* will scarce serve thy turn."

I have placed the last two lines, spoken, as I take it, by Love, within inverted commas.

LII. The joy of hope, the hope of meeting his friend spoken of in the last sonnet (LI.).

4. *For blunting*, because it would blunt. So *The Two Gentlemen of Verona*, Act I. sc. 2, l. 136, " Yet here they shall not lie, *for* catching cold."

7–12. So 1 *King Henry IV.*, Act III. sc. 2, ll. 55–59 :—

> *Thus did I keep my person fresh and new ;*
> *My presence, like a robe pontifical,*
> *Ne'er seen but wonder'd at : and so my state,*
> Seldom *but sumptuous, showed* like a feast
> *And won by rareness such solemnity.*

8. *Captain*, chief. So *Timon of Athens*, Act III. sc. 5, l. 49 (Dyce ; but qu :? " captain " substantive) :—" The ass more *captain* than the lion."

Carcanet, necklace, or collar of jewels. *Comedy of Errors*, Act III. sc. 1, l. 4.

LIII. Not being able, in absence, to possess his friend, he finds his friend's shadow in all beautiful things.

4. You, although but one person, can give off all manner of shadowy images. Shakspere then, to illustrate this, chooses the most beautiful of men, Adonis, and the most beautiful of women, Helen ; both are but shadows or counterfeits (*i.e.*, pictures, as in Sonnet XVI.) of the " master-mistress " of his passion.

8. *Tires*, head-dresses, or, generally, attire.

9. *Foison*, abundance, as in *The Tempest*, Act IV. sc. 1, l. 110 :—

> *Earth's increase,* foison *plenty,*
> *Barns and garners never empty.*

Compare *Antony and Cleopatra*, Act v. sc. 2, l. 86 :—

> *For his* bounty
> *There was no winter in 't ; an* autumn *'twas*
> *That grew the more by reaping.*

12. *Blessed.* The fancy Shakspere has taken for this word in LII. 1, 11, 13, runs on into this sonnet.

LIV. Continues the thought of LIII. There Shakspere declared that over and above external beauty, more real than that of Helen and Adonis, his friend was pre-eminent for his constancy, his truth. Now he proceeds to show how this truth enhances the beauty.

5. *Canker-blooms,* blossoms of the dog-rose. *Much Ado about Nothing,* Act I. sc. 3, l. 28, "I had rather be a *canker* in a hedge than a rose in his grace." Steevens writes, "Shakspere had not yet begun to observe the productions of nature, or his eyes would have convinced him that the *cynorhodon* is by no means of as deep a colour as the *rose.* But what has truth or nature to do with Sonnets?" R. C. A. Prior, in *Popular Names of British Plants* (ed. 1870), gives "*Canker-rose,* from its red colour and its detriment to arable land, the field poppy."

8. *Discloses,* opens, as in *Hamlet,* Act I. sc. 3, l. 40 :—

> *The canker galls the infants of the spring*
> *Too oft before their buttons be* disclosed.

9. *For their virtue,* because their virtue. *For* as in *Othello,* Act III. sc. 3, l. 263, " Haply, *for* I am black."

10. *Unrespected,* unregarded.

11, 12. See the quotation from *A Midsummer Night's Dream*, in note on Sonnet v. 9.

14. *When that*, beauty, the general subject of the sonnet; or youth, taken from " sweet and lovely youth " of L. 13.

Vade, fade, as in *Passionate Pilgrim*, x. 1.

By verse. So the Quarto. Malone reads " my verse."

LV. A continuation of LIV. This looks like an *Envoy*, but LVI. is still a sonnet of absence. See on this sonnet, Introduction, p. 22.

1. *Monuments*. The Quarto has *monument*.

4. Stengel changes *unswept* to *in swept*.

6. *These contents*, what is contained in this rhyme.

14. *Till the judgment that yourself arise*, till the decree of the judgment-day that you arise from the dead.

LVI. This, like the sonnets immediately preceding, is written in absence (ll. 9, 10). The "love" Shakspere addresses, "Sweet love, renew thy force," is the love in his own breast. Is the sight of his friend, of which he speaks, only the imaginative seeing of love; such fancied sight as two betrothed persons may have although severed by the ocean ?

6. *Wink*. See note on XLIII. 1. Here, to sleep, as after a full meal.

8. *Dullness*. Taken in connection with "wink," meaning sleep, *dullness* seems to mean *drowsiness*, as when Prospero says of Miranda's slumber (*The Tempest*, Act I. sc. 2, l. 185), " 'Tis a good dulness."

13. *Or*. The Quarto has *As*. Mr. Palgrave reads *Else*.

LVII. The absence spoken of in this sonnet seems to be voluntary absence on the part of Shakspere's friend.

5. *World-without-end hour,* the tedious hour, that seems as if it would never end. So *Love's Labour's Lost,* Act v. sc. 2, l. 799 :—

> *A time, methinks, too short*
> *To make a* world-without-end *bargain in.*

13. *Will.* The Quarto has Will (capital W, but not italics). If a play on words is intended, it must be " Love in your Will (*i.e.,* your Will Shakspere) can think no evil of you, do what you please ; " and also " Love can discover no evil in your will."

LVIII. A close continuation of LVII. ; growing distrust in his friend, with a determination to resist such a feeling. Hence the attempt to disqualify himself for judging his friend's conduct, by taking the place of a vassal, a servant, a slave, in relation to a sovereign.

6. *The imprison'd absence of your liberty,* the separation from you, which is proper to your state of freedom, but which to me is imprisonment. Or the want which I, a prisoner, suffer of such liberty as you possess.

8. *Tame to sufferance,* bearing tamely even cruel distress ; or, tame even to the point of entire submission.

11. *To what you will.* Malone reads " time : Do what you will."

LIX. Is this connected with the preceding sonnet ? or a new starting-point ? Immortality conferred by verse, LIV.–LV., is again taken up in Sonnet LX., connected with LIX., and jealousy (see LVII.) in LXI.

6. Stengel changes *hundred* to *thousand.*

8. *Since mind,* etc., " Since thought was first expressed in writing."—SCHMIDT.

11. *Whether,* etc. " Whether " is often monosyllabic in Elizabethan verse. In this line the Quarto prints the second "whether" *where;* so in *Venus and Adonis,* l. 304, " And *where* he run or fly they know not whether." The Cambridge editors read, "Whether we are mended, or whether better they." Dyce reads, " Whether we're mended or whêr better they."

12. *Or whether,* etc., *i.e.,* whether the ages, revolving on themselves, return to the same things.

LX. The thought of revolution, the revolving ages, LIX. 12, sets the poet thinking of changes wrought by Time.

5. *The main of light.* The entrance of a child into the world at birth is an entrance into the main or ocean of light; the image is suggested by l. 1, where our minutes are compared to waves.

9. *Flourish set on youth,* external decoration of youth. *Love's Labour's Lost,* Act II. sc. 1, l. 14, "The painted *flourish* of your praise." So in Nash's *Summer's Last Will and Testament* (Hazlitt's *Dodsley,* vol. viii. p. 73), " Folly Erasmus *sets a flourish on.*"

10. Compare Sonnet II. 1, 2.

13. *Times in hope,* future times.

LXI. The jealous feeling of LVII. reappears in this sonnet.

7. *Idle hours.* So in the dedication of *Venus and Adonis,*

"I . . . vowe to take advantage of all *idle hours,* till I have honoured you with some graver labour."

11. *Defeat,* destroy. *Othello,* Act IV. sc. 2, l. 150, "His unkindness may *defeat* my life."

LXII. Perhaps the thought of jealousy in LXI. suggests this. "How self-loving to suppose my friend could be jealous of such an one as I—beated and chopp'd with tann'd antiquity! My apology for supposing that others could make love to me is that my friend's beauty is mine by right of friendship."

7. *And for myself,* etc. Sidney Walker conjectures "*so* define;" Lettsom, "And *so* myself." Does "for myself" mean "for my own satisfaction"?

8. *As I,* [define] in such a way that I.

10. *Beated and chopp'd.* "*Beated* was perhaps a misprint for *'bated.* *'Bated* is properly *overthrown; laid low.;* *abated;* from *abattre,* Fr. . . . *Beated,* however, the regular participle from the verb to *beat,* may be right. . . . In *King Henry V.* we find *casted,* and in *Macbeth, thrusted.*"— MALONE.

Steevens conjectured *blasted;* Collier, *beaten.* Compare *The Merchant of Venice,* Act III. sc. 3, l. 32, "These griefs and losses have so *bated* me."

The word *tann'd* led me to turn to the article "Leather," in Chambers's Encyclopædia, where I met the following passage: "Hides or skins intended for dressing purposes . . . have to be submitted to a process called 'bating'." Perhaps my find may rank with that of Steevens or Farmer, who discovered that in the line, "There's a divinity that *shapes our ends,*" Shakspere was thinking of the skewers whose ends his father shaped when a butcher!

Chopp'd. Dyce reads *chapp'd.*

13. *'Tis thee, myself,* etc. 'Tis thee, my *alter ego,* my second self, that I praise as if myself.

LXIII. Obviously in close continuation of LXII.

2. *Crush'd.* Steevens, with no good reason, suggested *frush'd, i.e.,* bruised or battered.

5. *Steepy night.* So *King Richard III.,* Act IV. sc. 4, l. 16; "dimm'd your *infant morn* to *aged night.*" The epithet "steepy" is explained by Sonnet VII. 5, 6.

> *Lo! in the orient when the gracious light*
>
> · · · · ·
>
> *. . . having climb'd the* steep-up *heavenly hill*
> *Resembling strong youth.*

Youth and age are on the steep ascent and the steep decline of heaven. Malone conjectured and withdrew "sleepy night" and "steepy height."

9. *For such a time.* In anticipation of such a time.

Fortify, erect defensive works. Compare "the wreckful siege of battering days," Sonnet LXV. 6.

LXIV. In LXIII. 12, the thought of the loss of his "lover's life" occurs; this sonnet (see l. 12) carries on the train of reflection there started. "Time's fell hand," l. 1, repeats "Time's injurious hand" of LXIII. 2.

5-9. Compare 2 *King Henry IV.,* Act III. sc. 1, ll. 45–53:—

> *O God! that one might read the book of fate,*
> *And see the revolution of the times*

Make mountains level, and the continent,
Weary of solid firmness, melt itself
Into the sea ! and, other times, to see
The beachy girdle of the ocean
Too wide for Neptune's hips.

The king goes on to meditate on the "interchange of state" in his time in England.

13. *Which cannot choose;* this thought, which cannot choose, etc., is as a death.

LXV. In close connection with LXIV. The first line enumerates the conquests of Time recorded in LXIV. 1–8.

3. *This rage.* Malone proposed " *his* rage."

4. *Action.* Is this word used here in a legal sense ? suggested perhaps by " hold a plea " of l. 3.

6. *Wreckful siege.* See Sonnet LXIII. 9, and note.

10. *Time's chest.* Theobald proposed "Time's *quest.*" Malone shows that the image of a jewel in its chest or casket is a favourite one with Shakspere. See Sonnet XLVIII., *King Richard II.,* Act I. sc. 1, l. 180 ; *King John,* Act v. sc. 1, l. 40.

12. *Of beauty.* The Quarto has *or,* a manifest error.

LXVI. From the thought of his friend's death Shakspere turns to think of his own, and of the ills of life from which death would deliver him.

The tone of this sonnet somewhat resembles that of Hamlet's soliloquies.

1. *All these.* The evils enumerated in the following lines.

R

2. *Beggar born.* Staunton proposes " beggar lorn."

3. *Needy nothing.* Staunton proposes " empty nothing."

4. *Unhappily,* evilly. See in Schmidt's Shakespeare Lexicon the words, *unhappied, unhappily, unhappiness,* and *unhappy.*

9. *Art made tongue-tied by authority ; art* is commonly used by Shakspere for letters, learning, science. Can this line refer to the censorship of the stage ?

11. *Simplicity, i.e.,* in the sense of folly.

LXVII. In close connection with LXVI. Why should my friend continue to live in this evil world ?

4. *Lace,* embellish, as in *Macbeth,* Act II. sc. 3, l. 118 :—

His silver skin laced *with his golden blood.*

6. *Dead seeing.* Why should painting steal the *lifeless appearance* of beauty from his living hue ? Capell and Farmer conjecture *seeming.*

12. *Proud of many lives,* etc. Nature, while she boasts of many beautiful persons, really has no treasure of beauty except his.

13. *Stores.* See note on Sonnet XI. 9.

LXVIII. Carries on the thought of LXVII. 13, 14 ; compare the last two lines of both sonnets.

1. *Map of days out-worn.* Compare *Lucrece,* l. 1350, " this pattern of the worn-out age." " Map," a picture or outline. *King Richard II.,* Act V. sc. 1, l. 12, " Thou *map* of honour."

3. *Fair,* beauty.

Born. The Quarto prints *borne,* and so Malone. But

the Quarto *borne* probably is our *born*, the word " bastard "
suggesting the idea of birth.

5, 6. Malone notes that Shakspere has inveighed against
the practice of wearing false hair in *The Merchant of
Venice*, Act III. sc. 2, ll. 92–96 :—

> *So are those crisped snaky golden locks*
> *Which make such wanton gambols with the wind*
> *Upon supposed fairness, often known*
> *To be the dowry of a second head,*
> *The skull that bred them in the sepulchre.*

And again in *Timon of Athens*, Act IV. sc. 3, l. 144.

10. *Without all ornament*, all, *i.e.*, any, as Sonnet LXXIV.
2, " without all bail."

Itself. Malone proposed *himself*.

LXIX. From the thought of his friend's external
beauty Shakspere turns to think of the beauty of his
mind, and the popular report against it.

3. *Due.* The Quarto has *end*, which, Malone observes,
arose from the printer transposing the letters of *due*, and
inverting the *u ;* but more probably the printer's eye
caught the *end* of " mend," l. 2, and his fingers repeated
it in the next line.

5. *Thy outward.* The Quarto has *Their outward.*
Malone read *Thine,* but *thy* is sometimes found before a
vowel, and the mistake " their " for " thy " is of frequent
occurrence in the Quarto.

14. *The soil is this.* The Quarto has *solye.* Malone
and Dyce read *solve.* Caldecott conjectures *foil.* The
Cambridge editors write : " As the verb ' to soil ' is not

uncommon in Old English, meaning ''to solve,' as for
example, 'This question could not one of them all soile'
(Udal's *Erasmus, Luke,* fol. 154 *b*), so the substantive
'soil' may be used in the sense of 'solution.' The play
upon words thus suggested is in the author's manner."

LXX. Continues the subject of the last sonnet, and
defends his friend from the suspicion and slander of the
time.

3. *Suspect,* suspicion, as in l. 13, and *Venus and Adonis,*
l. 1010. . "Her rash *suspect* she doth extenuate."

6. *Thy worth.* The Quarto has *their.*

Being woo'd of time. "Time is used by our early
writers as equivalent to the modern expression, *the times.*"
—HUNTER, *New Illustrations of Shakespeare,* vol. ii. p. 240.
Hunter quotes *King Richard III.,* Act IV. sc. 4, l. 106 :—

> *Thus hath the course of justice wheel'd about,*
> *And left thee but a very prey to time;*

where, however, the proposed meaning seems doubtful.
Steevens quotes from Ben Jonson, *Every Man out of his
Humour,* Prologue, "Oh, how I hate the monstrousness of
time," *i.e.,* the times. "Being woo'd of time" seems, then,
to mean being solicited or tempted by the present times.
Malone conjectured and withdrew "being void of crime."
C. [probably Capell] suggested "being *wood* of time," *i.e.,*
slander being *wood,* or *frantic* (1790), and previously
"being wood oftime," *i.e.* oft-time (1780). Delius proposes
"*weigh'd* of time;" Staunton, "being woo'd of crime."

7. *For canker vice,* etc. So *The Two Gentlemen of Verona,*
Act I. sc. 1, l. 43 :—

> *As in the* sweetest bud
> *The eating* canker *dwells, so eating love*
> *Inhabits in the finest wits of all.*

12. *To tie up envy evermore enlarged.* Prof. Hales writes to me: "Surely a reference here to the *Faerie Queene*, end of Book VI. Calidore ties up the Blatent Beast; after a time he breaks his iron chain, 'and got into the world at liberty again,' *i.e.*, is 'evermore enlarged.'"

14. *Owe,* own, possess.

LXXI. Shakspere goes back to the thought of his own death, from which he was led away by LXVI. 14, "to die, I leave my love alone." The world in this sonnet is the "vile world" described in LXVI.

2. *The surly sullen bell.* Compare 2 *King Henry IV.*, Act I. sc. 1, l. 102:—

> *His tongue*
> *Sounds ever after as a* sullen bell,
> *Remember'd knolling a departed friend.*

10. *Compounded am with clay.* 2 *King Henry IV.*, Act IV. sc. 5, l. 116:—

> *Only* compound *me with forgotten* dust.

LXXII. In close continuation of LXXI. "When I die let my memory die with me."

LXXIII. Still, as in LXXI., LXXII., thoughts of approaching death.

2. Compare *Macbeth*, Act v. sc. 3, l. 23 :—

> *My way of life*
> *Is fall'n into the sear, the yellow leaf.*

3. *Bare ruin'd choirs.* The Quarto has "*rn'wd* quiers." The edition of 1640 made the correction. Capell proposed "Barren'd of quires." Malone compares with this passage *Cymbeline*, Act III. sc. 3, ll. 60-64 :—

> *Then was I as a tree*
> *Whose boughs did bend with fruit, but in one night,*
> *A storm or robbery, call it what you will,*
> *Shook down my mellow hangings, nay, my leaves,*
> *And left me bare to weather ;*

and *Timon of Athens*, Act IV. sc. 3, ll. 263–266 :—

> *That numberless upon me stuck as leaves*
> *Do on the oak, have with one winter's brush*
> *Fell from their boughs and left me open, bare*
> *For every storm that blows.*

7. So in *The Two Gentlemen of Verona*, Act I. sc. 3, l. 87 :—

> *And by and by a cloud takes all away.*

12. *Consumed*, etc. Wasting away on the dead ashes which once nourished it with living flame.

LXXIV. In immediate continuation of LXXIII.
1, 2. The Quarto has no stop after *contented*.
That fell arrest. So *Hamlet*, Act v. sc. 2, ll. 347, 348 :—

> *Had I but time—as this* fell *sergeant, death,*
> *Is strict in his* arrest.

11. *The coward conquest,* etc.   Does Shakspere merely
speak of the liability of the body to untimely or violent
mischance ?   Or does he meditate suicide ?   Or think of
Marlowe's death, and anticipate such a fate as possibly his
own ?   Or has he, like Marlowe, been wounded?   Or does
he refer to the dissection of dead bodies ?   Or is it "con-
founding age's cruel knife " of LXIII. l. 10 ?

13, 14. *The worth,* etc.   The worth of that (my body)
is that which it contains (my spirit), and that (my spirit)
is this (my poems).

LXXV.   The last sonnet, LXXIV., seems to me like an
Envoy, and perhaps a new manuscript book of sonnets
begins with LXXV.–LXXVII.

3. *And for the peace of you,* the peace, content, to be
found in you ; antithesis to *strife.*   Malone, while receiving
the present text, thought the context required " for the
price of you," or " for the *sake* of you."

6. *Doubting the filching age,* etc.   Perhaps this is the
first allusion to the poet, Shakspere's rival in his friend's
favour.

10. *Clean starved for a look.*   See Sonnet XLVII. 3, and
note.

11, 12. Possessing no delight save what is had from
you, pursuing none save what must be took from you.

14. " That is, either feeding on various dishes, or having
nothing on my board—*all* being *away.*"—MALONE.

LXXVI.   Is this an apology for Shakspere's own Son-
nets—of which his friend begins to weary—in contrast
with the verses of the rival poet, spoken of in LXXVIII.–
LXXX. ?

4. Compare Sidney, *Astrophel and Stella*, 3 :—

> *Let dainty wits crie on the Sisters nine.*
>
> . . . . .
>
> *Ennobling new-found tropes with problemes old,*
> *Or with strange similies enrich each line.*

6. *Keep invention in a noted weed*, keep imagination, or poetic creation, in a dress which is observed and known.

7. *Tell.* The Quarto has *fel.*

8. *Where.* Capell proposed *whence.*

LXXVII. "Probably," says Steevens, "this sonnet was designed to accompany the present of a book consisting of blank paper." "This conjecture," says Malone, "appears to me extremely probable." If I might hazard a conjecture, it would be that Shakspere, who had perhaps begun a new manuscript-book with Sonnet LXXV., and who, as I suppose, apologised for the monotony of his verses in LXXVI., here ceased to write, knowing that his friend was favouring a rival, and invited his friend to fill up the blank pages himself (see note below, l. 12). Beauty, Time, and Verse formed the theme of many of Shakspere's sonnets ; now that he will write no more, he commends his friend to his *glass*, where he may discover the truth about his *beauty ;* to the *dial*, where he may learn the progress of *time ;* and to this *book*, which he himself—not Shakspere —must fill. C. A. Brown and Henry Brown treat this sonnet as an *Envoy.*

4. *This book.* Malone proposed "*thy* book."

6. *Mouthed graves.* So *Venus and Adonis*, l. 757, " A swallowing grave."

10. *Blanks.* The Quarto has *blacks*: the correction is from Theobald.

12. Perhaps this is said with some feeling of wounded love—my verses have grown monotonous and wearisome; write yourself, and you will find novelty in your own thoughts when once delivered from your brain and set down by your pen. Perhaps, also, "this learning mayst thou taste," l. 4, is suggested by the fact that Shakspere is unlearned in comparison with the rival. I cannot bring you learning; but set down your own thoughts, and you will find learning in them.

LXXVIII. Shakspere, I suppose, receives some renewed profession of love from his friend, and again addresses him in verse, openly speaking of the cause of his estrangement, the favour with which his friend regards the rival poet.

3. *Got my use*, acquired my habit [of writing verse to you].

6. *Heavy ignorance.* So *Othello*, Act II. sc. 1, l. 144, "O *heavy ignorance!*"

Fly. The Quarto has *flee.*

7. *The learned's wing.* "Compare Spenser's *Teares of the Muses*:—

> *Each idle wit at will presumes to make,*
> *And doth the* learneds *task upon him take.*"
>
> DYCE.

9. *Compile*, write, compose. So Sonnet LXXXV. 2, "Comments of your praise, richly *compiled*." *Love's Labour's Lost*, Act IV. sc. 3, l. 134:—

> *Longaville*
> *Never did sonnet for her sake* compile.

12. *Arts,* learning, scholarship. *Love's Labour's Lost,* Act II. sc. 1, l. 45 :—

> *A man of sovereign parts he is esteem'd ;*
> *Well fitted in* arts, *glorious in arms.*

13. *Advance,* lift up. As in *The Tempest,* Act I. sc. 2, l. 408 :—

> *The fringed curtains of thine eyes* advance.

LXXIX. In continuation of Sonnet LXXVIII.

5. *Thy lovely argument,* the lovely theme of your beauty and worth.

LXXX. Same subject continued.

2. *A better spirit.* For the conjectures made with respect to this " better spirit," see the Introduction, pp. 19, 20.

6, 7. *The humble,* etc. Compare *Troilus and Cressida,* Act I. sc. 3, ll. 34—42 :—

> *The sea being smooth,*
> *How many shallow bauble boats dare sail*
> *Upon her patient breast, making their way*
> *With those of nobler bulk !*
> *But let the ruffian Boreas once enrage*
> *The gentle Thetis . . . .*
> *. . . where's then the* saucy boat ?

LXXXI. After depreciating his own verse in comparison with that of the rival poet, Shakspere here takes heart, and asserts that he will by verse confer immortality on his friend, though his own name may be forgotten.

1. *Or I.* Staunton proposes "Wh'er I," *i.e.,* Whether I.

12. *Breathers of this world;* this world, *i.e.,* this age. Compare *As You Like It,* Act III. sc. 2, l. 297, "I will chide no *breather in the world* but myself." Sidney Walker proposes to point as follows :—

> *shall o'er-read,*
> *And tongues to be your being shall rehearse ;*
> *When all the breathers of this world are dead,*
> *You still shall live,* etc.

It is rare, however, with Shakspere to let the verse run on without a pause at the twelfth line of the sonnet.

14. *Where breath most breathes.* Staunton proposes "most kills," slanderous breath being poisonous.

LXXXII. His friend had perhaps alleged in playful self-justification that he had not married Shakspere's Muse, vowing to forsake all other, and keep only unto her.

3. *Dedicated words.* This may only mean *devoted words,* but probably has reference, as the next line seems to show, to the words of some dedication prefixed to a book.

5. *Thou art as fair in knowledge as in hue.* Shakspere had celebrated his friend's beauty (hue); perhaps his learned rival had celebrated the patron's knowledge; such excellence reached "a limit past the praise" of Shakspere, who knew small Latin and less Greek.

11. *Sympathized,* answered to, tallied. So *Lucrece,* 1113 :—

> *True sorrow then is feelingly sufficed*
> *When with like semblance it is* sympathized.

Notes.

13, 14. Compare with the rhyming of these lines, *Love's Labour's Lost*, Act II. sc. 1, ll. 226, 227 :—

> *This civil war of wits were much better used*
> *On Navarre and his book-men ; for here 'tis abused.*

LXXXIII. Takes up the last lines of LXXXII., and continues the same theme.

2. *Fair,* beauty.

5. *Slept in your report,* neglected to sound your praises.

7. *Modern,* trite, ordinary, common. So *Antony and Cleopatra,* Act V. sc. 2, l. 167 :—

> *Immoment toys, things of such dignity*
> *As we greet* modern *friends withal.*

8. *What worth.* Malone suggested " that worth." For " being dumb " Staunton proposes " thinking dumb " or " praising dumb."

12. *Bring a tomb.* Compare Sonnet XVII. 3.

> *It* [my verse] *is but as a tomb*
> *Which hides your life and shows not half your parts.*

LXXXIV. Continues the same theme. Which of us, the rival poet or I, can say more than that you are you ?

1–4. Staunton proposes to omit the note of interrogation after *most* (l. 1), and to introduce one after *grew* (l. 4).

8. *Story.* W. S. Walker proposes to retain the period of the Quarto after *story ;* so also Staunton—perhaps rightly.

9. *Let him but copy,* etc. Compare Sidney, *Astrophel and Stella,* 3 :—

> *In Stella's face I read*
> *What Love and Beauty be, then all my deed*
> *But copying is what in her nature writes.*

10. *Worse.* Staunton proposes *gross.*

14. *Being fond on praise,* doting on praise. *A Midsummer Night's Dream,* Act II. sc. 1, l. 266 :—

> *That he may prove*
> *More* fond on *her than she upon her love.*

Palgrave has " *of* praise."

LXXXV. Continues the subject of LXXXIV. Shakspere's friend is fond on praise; Shakspere's Muse is silent while others compile comments of his praise.

1. *My tongue-tied Muse.* Compare Sonnet LXXX. 4.

2. *Compiled.* See note on Sonnet LXXVIII. 9.

3. *Reserve their character. Reserve* has here, says Malone, the sense of preserve; see Sonnet XXXII. 7. But what does " preserve their character " mean? An anonymous emender suggests " Rehearse thy " or " Rehearse your." Possibly " *Deserve* their character " may be right, *i.e.,* " deserve to be written."

4. *Fil'd,* polished, refined (as if rubbed with a file). *Love's Labour's Lost,* Act V. sc. 1, l. 11, " His humour is lofty, his discourse peremptory, his tongue *filed.*" See note on Sonnet LXXXVI. 13.

11. *But that, i.e.,* that which I add.

LXXXVI. Continues the subject of LXXXV., and explains the cause of Shakspere's silence.

1. *Proud full sail.* The same metaphor which appears in Sonnet LXXX.

4. *Making their tomb the womb,* etc. So *Romeo and Juliet,* Act II. sc. 3, l. 9 :—

> The earth that's nature's mother is her tomb ;
> What is her burying grave that is her womb.

5–10. See Introduction, pp. 19, 20.

8. *Astonished,* stunned as by a thunder-stroke, as in *Lucrece,* l. 1730.

> *Stone-still,* astonish'd *with this deadly deed,*
> *Stood Collatine.*

13. *Fill'd up his line.* Malone, Steevens, Dyce, read *fil'd, i.e.,* polished. Steevens quotes Ben Jonson's *Verses on Shakespeare* :—

> *In his well-torned and true-*filed *lines.*

But "fill'd up his line" is opposed to "then lack'd I matter." *Filed* in LXXXV. 4, is printed in the Quarto *fil'd; filled* is printed XVII. 2 ; LXIII. 3, as it is in this passage, *fild.*

LXXXVII. Increasing coldness on his friend's part brings Shakspere to the point of declaring that all is over between them. This sonnet in form is distinguished by double-rhymes throughout.

4. *Determinate,* limited ; or out of date, expired. " The term is used in legal conveyances."—MALONE.

6. *That riches.* Rightly a substantive singular; Fr. *richesse.*

8. *Patent,* privilege. As in *A Midsummer Night's Dream,* Act I. sc. 1, l. 80:—

> *So will I grow, so live, so die, my lord,*
> *Ere I will yield my virgin* patent *up*
> *Unto his lordship.*

11. *Upon misprision growing,* a mistake having arisen. 1 *King Henry IV.,* Act I. sc. 3, l. 27, "misprision is guilty of this fault."

> *Either envy, therefore, or* misprision
> *Is guilty of this fault, and not my son.*

13. *As some dream doth flatter.* So *Romeo and Juliet,* Act v. sc. 1, ll. 1, 2:—

> *If I may trust the* flattering *truth of sleep,*
> *My* dreams *presage some joyful news at hand.*

LXXXVIII. In continuation. Shakspere still asserts his own devotion, though his unfaithful friend not only should forsake him, but even hold him in scorn.

1. *Set me light,* esteem me little. So *King Richard II.,* Act I. sc. 3, l. 293 :—

> *For gnarling sorrow hath less power to bite*
> *The man that mocks at it and* sets it light.

7. So *Hamlet,* Act III. sc. 1, ll. 23–26, "I am myself indifferent honest; but yet I could accuse me of such things that it were better my mother had not borne me."

8. *Shalt.* Quarto, *shall.*

LXXXIX. Continues the subject of LXXXVIII., show-ing how Shakspere will take part with his friend against himself.

3. *My lameness.* See note on Sonnet XXXVII. 3.

6. *To set a form,* etc., to give a becoming appearance to the change which you desire. So *A Midsummer Night's Dream,* Act I. sc. 1, l. 233 :—

> *Things base and vile, holding no quantity,*
> *Love can transpose to* form *and dignity.*

8. *I will acquaintance strangle,* put an end to our familiarity. So *Twelfth Night,* Act V. sc. 1, l. 150 :—

> *Alas, it is the baseness of thy fear*
> *That makes thee* strangle *thy propriety.*

I. e., disown your personality. *Antony and Cleopatra,* Act II. sc. 6, l. 130, " You shall find, the band that seems to tie their friendship together will be the very *strangler* of their amity."

13. *Debate,* contest, quarrel. 2 *King Henry IV.,* Act IV. sc. 4, l. 2, " this *debate* that bleedeth at our door."

XC. Takes up the last word of LXXXIX., and pleads pathetically for hatred ; for the worst, speedily, if at all.

6. *The rearward of a conquer'd woe.* *Much Ado About Nothing,* Act IV. sc. 1, l. 128 :

> *Thought I thy spirit were stronger than thy shames,*
> *Myself would, on the rearward of reproaches,*
> *Strike at thy life.*

13. *Strains of woe,* inward motions of woe. So *Much Ado About Nothing,* Act v. sc. 1, l. 12 :—

> *Measure his woe the length and breadth of mine,*
> *And let it answer every* strain for strain.

XCI. Having in xc. thought of his own persecution at the hand of Fortune, Shakspere here contrasts his state with that of the favourites of Fortune, maintaining that, if he had but assured possession of his friend's love, he would lack none of their good things.

4. *Horse.* Probably the plural, meaning *horses,* as in *The Taming of the Shrew, Induction,* l. 61 :—

> *Another tell him of his hounds and* horse.

1 *King Henry VI.,* Act i. sc. 5, l. 31 :—

> *Sheep run not half so treacherous from the wolf,*
> *Or* horse *or oxen from the leopard.*

10. *Richer than wealth, prouder than garments' cost.* So *Cymbeline,* Act iii. sc. 3, ll. 23, 24 :—

> *Richer than doing nothing for a bauble,*
> *Prouder than rustling in unpaid-for silk.*

XCII. In close connection with xci. This sonnet argues for the contradictory of the last two lines of that immediately preceding it. No : you cannot make me wretched by taking away your love, for, with such a loss, death must come and free me from sorrow.

10. *My life on thy revolt doth lie,* my life hangs upon, is dependent on, your desertion. *All's Well that Ends Well,*

Act IV. sc. 3, l. 204, " With well-weighing sums of gold to corrupt him to a *revolt.*" *Macbeth*, Act v. sc, 4, l. 12 :—

> *Both more and less have given him the* revolt,
> *And none serve with him but constrained things*
> Whose hearts are absent too.

Compare Sonnet XCIII. 4.

XCIII. Carries on the thought of the last line of XCII. 11, 12. So *Macbeth*, Act I. sc. 4, l. 12 :—

> *There's no art*
> *To find the mind's construction in the face.*

XCIV. In XCIII. Shakspere has described his friend as able to show a sweet face while harbouring false thoughts ; the subject is enlarged on in the present sonnet. They who can hold their passions in check, who can refuse to wrath its outbreak, who can seem loving yet keep a cool heart, who move passion in others, yet are cold and un-moved themselves—they rightly inherit from heaven large gifts, for they husband them ; whereas passionate intemperate natures squander their endowments ; those who can assume this or that semblance as they see reason are the masters and owners of their faces ; others have no property in such excellences as they possess, but hold them for the advantage of the prudent self-contained persons. True, these self-contained persons may seem to lack generosity ; but then, without making voluntary gifts, they give inevitably, even as the summer's flower is sweet to the summer, though it live and die only to itself.

Yet let such an one beware of corruption, which makes odious the sweetest flowers.

6. *Expense*, expenditure, and so loss.

11. *Base.* Staunton proposes *foul*.

12. *The basest weed.* Sidney Walker proposes " the *barest* weed," a more legitimate kind of emendation than Staunton's.

14. *Lilies*, etc. This line occurs in *King Edward III.*, Act II. sc. 1 (near the close of the scene). I quote the passage that the reader may see how the line comes into the play, and form an opinion as to whether play or sonnet has the right of first ownership in it.

> *A spacious field of reasons could I urge*
> *Between his glory, daughter, and thy shame :*
> *That poison shows worst in a golden cup ;*
> *Dark night seems darker by the lightning flash ;*
> *Lilies, that fester, smell far worse than weeds ;*
> *And every glory, that inclines to sin,*
> *The same is treble by the opposite.*

It should be remembered that several critics assign to Shakspere a portion of this play, which was first printed in 1596. In a scene ascribed to Shakspere occur the lines which have been quoted.

Fester, rot. As in *Romeo and Juliet*, Act IV. sc. 3, l. 43 :—

> *Where bloody Tybalt, yet but green in earth,*
> *Lies festering in his shroud.*

Compare with this Sonnet, *Twelfth Night*, Act III. sc. 4, ll. 399–404 :—

> *But O how vile an idol proves this god!*
> *Thou hast, Sebastian, done good feature shame.*
> *In nature there's no blemish but the mind;*
> *None can be called deform'd but the unkind:*
> *Virtue is beauty, but the beauteous evil*
> *Are empty trunks o'erflourish'd by the devil.*

XCV. Continues the warning of XCIV. 13, 14. Though now you seem to make shame beautiful, beware! a time will come when it may be otherwise.

1. *Naming thy name blesses*, etc.   *Antony and Cleopatra*, Act II. sc. 2, ll. 243–245 :—

> *Vilest things*
> *Become themselves in her; that the holy priests*
> *Bless her when she is riggish.*

XCVI. Continues the subject of XCV.   Pleads against the misuse of his friend's gifts, against youthful licentiousness.

2. *Gentle sport.*   As in the last sonnet, " Making lascivious comments on thy *sport.*"

3. *More and less*, great and small, as in 1 *King Henry IV.*, Act IV. sc. 3, l. 68 :—

> *The* more and less *came in with cap and knee.*

9, 10. The same thought expressed in different imagery appears in XCIII.

Translate, transform ; as in *Hamlet*, Act III. sc. 1, l. 113, " For the power of beauty will sooner transform honesty from what it is to a bawd than the force of honesty can *translate* beauty into his likeness."

12. *The strength of all thy state,* the strength of all thy majesty, splendour. Schmidt says " used periphrastically, and = all thy strength."

13, 14. The same couplet closes Sonnet XXXVI. See Introduction, p. 32, note.

XCVII. A new group of Sonnets seems to begin here.
5. *This time removed.* This time of absence. *Twelfth Night,* Act v. sc. 1, l. 92 :—

> *Taught him to face me out of his acquaintance,*
> *And grew a twenty years* removed *thing.*

6. *The teeming autumn,* etc. So *A Midsummer Night's Dream,* Act II. sc. 1, ll. 111–114 :—

> *The spring, the summer,*
> *The childing autumn, angry winter, change*
> *Their wonted liveries, and the mazed world,*
> *By their increase now knows not which is which.*

7. *Prime,* spring.
10. *Hope of orphans,* expectation of the birth of children whose father is dead; or, such hope as orphans bring. Staunton proposes " *crop* of orphans."

XCVIII. The subject of XCVII. is Absence in Summer and Autumn; the subject of XCVIII., IX., Absence in Spring.
2, 3. *Proud-pied April,* etc. So *Romeo and Juliet,* Act I. sc. 2, l. 27 :—

> *Such comfort as do lusty* young men *feel*
> *When* well-apparell'd April *at the heel*
> *Of limping winter treads.*

4. *That.* So that.

7. *Summer's story.* " By a *summer's story* Shakspeare seems to have meant some *gay fiction.* Thus, his comedy founded on the adventures of the king and queen of the fairies, he calls *A Midsummer Night's Dream.* On the other hand, in *The Winter's Tale* he tells, ' a *sad tale's* best for *winter.*' So also in *Cymbeline,* Act III. sc. 4, ll. 12–14:—

> —*if it be* summer *news,*
> *Smile to it before : if winterly, thou need'st*
> *But keep that countenance still.*"

MALONE.

But is not *A Midsummer Night's Dream* so named because on Midsummer Eve men's dreams ran riot, ghosts were visible, maidens practised divination for husbands, and " midsummer madness " (*Twelfth Night,* III. 4, 61) reached its height ?

8. *The lily's white.* The Quarto has *lilies;* so Malone and other editors.

11. *They were but sweet.* Malone proposed " they were, my sweet, but," etc. The poet declares, as Steevens says, that the flowers " are *only* sweet, *only* delightful, so far as they resemble his friend." Lettsom proposes, " They were but fleeting figures of delight."

XCIX. In connection with the last line of Sonnet XCVIII. The present sonnet has fifteen lines, as also has one of the sonnets in Barnes's *Parthenophil and Parthenophe.*

6. *Condemned for thy hand,* condemned for theft of the whiteness of thy hand.

7. *And buds of marjoram,* etc. Compare Suckling's *Tragedy of Brennoralt,* Act IV. sc. 1 :—

Hair curling, and cover'd like buds of marjoram ;
Part tied in negligence, part loosely flowing.

Mr. H. C. Hart tells me that buds of marjoram are dark purple-red before they open, and afterwards pink ; dark auburn, I suppose, would be the nearest approach to marjoram in the colour of hair. Mr. Hart suggests that the marjoram has stolen not colour but *perfume* from the young man's hair. Gervase Markham gives sweet marjoram as an ingredient in "The water of sweet smells," and Culpepper says "marjoram is much used in all odoriferous waters." Cole (*Adam in Eden,* ed. 1657) says, "Marjerome is a chief ingredient in most of those powders that Barbers use, in whose shops I have seen great store of this herb hung up."

8. *On thorns did stand.* To "stand on thorns" is an old proverbial phrase.

Mr. Massey compares with these flower sonnets Constable's *Diana* (before 1594), First Decade, Sonnet 9 :—

My Lady's presence makes the Roses red,
Because to see her lips they blush for shame.
The Lily's leaves, for envy, pale became ;
And her white hands in them this envy bred.
The Marigold the leaves abroad doth spread ;
Because the sun's and her power is the same.
The Violet of purple colour came,
Dyed in the blood she made my heart to shed.

In brief, all flowers from her their virtue take,
From her sweet breath their sweet smells do proceed.

Compare also Spenser, *Amoretti*, 64.

9. *One.* The Quarto has "*our.*"

12. *A vengeful canker eat him*, etc. So *Venus and Adonis*, l. 656 :—

This canker that eats up *Love's tender spring.*

The metaphor of the canker appears also in a sonnet not far distant, xcv.

14. *But sweet.* Sidney Walker proposes *scent.*

C. Written after a cessation from sonnet-writing, during which Shakspere had been engaged in authorship,— writing plays for the public as I suppose, instead of poems for his friend.

3. *Fury*, poetic enthusiasm, as in *Love's Labour's Lost*, Act IV. sc. 3, l. 229.

9. *Resty*, torpid. "Resty, *piger, lentus,*" Coles's *Latin and English Dictionary* (quoted by Dyce). Compare "Resty-stiff," *Edward III.*, Act II. sc. 3 (p. 51, ed. Delius). "Resty" in *Cymbeline*, Act III. sc. 6, l. 34, may mean uneasy. In *Troilus and Cressida*, Act I. sc. 3, l. 263, the Folios have *rusty.*

11. *Satire.* "*Satire* is satirist. Jonson, *Masque of Time Vindicated*, Gifford, vol. viii. p. 5 :—

Who's this?
EARS. *'Tis Chronomastix, the brave satyr.*
NOSE. *The gentleman-like satyr, cares for nobody.*

Poetaster, V. I. vol. ii. p. 524 :—

> *The honest satyr hath the happiest soul."*
>
> W. S. WALKER.

14. *Prevent'st*, dost frustrate by anticipating.

CI. Continues the address to his muse, calling on her to sing again the praises of his friend; c. calls on her to praise his beauty; CI. his " truth in beauty dyed."

6. *His colour*, the colour of my love (*i.e.*, my friend).

7. *To lay*, to spread on a surface, to lay on. *Twelfth Night*, Act I. sc. 5, l. 258 :—

> *'Tis beauty truly blent, whose red and white*
> *Nature's own sweet and cunning hand* laid on.

CII. In continuation. An apology for having ceased to sing.

3. *That love is merchandiz'd*, etc. So in *Love's Labour's Lost*, Act II. sc. 1, ll. 13–16 :—

> *My beauty, though but mean,*
> *Needs not the painted flourish of your praise :*
> *Beauty is bought by judgement of the eye,*
> *Not utter'd by base sale of chapmen's tongues.*

7. *Summer's front.* So *The Winter's Tale*, Act IV. sc. 4, l. 3 :—

> *No shepherdess, but Flora*
> *Peering in* April's front.

Coriolanus, Act II. sc. 1, l. 57, " One that converses . . . with the *forehead of the morning.*"

8. *Her pipe.* The Quarto has "*his* pipe." Corrected by Housman in his *Collection of English Sonnets* (1835). Compare *Twelfth Night*, Act I. sc. 4, l. 32 :—

> *Thy small pipe*
> *Is as the maiden's organ.*

CIII. Continues the same apology.

3. *The argument, all bare,* the theme of my verse merely as it is in itself.

6, 7. So *The Tempest*, Act IV. sc. 1, l. 10 :—

> *For thou shalt find she will* outstrip *all praise*
> *And make it halt behind her.*

9, 10. So *King Lear*, Act I. sc. 4, l. 369 :—

> *Striving to better, oft we mar what's well.*

And *King John*, Act IV. sc. 2, ll. 28, 29 :—

> *When workmen strive to do better than well,*
> *They do confound their skill in covetousness.*

CIV. Resumes the subject from which the poet started in Sonnet C. After absence and cessation from song, he resurveys his friend's face, and inquires whether Time has stolen away any of its beauty. Note the important reference to time—three years "since first I saw you fresh."

2. *Eyed.* So in *The Two Noble Kinsmen*, " I *ear'd* her language."

3. *Three winters cold.* Dyce reads, perhaps rightly, "*winters'* cold." The Quarto in 3, 4, has " Winters cold . . . summers pride."

4. *Three summers' pride.* So *Romeo and Juliet*, Act I. sc. 2, l. 10 :—

Let two more summers wither in their pride.

10. *Steal from his figure,* creep from the figure on the dial. So in Sonnet LXXVII., "thy *dial's* shady *stealth.*"

13. *For fear of which,* because I fear which.

CV. To the beauty praised in C., and the truth and beauty in CI., Shakspere now adds a third perfection, kindness ; and these three sum up the perfections of his friend.

1, 4. *Let not my love,* etc. "Because the continual repetition of the same praises seemed like a form of worship."—W. S. WALKER. Compare CVIII. 1–8.

CVI. The last line of Sonnet CV. declares that his friend's perfections were never before possessed by one person. This leads the poet to gaze backward on the famous persons of former ages, men and women, his friend being possessor of the united perfections of both man and woman (as in Sonnets XX. and LIII.).

1. *Chronicle.* Prof. Hales asks, "What *chronicle* is he thinking of ? The *Faerie Queene ?*"

8. *Master,* possess, own as a master. So *King Henry V.,* Act II. sc. 4, l. 137 :—

> *You'll find a difference*
>
> .   .   .   .   .
>
> *Between the promise of his greener days*
> *And these he* masters *now.*

9. Compare Constable's *Diana* :—

> *Miracle of the world I never will deny*
> *That former poets praise the beauty of their days;*
> *But all those beauties were but figures of thy praise,*
> *And all those poets did of thee but prophecy.*

12. *They had not skill enough.* The Quarto has "*still* enough," on which a meaning may be forced: "Only divining your beauty, they did not as yet possess enough to sing your worth."

CVII. Continues the celebration of his friend, and rejoices in their restored affection. Mr. Massey explains this sonnet as a song of triumph for the death of Elizabeth, and the deliverance of Southampton from the Tower. Elizabeth (Cynthia) is the eclipsed mortal moon of l. 5. Compare *Antony and Cleopatra*, Act III. sc. 13, l. 153 :—

> *Alack, our* terrene moon (*i.e., Cleopatra*)
> *Is now* eclipsed.

But an earlier reference to a moon-eclipse (XXXV. l. 3) has to do with his friend, not with Elizabeth, and in the present sonnet the moon is imagined as having endured her eclipse, and come out none the less bright. I interpret (agreeing with Mr. Simpson, *Philosophy of Shakspere's Sonnets*, p. 78) : "Not my own fears (that my friend's beauty may be on the wane, Sonnet CIV. 9–14) nor the prophetic soul of the world, prophesying in the persons of dead knights and ladies your perfections (Sonnet CVI.), and so prefiguring your death (or, possibly, divining other future perfections higher than yours), can confine my lease of love to a brief term of years. Darkness and fears are past, the augurs of ill find their predictions falsified, doubts are over, peace has come in place of strife; the love in my heart is fresh and young (see CVIII. l. 9), and I have conquered Death, for in this verse we both shall find life in the memories of men."

4. *Supposed*, etc., supposed to be a lease expiring within a limited term.

10. *My love looks fresh.* I am not sure whether this means "the love in my heart," or "my love," my friend. Compare CIV. l. 8, and CVIII. l. 9.

Subscribes, submits. As in *The Taming of the Shrew*, Act I. sc. 1, l. 81:—

Sir, to your pleasure humbly I subscribe.

12. *Insults o'er*, triumphs over. As in 3 *King Henry VI.*, Act I. sc. 3, l. 14:—

And so he [the lion] walks insulting o'er his prey.

CVIII. How can "this poor rhyme," which is to give us both unending life (CVII. 10–14), be carried on? Only by saying over again the same old things. But eternal love, in "love's fresh case" (an echo of "my love looks fresh," CVII. 10), knows no age, and finds what is old still fresh and young.

3. *What new to register.* So Malone and other editors. The Quarto has "What *now*." Sidney Walker conjectures, "What's *now* to speak, what now," etc.

5. *Nothing sweet boy.* Altered in ed. 1640 to "Nothing sweet *love.*'

9. *Love's fresh case,* love's new condition and circumstances, the new youth of love spoken of in CVII. 10. But Schmidt explains " case " here as " question of law, cause, question in general; " and Malone says, " By the *case* of *love* the poet means his own compositions."

13, 14. Finding the first conception of love, *i.e.,* love as passionate as at first, excited by one whose years and outward form show the effects of age.

CIX. The first ardour of love is now renewed as in the days of our early friendship (CVIII. 13, 14). But what of the interval of absence and estrangement? Shakspere confesses his wanderings, yet declares that he was never wholly false.

2. *Qualify,* temper, moderate, as in *Troilus and Cressida,* Act II. sc. 2, l. 118 :—

Is your blood
So madly hot that no discourse of reason

.   .   .   .   .

Can qualify *the same ?*

4. *My soul which in thy breast doth lie.* So *King Richard III.,* Act I. sc. 1, l. 204 :—

Even so thy breast encloseth my poor heart.

7, *Just to the time, not with the time exchanged,* punctual to the time, not altered with the time. So Jessica in her boy's disguise, *Merchant of Venice,* Act II. sc. 6, l. 35 :—

I am glad 'tis night, you do not look on me,
For I am much ashamed of my exchange.

Mr. H. C. Hart suggests to me—over-ingeniously I think—that Shakspere here alludes to the practice, when travel was more dangerous than at present, of "putting out upon return," when if the traveller did not come home true to the time, he had as it were *exchanged* for his journey whatever sum he staked, forfeiting both the principal and the large interest to be paid on a punctual return home, and getting in exchange only his travels. Shakspere alludes to this in *The Tempest*, and Massinger, *Devil's Law Case*, v. 4:—

> *Do you remember the Welsh gentleman*
> *That was* travelling *to Rome upon* returns?

11. *Stain'd.* Staunton proposes *strain'd.*

14. *My rose.* Shakspere returns to the loving name which he has given his friend in Sonnet I.

CX. In CIX. Shakspere has spoken of having wandered from his "home of love;" here he continues the subject, "Alas, 'tis true I have gone here and there." This sonnet and the next are commonly taken to express distaste for his life as a player.

2. *A motley*, a wearer of motley, a fool or jester.

3. *Gored mine own thoughts*, deeply wounded my own thoughts. *Troilus and Cressida*, Act III. sc. 3, l. 228, "My fame is shrewdly *gored.*" *King Lear*, Act v. sc. 3, l. 320:—

> *Friends of my soul, you twain*
> *Rule in this realm, and the* gored *state sustain.*

4. *Made old offences*, etc., entered into new friendships and loves, which were transgressions against my old love

6. *Strangely,* in a distant, mistrustful way. I have regarded your truth with mistrustful side-glances.

7. *Blenches,* starts aside, aberrations, inconstancies. *Measure for Measure,* Act iv. sc. 5, l. 5 :—

> And hold you ever to our special drift,
> Though sometimes you do blench *from this to that,*
> As cause doth minister.

Troilus and Cressida, Act ii. sc. 2, l. 68 :—

> There can be no evasion
> To blench *from this, and to stand firm by honour.*

9. *Now all is done, have what shall have no end.* Malone accepted Tyrwhitt's conjecture, "Now all is done *save,*" etc.; but the meaning is, "Now all my wanderings and errors are over, take love which has no end."

10. *Grind, i.e.,* whet.

11. *Newer proof,* newer trial or experiment.

12. This line seems to be a reminiscence of the thoughts expressed in Sonnet cv., and to refer to the First Commandment.

CXI. Continues the apology for his wanderings of heart, ascribing them to his ill fortune—that, as commonly understood, which compels him to a player's way of life.

1. *With Fortune.* The Quarto has "*wish* fortune."

3. "The author seems here to lament his being reduced to the necessity of appearing on the stage, or writing for the theatre."—MALONE.

10. *Eisel, 'gainst my strong infection. Eisel* or *eysell* is vinegar. O. Fr. *aissel*, Gr. ὀξαλίς. Skelton (quoted in Nares's Glossary) says of Jesus :—

> *He drank* eisel *and gall*
> *To redeeme us withal.*

" Vinegar is esteemed very efficacious in preventing the communication of the plague and other contagious distempers."—MALONE.

CXII. Takes up the word " pity " from CXI. 14, and declares that his friend's love and pity compensate the dishonours of his life, spoken of in the last sonnet.

4. *Allow,* approve, as in *King Lear,* Act II. sc. 4, l. 194 :—

> *O heavens,*
> *If you do love old men, if your sweet sway*
> Allow *obedience.*

7, 8. No one living for me except you, nor I alive to any, who can change my feelings fixed as steel either for good or ill (either to pleasure or pain). Malone proposed " *e'er* changes." Knight, " *so* changes." " Sense " may be the plural.

11. *Critic,* censurer, as in *Troilus and Cressida,* Act v. sc. 2, l. 131 :—

> *Do not give advantage*
> *To stubborn* critics, *apt, without a theme*
> *For depravation, to square the general sense*
> *By Cressid's rule.*

T

12. *Dispense with,* excuse, pardon. So *Lucrece,* l. 1070:—

> *I am mistress of my fate,*
> *And with my trespass never will* dispense;

and l. 1279 :—

> *Yet with the fault I thus far can* dispense.

13. *So strongly in my purpose bred.* Schmidt gives as an explanation : " So kept and harboured in my thoughts."

14. *They're dead.* The Quarto has "*y'are;*" Malone (1780) reads " are," (1790) " they are ; " Dyce, " they're." The Quarto *y'* = th' = they.

CXIII. In connection with CXII.; the writer's mind and senses are filled with his friend; in CXII. he tells how his ear is stopped to all other voices but one beloved voice; here he tells how his eye sees things only as related to his friend.

1. *Mine eye is in my mind.* *Hamlet,* Act I. sc. 2, l. 185, " In my *mind's eye,* Horatio." So too *Lucrece,* l. 1426.

3. *Part his function,* divide its function.

6. *Latch,* catch, seize. *Macbeth,* Act IV. sc. 3, l. 195 :—

> *I have words*
> *That would be howl'd out in the desert air*
> *Where hearing should not* latch *them.*

The Quarto has "*lack.*"

10. *Favour,* aspect, appearance, countenance, as in *Measure for Measure,* Act IV. sc. 2, l. 185.

14. *Mine untrue.* If we accept this, the text of the Quarto, we must hold "untrue" to be a substantive; explaining, with Malone: "The sincerity of my affection is the cause of my untruth, *i.e.*, my not seeing objects truly, such as they appear to the rest of mankind." So in *Measure for Measure,* Act II. sc. 4, l. 170:—

> *As for you,*
> *Say what you can, my false o'erweighs your* true.

Malone proposed and withdrew "makes mine *eye* untrue." Collier, " maketh my eyne untrue ; " Lettsom, " mak'th mine eye untrue ; " Cartwright, " maketh m'eye " or " m'eyne ; " Tschischwitz, " maketh my mine," *i.e.*, mien.

CXIV. Continues the subject treated in CXIII., and inquires why and how it is that his eye gives a false report of objects.

5. *Indigest,* chaotic, formless. As in 2 *King Henry IV.,* Act v. sc. 1, l. 157 :—

> *Hence, heap of wrath, foul* indigested *lump,*
> *As crooked in thy manners as thy shape.*

So 3 *King Henry VI.,* Act v. sc. 6, l. 51.

9, Compare *Twelfth Night,* Act I. sc. 5, l. 328:—

> *I do I know not what, and fear to find*
> *Mine eye too great a flatterer for my mind.*

11. *What with his gust is 'greeing,* what is pleasing to his (the eye's) taste ; *'gree ;* to agree.

13, 14. " The allusion here is to the tasters to princes. So in *King John* :—

> who did taste to him ?
>
> HUB. *A monk whose bowels suddenly burst out.*"
>
> STEEVENS.

CXV. Shakspere now desires to show that love has grown through error and seeming estrangement. Before trial and error love was but a babe.

4. *My flame.* So in CIX. 1. 2, "absence seemed my flame to qualify."

11, 12. *Certain o'er incertainty, crowning the present.* So Sonnet CVII. 7 :—

> Incertainties *now* crown *themselves assured.*

CXVI. Admits his wanderings, but love is fixed above all the errors and trials of man and man's life.

2. *Impediments* (to the marriage of true minds). So *Form of Solemnization of Matrimony* in Book of Common Prayer : " If any of you know cause or just *impediment*," etc.

2, 3. *Love is not love*, etc. So *King Lear*, Act I. sc. 1, l. 241 :—

> *Love's not love*
> *When it is mingled with regards that stand*
> *Aloof from the entire point.*

4. *With the remover to remove.* So Sonnet XXV. 13, 14 :—

> *Then happy I, that love and am beloved*
> *Where I cannot remove nor be removed.*

5, 6. *An ever-fixed mark that looks on tempests,* etc. So
Coriolanus, Act v. sc. 3, l. 74:—

> *Like a great sea-mark standing every flaw.*

7. *It is the star,* etc. "Apparently, whose stellar in-
fluence is unknown, although his angular altitude has
been determined."—F. T. PALGRAVE. Schmidt explains
unknown here as *inexpressible, incalculable, immense.* The
passage seems to mean, "As the star, over and above
what can be ascertained concerning it for our guidance at
sea, has unknowable occult virtue and influence, so love,
beside its power of guiding us, has incalculable poten-
cies." This interpretation is confirmed by the next son-
net (CXVII.), in which the simile of sailing at sea is
introduced. Shakspere there confesses his wanderings,
and adds as his apology,

> *I did strive to prove*
> *The* constancy *and* virtue *of your love.*

Constancy, the guiding fixedness of love; *virtue,* the "un-
known worth." Sidney Walker proposed "whose *north's*
unknown;" explaining, "As by following the guidance of
the northern star, a ship may sail an immense way, yet
never reach the true north, so the limit of love is
unknown. Or can any other good sense be made of
'*north*'? *Judicent rei astronomicæ periti.*" Dr. Ingleby
(*The Soule Arayed,* 1872, pp. 5, 6, note), after quoting in
connection with this passage the lines in which Cæsar
speaks of himself (*Julius Cæsar,* III. 1) as "constant as
the northern star," writes: "Here human virtue is
figured under 'the true-fix'd and resting quality' of the

northern star. Surely, then, the 'worth' spoken of must be *constancy* or *fixedness.* The sailor must know that the star has this worth, or his latitude would not depend on its altitude. Just so, without the knowledge of this worth in love, a man 'hoists sail to all the winds,' and is 'frequent with unknown minds.'"

Height, it should be observed, was used by Elizabethan writers in the sense of value, and the word may be used here in a double sense, *altitude* (of the star) and *value* (of love), " love whose worth is unknown, however it may be valued."

9. *Time's fool,* the sport or mockery of Time. So 1 *King Heny IV.*, Act v. sc. 4, l. 81 :—

But thought's the slave of life, and life time's fool.

11. *His brief hours, i.e.,* Time's brief hours.

12. *Bears it out even to the edge of doom.* So *All's Well that Ends Well,* Act III. sc. 3, ll. 5, 6 :—

We'll strive to bear it *for your worthy sake*
To the extreme edge *of hazard.*

CXVII. Continues the confession of his wanderings from his friend, but asserts that it was only to try his friend's constancy in love.

5. *Frequent,* conversant, intimate.

With unknown minds, persons who may not be known, or obscure persons.

6. *Given to time,* given to society, to the world. See note on Sonnet LXX. l. 6. Or, given away to temporary

occasion what is your property, and therefore an heirloom for eternity. Staunton proposes " given to *them.*"

11. *Level,* the direction in which a missive weapon is aimed, as in *The Winter's Tale,* Act II. sc. 3, l. 6 :—

> The harlot king
> Is quite beyond mine arm, out of the blank
> And level of my brain.

CXVIII. Continues the subject; adding that he had sought strange loves, only to quicken his appetite for the love that is true.

Herr Krauss compares Sidney, *Arcadia,* lib. III. (p. 338, ed. 1613) :—

> Like those sicke folkes, in whom strange humours flowe,
> Can taste no sweets, the sower only please :
> So to my mind while passions daily growe,
> Whose fierie chaines upon his freedome seaze,
>> Joyes strangers seem, I cannot bide their show,
>> Nor brooke ought else but well acquainted woe.
>> Bitter griefe tastes me best, paine is my ease,
>> Sick to the death, still loving my disease.

2. *Eager, sour, tart, poignant.* Aigre, Fr., as in *Hamlet,* Act I. sc. 5, l. 69 :—

> Did curd, like eager droppings into milk.

9. *Policy,* prudent management of affairs.

12. *Rank,* " sick (of hypertrophy)."—SCHMIDT. So 2 *King Henry IV.,* Act IV. sc. 1, l. 64:—

> *To diet* rank *minds sick of happiness,*
> *And purge the obstructions which begin to stop*
> *Our very veins of life.*

CXIX. In close connection with the preceding sonnet; showing the gains of ill, that strange loves have made the true love more strong and dear.

2. *Limbecks*, alembics, stills. *Macbeth*, Act I. sc. 7, l. 67.

4. Either, losing in the very moment of victory, or gaining victories (of other loves than those of his friend) which were indeed but losses.

7. *How have mine eyes out of their spheres been fitted*, etc., how have mine eyes started from their hollows in the fever-*fits* of my disease. Compare *Hamlet*, Act I. sc. 5, l. 17:—

> *Make thy two eyes, like stars, start from their* spheres.

Lettsom would read "been *flitted.*"

11. *Ruin'd love . . . built anew.* Note the introduction of the metaphor of rebuilt love, reappearing in later sonnets. Compare *The Comedy of Errors*, Act III. sc. 2, l. 4:—

> *Shall* love, in building, *grow so* ruinate.

And *Antony and Cleopatra*, Act III. sc. 2, ll. 29, 30.

14. *Ills.* So the Quarto; altered by Malone and other editors, perhaps rightly (see l. 9), to *ill.*

CXX. Continues the apology for wanderings in love; not Shakspere alone has so erred, but also his friend.

3. I must needs be overwhelmed by the wrong I have

done to you, knowing how I myself suffered when you were the offender.

6. *A hell of time.* So in *Othello*, Act III. sc. 3, ll. 169, 170 :—

> *But O, what* damned minutes *tells he o'er*
> *Who dotes, yet doubts, suspects, yet strongly loves.*

And *Lucrece*, ll. 1286, 1287 :—

> *And that deep torture may be call'd* a hell,
> *When more is felt than one hath power to tell.*

9. *Our night.* Staunton proposes "*sour* night."
Remember'd, reminded, an active verb governing *sense* in l. 10. So *The Tempest*, Act I. sc. 2, l. 243.

11. *And soon to you, as you to me, then tender'd.* "Surely the sense requires that we should point—

> *And soon to you, as you to me then, tender'd.*"
> W. S. WALKER.

Staunton proposes—

> *And* shame *to you—as you to me then—tender'd.*

12. *Salve.* Compare Sonnet XXXIV. l. 7.

CXXI. Though admitting his wanderings from his friend's love (CXVIII.–CXX.), Shakspere refuses to admit the scandalous charges of unfriendly censors.

Dr. Burgersdijk regards this sonnet as a defence of the stage against Puritans.

2. *Not to be, i.e.,* not to be vile.

3, 4. And the legitimate pleasure lost, which is deemed

vile, not by us who experience it, but by others who look on and condemn.

6. *Give salutation to my sportive blood.* Compare *King Henry VIII.*, Act II. sc. 3, l. 103:—

> *Would I had no being,*
> *If this* salute my blood *a jot.*

8. *In their wills,* according to their pleasure.

9. *No, I am that I am.* Compare *Othello,* Act I. sc. 1, l. 65, " I am not what I am."

Level. See note on Sonnet CXVII. 11.

11. *Bevel,* " *i.e.,* crooked; a term used only, I believe, by masons and joiners."—STEEVENS.

CXXII. An apology for having parted with the tables (memorandum-book) given to Shakspere by his friend.

1, 2. So in *Hamlet,* Act I. sc. 5, ll. 98–103:—

> *Yea, from the* table *of my memory*
> *I'll wipe away all trivial fond records;*
> .   .   .   .   .
> *And thy commandment all alone shall live*
> *Within the* book *and* volume *of my* brain;

and in the same play, Act I. sc. 3, l. 58:—

> *And these few precepts in thy* memory
> *Look thou* character.

So also *Two Gentlemen of Verona,* Act II. sc. 7, ll. 3, 4.

3. *That idle rank,* that poor dignity (of tables written upon with pen or pencil).

9. *That poor retention*, that poor means of retaining impressions, *i.e.*, the tables given by his friend.

10. *Tallies*, sticks on which notches and scores are cut to keep accounts by. So 2 *King Henry VI.*, Act IV. sc. 7, l. 39.

CXXIII. In the last sonnet Shakspere boasts of his "lasting memory" as the recorder of love; he now declares that the registers and records of Time are false, but Time shall impose no cheat upon his memory or heart.

2. *Thy pyramids.* I think this is metaphorical; all that Time piles up from day to day, all his new stupendous erections, are really but "dressings of a former sight." Is there a reference to the new love, the "ruined love built anew" (Sonnet CXIX.), between two friends? The same metaphor appears in the next Sonnet (CXXIV.), " No, it [his love] was *builded* far from accident;" and again in CXXV., "Laid great bases for eternity," etc. Does Shakspere mean here that this new love is really the same with the old love; *he* will recognize the identity of new and old, and not wonder at either the past or present?

5. *Admire*, wonder at, as in *Twelfth Night*, Act III. sc. 4, l. 165, "Wonder not nor *admire* not in thy mind why I do call thee so."

7. *And rather make them.* "Them" refers to "*what* thou dost foist," etc.; we choose rather to think such things new, and specially created for our satisfaction, than, as they really are, old things of which we have already heard.

CXXIV. Continues the thought of CXXIII. 13, 14. The writer's love being unconnected with motives of self-interest, is independent of Fortune and Time.

1. *The child of state,* born of place and power and pomp.

4. *Weeds,* etc. My love might be subject to Time's hate, and so plucked up as a weed, or subject to Time's love, and so gathered as a flower.

7, 8. When time puts us, who have been in favour, out of fashion.

9. *Policy, that heretic,* the prudence of self-interest, which is faithless in love. Compare *Romeo and Juliet,* Act I. sc. 2, l. 95. Romeo, speaking of eyes unfaithful to the beloved :—

> *Transparent* heretics *be burnt for liars.*

11. *Hugely politic,* love itself is infinitely prudent, prudent for eternity.

12. *That it nor grows.* Steevens proposes *glows.*

13, 14. Does this mean, " I call to witness the transitory unworthy loves (fools of time = sports of time. See CXVI. 9), whose death was a virtue since their life was a crime "?

CXXV. In connection with Sonnet CXXIV.; there Shakspere asserted that his love was not subject to time, as friendships founded on self-interest are ; here he asserts that it is not founded on beauty of person, and therefore cannot pass away with the decay of such beauty. It is pure love for love.

1. *Bore the canopy, i.e.,* rendered outward homage, as one renders who bears a canopy over a superior. The metaphor was not so far-fetched in Shakspere's day as it

would be in ours. At the funeral procession of Queen Elizabeth, a canopy over the corpse was borne by six knights. King James I. made his progress through London, 1603-4, under a canopy. In the account of the King and Queen's entertainment at Oxford, 1605, we read: " From thence was carried over the King and Queen a fair canopy of crimson taffety, by six of the Canons of the Church."—Nichol's *Progresses of King James*, vol. i. p. 546.

2. *The outward.* Compare Sonnet LXIX. 1-5. Staunton proposes " *thy* outward," or " *thee* outward."

3. *Or laid,* etc. The love of the earlier sonnets, which celebrated the beauty of Shakspere's friend, was to last for ever, and yet it has been ruined.

5. *Favour,* outward appearance, as in Sonnet CXIII. 10.

6. *Lose all and more,* cease to love, and through satiety even grow to dislike.

9. *Obsequious,* zealous, devoted, as in *Merry Wives of Windsor,* Act IV. sc. 2, l. 2, " I see you are *obsequious* in your love."

11. *Mix'd with seconds,* mixed with baser matter. " I am just informed by an old lady, that *seconds* is a provincial term for the *second kind of flour,* which is collected after the smaller bran is sifted. That our author's oblation was pure [an offering of fine flour], *unmixed with baser matter,* is all that he meant to say."—STEEVENS. Dyce, who at one time spoke of this note of Steevens as " preposterously absurd," believed then that the word *seconds* is a misprint.

13. *Suborn'd informer.* Does this refer to an actual person, one of the spies of Sonnet CXXI. 7, 8 ? Or is the

" informer " Jealousy, or Suspicion ? as in *Venus and Adonis,* l. 655 :—

> *This sour informer, this bate-breeding spy,*
> *This canker that eats up Love's tender spring,*
> *This carry-tale, dissentious Jealousy.*

CXXVI. This is the concluding poem of the series addressed to Shakspere's friend ; it consists of six rhymed couplets. In the Quarto, parentheses follow the twelfth line, thus :—

$$(\qquad\qquad\qquad\qquad)$$
$$(\qquad\qquad\qquad\qquad)$$

as if to show that two lines are wanting. But there is no good reason for supposing that the poem is defective. In William Smith's *Chloris,* 1596, a " sonnet " (No. 27) of this six-couplet form appears.

2. *Sickle, hour.* " Lintott reads ' fickle hour ; ' S. Walker conjectures ' sickle-hour ; ' Capell, in his copy of Lintott's edition, has corrected ' hower ' to ' hoar,' leaving ' fickle.' Doubtless he intended to read ' sickle hoar.' "—*Cambridge Shakespeare.*

12. *Quietus.* As in Hamlet's soliloquy, Act III. sc. 1, l. 75. " This is the technical term for the acquittance which every sheriff [or accountant] receives on settling his accounts at the Exchequer. Compare Webster, *Duchess of Malfi* [I. i. vol. i. p. 198, *Works,* ed. Dyce] :— ' And 'cause you shall not come to me in debt, being now my steward, here upon your lips I sign your *Quietus est.* ' "—STEEVENS. Quoted by Furness, in his edition of *Hamlet,* p. 212.

To render thee, to yield thee up, surrender thee. When Nature is called to a reckoning (by Time ?), she obtains her acquittance upon surrendering thee, her chief treasure.

CXXVII. The sonnets addressed to his lady begin here. Steevens called attention to the fact that "almost all that is said here on the subject of complexion is repeated in *Love's Labour's Lost,* Act IV. sc. 3, ll. 250–258 :—

> *O who can give an oath ? where is a book ?*
> *That I may swear beauty doth beauty lack,*
> *If that she learn not of her eye to look :*
> *No face is fair that is not full so black.*
>
> . . . . .
>
> *O, if in black my lady's brows be deck'd,*
> *It mourns that painting and usurping hair*
> *Should ravish doters with a false aspect ;*
> *And therefore is she born to make black fair."*

Herr Krauss points out several resemblances between Sonnets CXXVII.–CLII. and the Fifth Song of Sidney's *Astrophel and Stella,* that beginning,

While favour fed my hope, delight with hope was brought,

in which may be felt "the ground tone of the whole series" of later sonnets.

3. *Successive heir,* heir by order of succession, as in 2 *King Henry VI.,* Act III. sc. 1, l. 49 :—

> *As next the King he was* successive heir.

7. *No holy bower.* Malone reads "no holy *hour.*"
10. *Suited,* clad. *And they.* Dyce reads "*as* they." Walker proposes instead of "my mistress' *eyes*" in line 9

" my mistress' *hairs.*"   The editors of the Globe Shakespeare read, perhaps rightly, " My mistress' brows." " Her eyes so suited," etc., is confirmed by CXXXII. 3.

12. *Slandering creation,* etc., dishonouring nature with a spurious reputation, a fame gained by dishonest means.

13. *Becoming of,* gracing.   The word *of* is frequently used as here after the participles of transitive verbs.   So " fearing of," Sonnet CXV. l. 9 ; " licking of," *Venus and Adonis,* l. 915.   See Schimidt's Shakespeare Lexicon under " of," p. 797, col. i.

CXXVIII.

5. *Envy.*   The accent is on the last syllable.   So in Marlowe's *Edward II.* :—

> *If for the dignities thou be envý'd.*

Compare *Titus Andronicus,* Act II. sc. 4, l. 44 (of fingers on a lute) :—

> *And make the silken strings delight to kiss them.*

Jacks, keys of the virginal.   " The virginal jack was a small flat piece of wood, furnished on the upper part with a quill, affixed to it by springs of bristle.   These jacks were directed by the finger-key to the string, which was struck by the quill then forced past the string by the elastic spring, giving it liberty to sound as long as the finger rested on the key.   When the finger was removed, the quill returned to its place, and a small piece of cloth, fixed on the top of the jack, resting on the string, stopped its vibration."—FAIRHOLT (quoted by Dyce in his Glossary to Shakespeare under "jack ").

11. *Thy fingers.*   The Quarto has " their fingers."

CXXIX.

1. *Expense,* expenditure.

9. *Mad.* The Quarto has "*made.*"

11. *Proved, a very woe.* The Quarto has "proud *and* very wo."

CXXX. She is not beautiful to others, but beautiful she is to me, although I entertain no fond illusions, and see her as she is. For the sonneteer's conventional praise of beauty, compare Spenser, *Amoretti,* 9, 15; Sidney, *Astrophel and Stella,* 9; and Lodge, *Phillis,* 8, with reference to which H. Isaac supposes this sonnet to have been written.

9. *Lips' red.* The Quarto has "lips red."

CXXXI. Connected with Sonnet cxxx.; praise of his lady, black but, to her lover, beautiful.

3. *Dear doting.* Dyce reads "dear-doting."

14. *This slander.* The slander that her face has not the power to make love groan.

CXXXII. Connected with Sonnet cxxxi.; there Shakspere complains of the cruelty and tyranny of his lady; here the same subject is continued, and a plea made for her pity.

2. *Knowing thy heart torments me.* The Quarto has "heart torment," and Malone reads "Knowing thy heart, torment." The correction "torments" was made in ed. 1640.

5. Perhaps referring to cxxx. 1; after all, her eyes *are* like sun and stars in a dim sky (her black brows and hair).

9. *Mourning.* The Quarto has "*morning,*" and probably a play was intended on the words " morning sun " and " mourning eyes." This line has a ring like that of *Taming of the Shrew,* Act IV. sc. 5. l. 32 :—

> *What stars do spangle heaven with their beauty*
> *As those two eyes become that heavenly face.*

12. *Suit,* clothe, array.

CXXXIII. Here Shakspere's heart " groans " (see CXXXI.) for the suffering of his friend as well as his own.

8. *Crossed.* See Sonnet XXXIV. 12, and XLII. 12.

9. *Prison.* Delius says, " Für *prison* hat die Q [Quarto] *poison.*" I can find no evidence nor other authority for this statement.

CXXXIV. In close connection with Sonnet CXXXIII.

3. *That other mine,* that other myself, my *alter ego.*

5. *Wilt not,* wilt not restore him.

9. *Statute.* "*Statute* has here its legal signification, that of a security or obligation for money."—MALONE.

11. *A friend came,* etc., a friend who became, etc.

CXXXV. Perhaps suggested by the second line of the last sonnet, " I myself am mortgaged to thy *will.*"

1. *Will.* In this Sonnet, in the next, and in Sonnet CXLIII., the Quarto marks by italics and capital W the play on words, Will = William [Shakspere], *Will* = William, the Christian name of Shakspere's friend [? Mr. W. H.], and Will = desire, volition. Here " *Will* in over- plus " means Will Shakspere, as the next line shows, " More than enough am I." The first " Will " means

desire (but as we know that his lady had a husband, it is possible that he also may have been a "Will," and that the first "Will" here may refer to him, beside meaning "desire"); the second "Will" is Shakspere's friend.

"In Shakespeare's time quibbles of this kind were common. Compare the following in the Booke of Merry Riddles, ed. 1617 :—

THE LI. RIDDLE.

> *My love's will*
> *I am content for to fulfill.*
> *Within this rime his name is framed,*
> *Tell me then how he is named.*

['Will I am' (in lines 1, 2) = William.]"—HALLIWELL (Folio ed. of Shakespeare's Works, 1865).

9. Compare *Twelfth Night*, Act II. sc. 4, l. 103, and Act I. sc. 1, l. 11, "Thy [love's] capacity receiveth as the sea."

13. *Let no unkind, no fair beseechers kill.* If this be the true reading, we must take "unkind" as a substantive, meaning "unkind one" (*i.e.*, his lady). So in Daniel's *Delia*, Sonnet 2 :—

> *And tell th' Unkind how dearly I have loved her.*

But perhaps the line ought to be printed thus:—

> *Let no unkind "No" fair beseechers kill;*

i.e., let no unkind refusal kill fair beseechers. Mr. W. M. Rossetti proposes "skill" for "kill," meaning avail, profit.

CXXXVI. Continues the play on words of Sonnet cxxxv.

6. *Ay, fill.* The Quarto has " I fill," " I " being the usual way of printing our " *Ay* " at the time; but possibly there may here (as often elsewhere in Shakspere) be a play on the words " I "=ay, yes, and " *I* "=myself.

9. *Among a number one is reckon'd none.* See note on Sonnet viii. 13, 14.

10. *Store's.* The Quarto has " stores; " the Cambridge editors follow Malone in reading " *stores;* " Schmidt says of *Store:* " used only in the sing.; therefore in Sonnet cxxxvi. 10, *store's* not *stores'.*" Lines 9, 10, mean " You need not count me when merely counting the *number* of those who hold you dear, but when estimating the *worth* of your possessions, you must have regard to me." " To set *store* by a thing or person " is a phrase connected with the meaning of " store " in this passage.

12. *Something sweet.* Sidney Walker proposed, and Dyce reads, " something, sweet."

13, 14. Love only my name (something less than loving myself), and then thou lovest me, for my name is Will, and I myself am all will, *i.e.*, all desire.

CXXXVII. In cxxxvi. he has prayed his lady to receive him in the blindness of love; he now shows how Love has dealt with his own eyes.

6. *Anchor'd.* The same metaphor is found in *Antony and Cleopatra*, Act i. sc. 5, l. 33 :—

> *Great Pompey*
> *Would stand and make his eyes grow in my brow;*
> *There would he anchor his aspect.*

9, 10. *Several plot,* etc.   So *Love's Labour's Lost,* Act II. sc. 1, l. 223 :—

> *My lips are no common though several they be.*

" Fields that were enclosed were called *severals,* in opposition to commons, the former belonging to individuals, the others to the inhabitants generally. When commons were enclosed, portions allotted to owners of freeholds, copyholds, and cottages, were fenced in, and termed *severals.*"—HALLIWELL.

CXXXVIII. Connected with CXXXVII. The frauds practised by blind love, and the blinded lovers, Shakspere and his lady, who yet must strive to blind themselves. This sonnet appeared as the first poem of *The Passionate Pilgrim* (1599), in the following form :—

> *When my love swears that she is made of truth,*
> *I do believe her, though I know she lies,*
> *That she might think me some untutor'd youth,*
> *Unskilful in the world's false forgeries.*
> *Thus vainly thinking that she thinks me young,*
> *Although I know my years be past the best,*
> *I smiling credit her false-speaking tongue,*
> *Outfacing faults in love with love's ill rest.*
> *But wherefore says my love that she is young?*
> *And wherefore say not I that I am old?*
> *O, love's best habit is a soothing tongue,*
> *And age, in love, loves not to have years told,*
> > *Therefore I'll lie with love, and love with me,*
> > *Since that our faults in love thus smother'd be.*

11. *Habit,* bearing, deportment, or garb.

CXXXIX. Probably connected with CXXXVIII; goes on to speak of his lady's untruthfulness; he may try to believe her professions of truth, but do not ask him to justify the wrong she lays upon his heart.

8. *O'erpress'd defence*, efforts at defence too hard pressed by the assailant.

14. *Kill me outright*, etc. Compare Sidney, *Astrophel and Stella*, 48 :—

> *Dear killer, spare not thy sweet, cruell shot ;*
> *A kind of grace it is to slay with speed.*

CXL. In connection with Sonnet CXXXIX.; his lady's " glancing aside " of that sonnet (l. 6) reappears here, l. 14, " Bear thine eyes straight." He complains of her excess of cruelty.

6. *To tell me so*, " to tell me thou *dost* love me."— MALONE.

14. *Bear thine eyes straight*, etc. " That is (as it is expressed in a former Sonnet) :—

> *Thy looks with me*, thy heart in other place."
> MALONE.

CXLI. In connection with CXL.; the proud heart of line 14 of that sonnet reappears here, l. 12. His foolish heart loves her, and her proud heart punishes his folly by cruelty and tyranny. Compare with this sonnet, Drayton, *Idea*, 29.

5. *Tongue's tune*. So *Venus and Adonis*, l. 431, " Heavenly tune harsh-sounding ;" so too " the tune of Imogen."

9. *Five wits.* " The wits seem to have been reckoned
five, by analogy to the five senses, or the inlets of ideas."
—Johnson. " From Stephen Hawes's poem called
Graunde Amoure [*and La Belle Pucel*], ch. xxiv. edition
1554, it appears that the *five wits* were ' common wit,
imagination, fantasy, estimation [*i.e.*, judgment], and
memory.' *Wit* in our author's time was the general
term for the intellectual power."—Malone.—Dyce's
Glossary to Shakespeare, p. 507.

11, 12. My heart ceases to govern me, and so leaves
me no better than the likeness of a man—a man without
a heart—in order that it may become slave to thy proud
heart.

15. *Pain.* "*Pain* in its old etymological sense of
punishment."—W. S. Walker.

Compare with this sonnet Drayton's *Idea*, 29 :—

> *My hearing bribed with her tongue's harmony,*
> *My taste by her sweet lips drawn with delight,*
> *My smelling won with her breath's spicery,*
> *But when my touching came to play his part,* etc.

CXLII. In connection with cxli. ; the first line takes
up the word "sin" from the last line of that sonnet ;
" She that makes me sin," and "Love is my sin." "Those
whom thine eyes woo " (l. 10) carries on the complaint of
cxxxix. 6, and cxl. 14.

6. *Scarlet ornaments.* So in *King Edward III.* (printed
1596), Act ii. sc. 1, ll. 9, 10 :—

> *Anon, with reverent fear when she grew pale*
> *His cheeks put on their* scarlet ornaments.

This line occurs in the part of the play attributed by several critics to Shakspere.

7. *Seal'd false bonds of love*, given false kisses. So in *Venus and Adonis*, l. 511 :—

> *Pure* lips, *sweet* seals *in my soft lips imprinted,*
> *What bargains may I make, still to be* sealing ?

Again in *Measure for Measure*, Act IV. sc. 1, ll. 5, 6 :—

> *But my* kisses *bring again*
> Seals *of love, but seal'd in vain.*

And again in *The Merchant of Venice*, Act II. sc. 6, ll. 5, 6 :—

> *O ten times faster Venus' pigeons fly*
> To seal love's bonds *new made*, etc.

MALONE.

8. *Robb'd others' beds' revenues.* The Quarto has " beds revenues." Sewell (ed. 1) reads " beds, revenues." Capell MS. has " bed-revenues."

13, 14. *If thou dost seek to have*, etc. If you seek to possess love, and will show none, you may be denied on the precedent of your own example. Staunton proposes " chide " in place of " hide."

CXLIII. Perhaps .the last two lines of Sonnet CXLII. suggest this. In that sonnet Shakspere says, " If you show no kindness, you can expect none from those you love; " here he says, " If you show kindness to me, I shall wish you success in your pursuit of him you seek."

4. *Pursuit.* For examples of this pronunciation of

pursuit and *pursue* see W. S. Walker's *Critical Examination of the Text of Shakespeare*, vol. iii. pp. 366, 367.

8. *Not prizing*, "making no account of."—SCHMIDT.

13. *Will.* Possibly, as Steevens takes it, Will Shakspere; but it seems as likely, or perhaps more likely, to be Shakspere's friend "Will" [? W. H.]. The last two lines promise that Shakspere will pray for her success in the chase of the fugitive (Will ?), on condition that, if successful, she will turn back to him, Shakspere, her babe.

CXLIV. This sonnet appears as the second poem in *The Passionate Pilgrim*, with the following variations : l. 2, "That like;" l. 3, "*My* better angel;" l. 4, "*My* worser spirit;" l. 6, "From my *side;*" l. 8, "*fair* pride;" l. 11, "*For* being both *to* me;" l. 13, "The truth I shall not know." Compare with this sonnet the twentieth of Drayton's *Idea* :—

> *An evil spirit, your beauty, haunts me still,*
> .   .   .   .   .
> *Which ceaseth not to tempt me to each ill ;*
> .   .   .   .   .
> *Thus am I still provoked to every evil*
> *By that good-wicked spirit, sweet angel-devil.*

Compare also *Astrophel and Stella*, Fifth Song :—

> *Yet witches may repent, thou art far worse than they,*
> *Alas, that I am forst such evill of thee to say,*
> *I say thou art a Divill though cloth'd in Angel's shining :*
> *For thy face tempts my soule to leave the heaven for thee, etc.*

2. *Suggest,* tempt, as in *The Two Gentlemen of Verona,* Act III. sc. 1, l. 34 :—

Knowing that tender youth is soon suggested.

6. *From my side.* The Quarto has " from my *sight.*" The text of this sonnet as given in *The Passionate Pilgrim* supplies the correction.

11. *From me,* away from me.

14. Compare 2 *King Henry IV.*, Act II. sc. 4, l. 365 :—

PRINCE. *For the women ?*

FALSTAFF. *For one of them, she is in hell already, and burns poor souls.*

CXLV. The only sonnet written in eight-syllable verses. Some critics, partly on this ground, partly because the rhymes are ill-managed, reject it as not by Shakspere.

13, 14. Steevens proposes " away from hate she *flew,*" and explains the meaning thus : " having pronounced the words *I hate,* she left me with a declaration in my favour." Malone writes : "The meaning is—she removed the words *I hate* to a distance from hatred. . . . We have the same kind of expression in *The Rape of Lucrece* (ll. 1534–1537) :—

' *It cannot be,*' *quoth she,* ' *that so much guile*'
She would have said ' *can lurk in such a look ;* '
But Tarquin's shape came in her mind the while,
And from her tongue ' *can lurk* ' *from* ' *cannot* ' *took.*"

Malone's explanation is probably the right one ; it is

. however possible that the meaning may be—from hatred to such words as " I hate," " she threw them away."

CXLVI. Herr Krauss compares with this sonnet the last of Sidney's Sonnets not included in *Astrophel and Stella,* beginning :—

> *Leave me O Love which reachest but to dust,*
> *And thou my mind aspire to higher things :*
> *Grow rich in that which never taketh rust :*
> *Whatever fades, but fading pleasure brings.*

1. *Centre of my sinful earth.* So *Romeo and Juliet,* Act II. sc. 1, ll. 1, 2 :—

> *Can I go forward when my heart is here ?*
> *Turn back, dull earth, and find thy centre out.*

2. The Quarto reads as line 2, *My sinful earth these rebel powers that thee array,* but the line is manifestly corrupt. Probably, as Malone suggests, the compositor inadvertently repeated the last three words of the first verse in the beginning of the second, omitting two syllables. Malone proposed " *Fool'd by those* rebel," etc. Steevens, " *Starv'd by the* rebel," etc. Dyce, " *Fool'd by these* rebel," etc. F. T. Palgrave, " *Foil'd by these* rebel," etc. Furnivall, " *Hemm'd with these* rebel," etc. Bullock, " *My sins these rebel,*" etc. An anonymous writer, " *Thrall to these* rebel." Cartwright, " *Slave of these* rebel," etc. Gerald Massey, " *My sinful earth these rebel powers array.*" What is the meaning of " array "? Does it mean to put raiment on ? So Malone seems to understand

it. "'Array' here," says Gerald Massey, "does not only mean dress. I think it also signifies that in the flesh these rebel powers set their battle in array against the soul."— *Shakspere's Sonnets never before interpreted :* 1866, p. 379. Dr. Ingleby, in his pamphlet, *The Soule Arayed,* 1872, endeavours to show that "*array*" here means *abuse, afflict, ill-treat.* There is no doubt the word "aray" or "array" was used in this sense by Elizabethan writers, and Shakspere, in *The Taming of the Shrew,* III. 2 and IV. 1, uses "raied," though nowhere "aray," except perhaps here, in this or a kindred sense. Taking "aray" to mean "afflict," Dr. Ingleby accepts Mr. A. E. Brae's suggestion, "*Leagu'd with these* rebel," etc. "It is," he writes, "the earth that is in league with the rebel powers, and the earth itself is therefore called 'sinful.' Here we have the flesh, and its resident lusts, represented as leagued or compacted in the work of defrauding the soul of her rightful nutriment, whereby she 'pines and suffers dearth'" (*The Soule Arayed,* p. 15). In support of the general opinion that "array" means invest in raiment, compare *The Merchant of Venice,* Act V. sc. 1, l. 64:—

> *Such harmony is in immortal souls ;*
> *But whilst* this muddy vesture *of decay*
> *Doth grossly close it in, we cannot hear it.*

The "rebel powers" and the "outward walls" perhaps receive some illustration from the following lines, *Lucrece,* ll. 722–728:—

> *She says her subjects with* foul insurrection
> *Have batter'd down* her consecrated wall,

And by their mortal fault brought in subjection
Her immortality, and made her thrall
To living death and pain perpetual.

It is curious to note that *siege* and *livery* are in close juxtaposition in Sonnet II.

Some emendation being necessary, I suggest *Pressed by.* Compare "o'er-pressed defence," CXXXIX. 8.

10. *To aggravate thy store.* "Malone says that the original copy and all the subsequent impressions read 'my' instead of 'thy.' The copies of the edition of 1609 in the Bodleian, one of which belonged to Malone himself, in the Bridgewater Library, and in the Capell collection, as well as Steevens's reprint, have 'thy.'"—*Cambridge Shakespeare.*

Aggravate, increase.

11. *Terms.* "*Terms* in the legal and academic sense. Long periods of time, opposed to hours."—W. S. WALKER.

CXLVII. In connection with CXLVI.; in that sonnet the writer exhorts the soul to feed and let the body pine, "within be fed," "so shalt thou feed on Death;" here he tells what the food of his soul actually is—the unwholesome food of a sickly appetite. Compare Drayton, *Idea*, 41, "Love's Lunacie."

5. *My reason, the physician to my love.* Compare *The Merry Wives of Windsor*, Act II. sc. 1, l. 5, "Ask me no reason why I love you; for though *Love* use *Reason* for his *physician* [so Farmer and most editors; *precisian*, Folio], he admits him not for his counsellor."

7, 8. *I desperate now approve Desire*, etc. The Quarto

has a comma after approve, which Malone retains. But
the meaning is, "I, who am desperate, now experience that
desire which did object (" except " = object) to physic, is
death."

9. *Past cure*, etc. " So *Love's Labour's Lost*, Act v. sc. 2,
l. 28 :—

> *Great reason ; for past cure is still past care.*

It was a proverbial saying. See *Holland's Leaguer*, a
pamphlet published in 1632 : ' She has got this *adage* in
her mouth; *Things past cure, past care.*' "—MALONE.

14. *Who art as black as hell, as dark as night.* So *Love's
Labour's Lost*, Act iv. sc. 3, ll. 254, 255 (the King speak-
ing of Rosaline) :—

> *Black is the badge of hell,*
> *The hue of dungeons and the suit of night.*

CXLVIII. Suggested apparently by the last two lines
of Sonnet CXLVII.: "I have thought thee bright who art
dark ; " " what eyes, then, hath love put in my head ? "

3. *Censures*, judge, estimate, as in *Julius Cæsar*, Act iii.
sc. 2, l. 16, " *Censure* me in your wisdom, and awake your
senses that you may the better judge."

8. *Love's eye is not so true as all men's : no.* Walker
writes, "Ought we not to affix a longer stop [than a comma]
to *no*? Otherwise the flow seems not to be Shake-
spearian; compare the context." Lettsom adds a note
to Walker's remark : " Ought we to stop here? Ought
we not to expunge the colon before *no*, and write :—

> *Love's eye is not so true as all men's no ?*

Shakspere seems to intend a pun on *eye* and *I*, i.e., *ay*."

13. *O cunning Love!* Here he is perhaps speaking of his mistress, but if so, he identifies her with "Love," views her as Love personified, and so the capital *L* seems right.

CXLIX. Connected with Sonnet CXLVIII., as appears from the closing lines of the two sonnets.

2. *Partake,* take part. So 1 *King Henry VI.*, Act II. sc. 4, l. 100, "Your *partaker* Pole," *i.e.*, partizan.

4. *All tyrant, i.e.,* thou complete tyrant! Malone conjectures "All *truant.*"

CL. Perhaps connected with Sonnet CXLIX.; "worship thy defect" in that sonnet (l. 11), may have suggested "with insufficiency my heart to sway" in this.

2. *With insufficiency,* etc., to rule my heart by defects.

5. *This becoming of things ill.* So *Antony and Cleopatra*, Act II. sc. 2, l. 243 :—

> *Vilest things*
> *Become themselves in her.*

7. *Warrantise of skill,* surety or pledge of sagacity and power. 1 *King Henry VI.*, Act I. sc. 3, l. 13 :—

> *Break up the gates, I'll be your* warrantise.

CLI. Mr. Massey, with unhappy ingenuity, misinterprets thus :—"The meaning of Sonnet CLI., when really mastered, is that he is betrayed into sin with others by her image, and in straying elsewhere he is in pursuit of her; it is on her account."

2. Compare *The Merry Wives of Windsor*, Act V. sc. 3, l. 31, "Why, now is Cupid a child of conscience."

3. *Then, gentle cheater.* Staunton writes, "'Cheater' here signifies *escheator*, an official who appears to have been regarded by the common people in Shakespeare's day much the same as they now look upon an informer." The more obvious meaning "rogue" makes better sense.

10. *Triumphant prize,* triumphal prize, the prize of his triumph. Walker cites Lord Brooke, *Alaham*, v. 1, l. 8, "this triumphant robe," *this robe in which I triumph.*

CLII. Carries on the thought of the last sonnet; she cannot justly complain of his faults, since she herself is as guilty or even more guilty.

11. *To enlighten thee gave eyes to blindness,* to see thee in the brightness of imagination I gave away my eyes to blindness, made myself blind.

13. *More perjured I.* The Quarto has "more perjurde *eye;*" corrected by Sewell.

CLIII. Malone writes: "This and the following sonnet are composed of the very same thoughts differently versified. They seem to have been early essays of the poet, who perhaps had not determined which he should prefer. He hardly could have intended to send them both into the world."

Herr Krauss believes these sonnets to be harmless trifles, written for the gay company at some Bathing-place.

Herr Hertzberg (*Jahrbuch der Deutschen Shakespeare-Gesellschaft*, 1878, pp. 158–162) has found a Greek source for these two sonnets. He writes: "Dann ging ich an die palatinische Anthologie und fand daselbst nach

Notes. 305

langem Suchen im ix. Buche (Ἐπιδεικτικά) unter N. 637 die ersehnte Quelle. . . . Es lautet."

Τᾷδ' ὑπὸ τὰς πλατάνους ἁπαλῷ τετρυμένος ὕπνῳ
εὗδεν Ἔρως, νύμφαις λαμπάδα παρθέμενος.
Νύμφαι δ' ἀλλήλῃσι, "τί μέλλομεν; αἴθε δὲ τούτῳ
σβέσσαμεν," εἶπον, "ὁμοῦ πῦρ κραδίης μερόπων."
Λαμπὰς δ' ὡς ἔφλεξε καὶ ὕδατα, θερμὸν ἐκεῖθεν
Νύμφαι Ἐρωτιάδες λουτροχοεῦσιν ὕδωρ.[1]

The poem is by the Byzantine Marianus, a writer probably of the fifth century after Christ. The germ of the poem is found in an Epigram by Zenodotus :—

Τίς γλύψας τὸν Ἔρωτα παρὰ κρήνῃσιν ἔθηκεν ;
Οἰόμενος παύσειν τοῦτο τὸ πῦρ ὕδατι.[2]

How Shakspere became acquainted with the poem of Marianus we cannot tell, but it had been translated into Latin: " Selecta Epigrammata, Basel, 1529," and again several times before the close of the sixteenth century.

I add literal translations of the epigrams: " Here 'neath the plane trees, weighed down by soft slumber, slept Love, having placed his torch beside the Nymphs. Then said the Nymphs to one another, 'Why do we delay? Would that together with this we had extinguished the fire of mortals' hearts!' But as the torch made the waters also to blaze, hot is the water the amorous Nymphs (or the Nymphs of the region of Eros[3]) draw from thence for their bath."

" Who was the man that carved [the statue of] Love,

---

[1] *Epigrammata* (Jacob), ix. 65.　　[2] Ibid. (Jacob), i. 57.
[3] See Hertzberg, *Sh.-Jahrbuch*, p. 61.

x

and set it by the fountains ? thinking to quench this fire with water."

6. *Dateless*, eternal, as in Sonnet xxx. l. 6.

Lively, living.

11. *The help of bath.* Steevens writes, "Query, whether we should read *Bath* (*i.e.*, the city of that name)." The Quarto does not print with capital *B*.

14. *Eyes.* The Quarto has " eye."

CLIV. A variation on the theme of Sonnet CLIII.

13. *This by that I prove,* this statement which follows (in l. 14).

THE END.

PRINTED BY WILLIAM CLOWES AND SONS, LIMITED, LONDON AND BECCLES.